Best wishes and kind regards

John T. Riddle

GOING TO COLLEGE MY WAY

GOING TO COLLEGE MY WAY

John T. Riddle, D.V.M.

with Virginia H. Meldrum

Sketches by Elsie Owenby

FAMILY PUBLISHING COMPANY
Marietta, Georgia 30060

Printed in the United States of America by
COPPLE HOUSE
LAKEMONT, GA. 30552

To Carolyn, the perfect prescription for this veterinarian.

CHAPTER 1

Feeding cows and chickens...carrying water to the fields...planting, chopping, and picking cotton...breaking corn...plowing...I hate it all. When I grow up, I'm not even going to look at a farm! Papa can have all the farms and dairies he wants to have—I don't even want a picture of one!

As a boy growing up on a dairy farm near Greenville, South Carolina, in the 1920's, I developed a wonderful vision of what I wanted to do when I grew up. I would get off that farm and become a veterinarian like Dr. Grear. That man had everything I wanted—a big car, a pretty wife, a lovely home, plenty of money, and the importance that goes with being a veterinarian in an agricultural community. When Dr. Grear came out to our farm, I followed him around like a hound puppy—hoping for scraps of attention and wary of getting in the way.

Papa was my idea of a cross between a chain-gang boss and a plantation overseer. I surely didn't want to spend the rest of my life chopping cotton, pulling corn, milking cows, feeding stock, cleaning barns, delivering milk, sterilizing dairy equipment, and doing the thousand and two other backbreaking jobs that made the farm successful. Papa worked hard himself and he made his children work hard from the time they were big enough to walk. No, sir, I definitely didn't want to grow up to be like Papa. Forget farming! I wanted to ride around in a big car and to be an important person in the community. I wanted to do the miracles that kept animals healthy or healed them when they were sick or hurt. Watching the pain and terror in an animal ease and relax as I helped Dr. Grear gave me an indescribable joy. Dr. Grear was quite often the difference between economic survival and disaster for the farmers of our area who were heavily dependent on their animals. To be able to help people and animals like he did ... and to make money at the same time ... oh, what a wonderful way to live. The dream grew until I wanted passionately to finish high school, to go to college, and to become a veterinarian.

Deciding what to do was the easy part—figuring out how to do it was going to be a lot harder. Nobody in my family except two of my sisters had graduated from high school and here I was daring to think about going to graduate school. This was definitely not the kind of dream to talk about around my brothers. They would decide that Johnny was getting too big for his britches. Then they would make it their business to cut him down to a more respectable size.

Greenville County in those days was sparsely settled, heavily wooded, and inhabited mostly by small farmers and their families. The roads were rutted red clay. Greenville, the county seat, was a small town. Money was scarce even before the Great Depression added its burdens to an area that was still recovering from the economic devastation of the Civil War. The rolling foothills of the Appalachian Mountains were beautiful and fertile, but life in the rural areas was hard. A good education was even scarcer than money. Men struggling to feed and clothe their families and to keep a roof over their heads had little time, strength, or inclination to worry about filling their children's heads with book learning. Many families feared education because it put ideas into youngsters' heads. Since it often encouraged and enabled children to leave the farm, education was frequently considered a luxury rather than a necessity. To suggest that education was a civil right would have been the rankest of heresies.

In 1918 Papa had bought 360 acres of land in Greenville County for $22.00 an acre. His first cash crop was timber. He and my older brothers cut and sold enough trees to pay for the land. Then they cut and milled enough lumber to build the house, barns, and other necessary outbuildings for a working farm. Papa made sure that it was a real working farm—he worked the dickens out of all eleven of us children and Mama, too.

Life for Papa wasn't easy. Like many other rural Southerners of his time, he had attended the local one-room school until he had learned all that the teacher could teach him. Then he had set out to put his knowledge to use earning a living and building a life for himself and his family.

Papa practiced "possibility thinking" long before the term was popularized. He would decide what he needed and then figure out how he could possibly make or get it—aided, of course, by his wife and children. When the size of the family necessitated a bigger house, he selected the site, drew the plans, cut and milled the lumber, and built the house. He got real help from his older sons and helpfully intended aggravation from the little ones. The plain, solidly built structure has sheltered four generations of the family for well over half a century. Planned obsolescence was abhorrent to Papa—he built things right and he built them to last. Slacking off and doing slip-shod work were mortal sins to him.

Our two-story house had eight rooms, four fireplaces, and three porches. A central hall or "dog trot" ran through the center of each floor from front to back. Upstairs were one huge bedroom for the boys, a smaller bedroom for the girls, and a storage room. Those upstairs bedrooms were as hot as a blacktop road in summer and colder than water from an artesian well in winter. Downstairs were the living room and guest bedroom which had windows opening onto the front porch. Behind the living room was the dining room, and beyond that was the kitchen. On the right side of the house behind the guest room were Mama and Papa's bedroom and a big back porch. On the left side were another small porch which opened off the living room and a cement porch which opened off the kitchen. The cement porch doubled as a summer dining room and a winter cold storage room. Our water was drawn from a well at the corner of the cement porch. We heated it on the wood-burning cookstove in the kitchen when we needed hot water. Two privies in the backyard provided our toilet facilities—we froze our fannies in the winter and held our noses in the summer. Reading in the bathroom was not one of our vices. Exterior paint, electric lights, indoor plumbing, carpets, and screens for doors and windows were not included on Papa's list of necessities. Despite our lack of the luxuries which today are considered absolute necessities, our rambunctious family thrived.

From Papa's big chicken house came eggs and chickens for our table and to sell, feathers for pillows, and an endless supply of manure for the garden. From Mama's huge garden came fruits and vegetables to eat, to can, to pickle, to preserve, to make jelly, or to sell in town. The extra vegetables and eggs were sold door to door in Greenville.

Eventually Papa replaced the chicken house with a dairy barn. Milk and dairy products became the chief cash crop for the Riddle family. Cotton was our other cash crop. We planted thirty to fifty acres and were lucky if we produced a bale to the acre. A bale contained five hundred pounds of cotton with a cash value of five to ten cents per pound. A lot of work and sweat went into producing that $25.00 to $50.00 cash and we still had to subtract the cost of seeds, fertilizer, and equipment. The rest of the land produced feed for the animals or was used for pasture or timberland.

As youngsters we despised chopping the weeds out of the cotton crop and picking cotton. These were the most hated chores on the farm. We thought Papa treated us worse than slaves. Working in the cotton fields gave me plenty of time to think and it got me started to thinking about my future. Mama and my older brothers had received a very minimal education before they dropped out of school to work full-time. Their formal education contained very little other than the basics of reading, writing and arithmetic. They would have to make their living as farmers because they didn't know how to do anything else. That prospect didn't suit me at all. I was definitely going to be something other than a farmer.

When I was twelve years old, I began watching Dr. Grear take care of our animals. The more I saw, the more interested I became. He was an excellent veterinarian and a good man. With his native skills with animals and his education, he could do many things that seemed miraculous to me. Being shy and having been moved out of the way less than gently by my older brothers on more than one occasion, I watched him from a safe distance at first. Gradually my curiosity, aided by Dr. Grear's warmth and friendliness, over-came my reticence. As he worked, I would watch for things to do to help him. Finally I got brave enough to ask him the question that had been burning inside me, "What would I have to do to be a veterinarian like you?"

He invited me to sit down beside him while he packed up his equipment. He told me that he had been watching me and had noticed how interested I was in what he did. We talked about the things he did and the things that I wanted to do. Apparently he had been aware of my fascination with veterinary medicine for quite some time. He knew, too, how difficult it would be for me do something so different from what the family expected. Finally he said, "Well, you keep all this in mind and we'll see what we can do to help you out."

Gosh! I had told him my dream and he hadn't laughed or made fun of me! Dredging up all of my courage, I mentioned my fear that the education I was getting would only produce another farmer. He understood the situation, but he told me to go on to school for two more years, study real hard, and then talk to him again.

We must have been quite a pair. Dr. Grear was a charming and handsome man. He was a shade over six feet tall, well muscled, and had big brown eyes and sandy hair. Even when he worked, he dressed well and moved gracefully. I was a rather small boy with curly brown hair, blue eyes that missed nothing, muscles hardened by working from before sun-up until after sun-down, and co-ordination honed by dodging whatever older brothers decided to throw at me. I wore the standard summer uniform for farm boys—bib overalls with no shoes and no other garments. Despite the contrasts, Dr. Grear and I became very close friends. My relationship with him enabled me to do many things that seemed almost impossible.

I kept on attending St. Alban's School and I kept on worrying that I wasn't learning anything that would help me to get off the farm. In desperation, I decided that I would have to talk to Papa about the problem. I wasn't sure what his reaction would be and I knew there would be trouble if he took offense at my uppity ambitions. My thoughts would spin round and round searching for answers, but they always came back to the same solution. If I were going to attend a different school, Papa would have to help me. Mama always encouraged me to make something of myself, but she couldn't help me out of this predicament.

Finally I convinced myself that I would just have to take my chances and talk to Papa. He was sitting under the chinaberry trees in the back yard when I approached him. Being outside, I at least had running room if he decided to take umbrage at the idea of changing schools. I told him that I just wasn't getting what I needed at St. Albans and that I wanted to go to a different school. To my surprise, he thought for a minute and then asked me what I needed. He listened quietly as I explained that I had to take certain courses in order to get into college and those courses were not being taught at St. Albans.

After what seemed an eternity, he said, "So you want to go to college, do you?"

I assured him that I certainly would like to go if we could figure out how to do it. He mulled the situation over for a little while and decided that if I wanted to go to college, he would help as much as he could. None of my brothers had finished high school nor mentioned going to college, but somehow we would find a way for me to go. The first thing he would do would be to get me out of St. Albans and into Simpsonville High School.

Papa didn't mind helping, but he sure wasn't going to make things too easy for me. He made the arrangements for me to attend the school and left it up to me to figure out a way to get the three miles from our house to the closest point to meet the city school bus.

Compared to talking to him, that didn't take much figuring. I would just ride Sonny Boy over to Mr. Lester's house, leave him in the Lester's barn during the day, and then ride him home in the afternoon. Sonny Boy was my bay horse. He was small, but he was pretty and he was smart. I had spent hours training him and grooming him. Papa had bought me a fine leather bridle and I had worked out a deal with an old black man down the road for a saddle. Uncle Joe had shown me how to oil the saddle and polish its brass and I kept it in prime condition. Sonny Boy could trot, canter, rack, and do all sorts of tricks as well as herd cattle. He would even let me balance my rifle on top of his head to sight and shoot. He responded to touch commands so that I could make him kneel on his left knee to be mounted, stand on his hind legs, or assume a show pose without saying a word. Between me and Sonny Boy, getting to the school bus would be no problem.

I rode Sonny Boy over to the Lesters' farm to discuss my plans with Mr. Lester. He agreed that I could leave Sonny Boy in one of his stalls during the day if I would just bring some feed over and store it in his barn.

When I told Papa what I had done, he reminded me that there were going to be some mighty cold mornings. If I was willing to ride that horse three miles every morning and every afternoon, the arrangement was all right with him. I was going to attend a real high school and then college!

With school, chores, homework, and a little social life, time flew by. I put everything I had into being a super student and participated in every activity I could squeeze in. My competitive spirit insisted that I be number one. From being president of the student body to having one of the top four academic averages in my class, I aimed for the top and achieved those goals. Papa agreed that I could apply for admission to Clemson College. When Clemson notified me of my acceptance, I knew that my farming days were numbered. Hooray and Halleleujah! Johnny Riddle was going to college to become a veterinarian.

I was the cockiest kid in the community for weeks before I left for Clemson. The girls in the community were all excited about my going to college. Carolyn, the curly haired little blonde who had been my special girl for almost two years, was particularly stirred up. We agreed to write to each other often and to see each other when I came home. I was so naive, I thought I would be back home in a week or two. Carolyn didn't know any more about Clemson than I did so she just accepted what I told her.

Mama and I carefully gathered up all the things on the list sent by the school and packed them into my trunk. According to the list, all that I would need to take with me were comfortable black dress shoes, black socks, plenty of underwear, two pairs of pajamas, sheets, towels, and other bedding including a wool blanket. What did they expect me to wear to class? Since I didn't know anybody to ask, I just kept my worries to myself. If I could just get to college, I could handle anything!

Papa and Dr. Grear had both assured me that I could make it through college and veterinary school, so I never doubted that I could handle whatever came along. With high hopes, big dreams, and very little idea of what college was all about, I set off to conquer the campus.

CHAPTER 2

Papa and my big brother Bly drove me the forty miles from our farm to the Clemson campus. I would never have admitted it, but I had a few butterflies in my stomach that didn't come from Mama's good breakfast.

I tried not to look excited as we pulled into the campus. The red brick buildings with their ivy covered towers, John C. Calhoun's beautiful columned mansion, the manicured lawns, paved walks, and smartly uniformed cadets were mighty impressive. Bly and Papa were impressed, too, but they tried not to show it. Clemson surely was different from our dairy farm. If I had realized just how different my life on campus would be, I might have turned tail right then and gone back to the farm.

Despite its gracious appearance, Clemson in those days was a military school—and I mean Military with a capital M. Clemson seemed to try to be tougher and more militaristic than West Point. If war came again, Clemson had no intention of being on the losing side. Her men were going to be the toughest guys around. That kind of discipline would make Clemson more like a prison than a college, but I was blissfully unaware of that.

As soon as we parked the car and got out, we were met by Sgt. Watson. Recognizing me as a green freshman, he introduced himself and offered to show me where to start the process of becoming a Clemson Cadet. With the innocence of a lamb going to the shearer, I followed him into the campus barber shop. I thought my hair looked extra nice, but I was a college man now and I was going to play the game the college way. Papa and Bly waited beside the car.

Before I realized what was happening, I was settled in the chair and the barber was running clippers over my head. I watched in stunned silence as my beautiful wavy hair fell to the floor. My naked scalp looked like a peeled onion. Sgt. Watson grinned, handed me a mirror, and asked, "Now what do you reckon your pretty little girl back home will think of that?"

I didn't answer him because I didn't dare to open my mouth. College was not working out at all like my dreams. I hadn't been

14

on campus fifteen minutes and my whole life was ruined. Carolyn would die if she could see me now ... and I would rather die than have her see me with my billiard ball hairstyle. My thoughts were swirling faster than Mama's butter churn as I followed Sgt. Watson back to the car.

There is no way to describe the expressions that flickered across Papa's face and Bly's when they got their first glimpses of my new appearance. By the time we got to them, Bly was about to kill himself laughing. Sgt. Watson added insult to injury by asking them if they thought I would look good in stripes. I don't remember what they answered because I was beginning to wonder which way those stripes were going to run. Would they run up the side of my pants like a military uniform or around them like a prisoner on the chain gang?

By now Sgt. Watson was asking Papa if he was going to pay my fees. Papa told him that he had come for that purpose. Bly was still laughing at my haircut. Turning so that Papa wouldn't hear me, I hissed, "You big old devil, I'll get even with you for this."

Just then a photographer appeared and asked if I wanted him to take my picture. I was making myself explicitly clear when Bly butted in and told him to go ahead and take the picture.

To my distress, the camera didn't break, the film was developed on the spot, and there was the clearest picture you ever saw of my bald head. I grabbed for the picture as Bly reached for his money to pay for it. The photographer had been through this routine before. He held the picture safely out my reach as he explained, "The one who pays gets the picture."

Bly gave him the money and got the picture while I fumed. That big rascal almost went into seizures from laughing so hard. I nearly panicked when he offered to take the picture to Carolyn. That was just what I needed to ruin my big shot college man image with all the girls. I vowed very fervently to kill him if he showed that picture to anybody.

Before Bly could respond, Sgt. Watson said, "All right, it's time to take you to the administration building and get you matriculated."

That word was not in my vocabulary, but castrated was. It sounded mighty similar. They had already cut off my hair ... God, I hoped they weren't going to castrate me, too.

We went up the long flight of steps, got into line, and gradually

moved forward. When we reached the desk, Papa laid out a pile
of money. Sgt. Watson looked at a sheet of yellow paper before
he turned to me and said, "You're a lucky rat. Yeah—a rat and
not a mouse. You are going to room in one of the four new barracks. They are at each corner of a large rectangle of concrete. Come
on now, Rat Riddle, and we will get you moved into your new
quarters."

As soon as we got outside, he spotted another bald-headed rat.
He yelled at him to come and help this rat get moved into the barracks. With Papa and Bly helping, we got my gear moved into my
room all too quickly. The building was definitely brand new, but
it didn't offer my bruised feelings much comfort. My room was
as coldly institutional as any cell in the penitentiary and there was
no sign of my roommate.

Sgt. Watson suggested that I take the top bunk and the study
desk next to the window. I thanked him sort of backhandedly because that bunk looked eight feet high to me. I hadn't ever slept
that high except the time one of my older brothers gave me a glass
of whiskey. After drinking the whiskey, the last thing I thought
about was that I was drifting off on a cloud—much later I had waked
up feeling awful. There was something definitely foreshadowing
about that memory.

Sgt. Watson assured my folks that I was in good hands now and
they could go on back home.

Boy, I sure did hate to see them drive away. Watson had already
told me that I couldn't see them again until late October. This was
the last week in August. October seemed a long way off to a boy
who had never been away from home. I have never felt so lonesome in my life. With two thousand other cadets on that campus,
I felt just as alone as if I had been stranded on an island in the
middle of the ocean.

CHAPTER 3

Sgt. Watson's voice broke through the waves of loneliness, misery, and homesickness. "Come on, Rat Riddle. Now we're going to meet your company officers."

His tone made it clear that this was a command rather than an invitation. Reluctantly I followed him down to the first floor and down a hall to a big fancy door. His knock was answered by a booming voice which ordered us to come in.

As we entered, Sgt. Watson came to attention and said, "Captain Ruff, sir, I want you to meet a new member of your company ..."

I stuck my hand out to shake his and Captain Ruff interrupted the introduction to bellow like an outraged bull, "Put that * *!# hand down, rat. Don't you know that a captain doesn't touch a lowly rat?"

Startled, I dropped my hand. He continued, "Now, rat, the first thing that you're going to do is learn to make your bed the right way. Sgt. Covington here is going to take you to your room and show you how to do it. And remember this ... it had better be made exactly that way at all times except when your lazy butt is in it."

He excused Sgt. Watson after thanking him for bringing fresh meat (me) for his dogs. Man, if this was an example of an officer and a gentleman, I would be better off back on the farm working for my daddy.

Sgt. Covington and I were also dismissed. As ordered, he accompanied me to my room and taught me to make my bed with mitered corners and linens pulled so tight a coin would bounce on it. This guy had more stripes on his sleeve than a convict. For most of my life I had handled animals that were bigger than I was, but I found dealing with these totally unpredictable cadets downright scary. None of the rules that had made me successful in high school were working here.

Sensing the tightness in my gut, Sgt. Covington showed a glimmer or two of humanity as he gave me my military manual and instructed me in both military courtesy and the rudiments of sur-

17

viving on campus. By now it was mid-afternoon and my stomach was reminding me that I hadn't eaten since breakfast. Sgt. Covington told me about a little restaurant approximately a quarter of a mile past the administration building and suggested that I walk up there and get a sandwich. With a firm reminder that when the big bell rang, I was to go directly to the mess hall for supper, he dismissed me.

I never saw so many ugly bald heads in my life as there were wandering around that campus. It was enough to make anybody wonder about the wisdom of going to college. On the way to the restaurant, I met a couple of friendly rats who were also starving. We ate together and talked a little. It helped to find out that they were just as miserable and scared as I was. It hurt to find out that this castration—no, matriculation—procedure was to go on for two more days. Oh, well, we might as well go back up the hill and see what was happening. None of us dared to express what we really thought - we might as well go back because we sure couldn't go home. How could we ever explain that we weren't men enough to handle even the first day?

Returning to campus was a bad tactical error. We were promptly recruited to help late comers find their quarters when we could hardly find our own backsides. Finally the bell rang and we hurried to the mess hall. At least we could eat and that was bound to improve the situation. If this had been a movie, the background music surely would have been "Dream, Dream, Dream."

The mess hall was nearly the size of a football field. Cadets were milling around inside like cows in a new barn. A sergeant told us to fill up the eight man tables and to be quiet. I was relieved to see that there was plenty of food on the tables. Running around toting trunks and suitcases up and down hills and stairs had made me ravenous.

A senior's voice came over the speaker system. He called us to attention and announced that freshmen would not be permitted to eat until they had been instructed in the proper technique by an upper classman. Finally he said grace and sat down. Dear Lord, we couldn't even eat in peace!

Pretty soon an upperclassman showed up at our table. He instructed us in the fine art of eating by the square. Food was to be picked up on the fork or spoon, raised straight up to mouth level, turned at a ninety degree angle, and inserted straight into the mouth.

The procedure was reversed to get the implement back down to the plate. Unfortunately, eating was not the only thing to be done "by the square"—everything a rat did was to be done by the square. Forgetting to observe the techniques of living by the square was punished by the enthusiastic application of a paddle to the unfortunate rat's behind. Those paddles were designed to make an impression. Each one was one inch thick, four inches wide, and four feet long and they definitely were not made from soft wood.

Most of us rats didn't eat much supper. The upperclassmen were much more enthusiastic about harassing than about helping and the climate was certainly not conducive to enjoying the meal.

After supper our company had a meeting in Capt. Ruff's office. He announced that it would be to our advantage to be in our rooms by eight o'clock and to remain there until reveille except for necessary trips to the latrine. That was another new word and I made the mistake of asking what and where it was.

Capt. Ruff bellowed, "The latrine is the shithouse, you ignorant country rat!"

Just as he roared, I remembered the advice given to me by one of my high school teachers who had graduated from Clemson: "Keep your mouth shut, your bowels open, and don't volunteer for a **#! thing."

I closed my mouth and resolved to keep it shut.

Capt. Ruff continued his harangue. "When you hear that bugle at 6:00 a. m., you will get the ***#! out of those sacks, make them up as you were instructed, get dressed, and be in this office promptly at 6:30 a.m. for further instructions. Company dismissed!"

My roommate still hadn't appeared so I spent the night alone. After all those years of sleeping in the same room with seven brothers and longing for a little privacy, I had too much privacy and too little security. It was a miserable night filled with strange noises and troubled dreams.

Promptly at 6:00 that wretched bugle sounded like Gabriel's trumpet. For us rats, it would be another day of judgement. At 6:30 in Capt. Ruff's office, we discovered that a night's sleep hadn't mellowed him out one bit. If anything, he had dreamed up ways to be more obnoxious. "Attention! You rats will report immediately to the mess hall. You will chow down by the square. Then you will get in line for uniform measurements. The lines will be alphabetical. If your last name is "A--hole," you will get in Line

A; if it's "Bastard," you will get in Line B; and so on. Now, move out on the double!"

We stood in lines for the next five days to get all the parts of our uniforms except the mackinaws. Those heavy wool coats would be shipped in later and we would have the privilege of standing in more lines to get them. Even getting uniforms was a traumatic experience. The guy measuring me for my pants asked which side I wore my credentials on. Baffled by the question, I answered, "I don't understand, sir."

The sergeant roared loud enough for Mama to hear him back at the farm, "Your balls are your credentials, you dumb country hick!"

Well, I never had thought much about that, but I sure wasn't going to ask any more questions. Since I was left-handed, I yelled back, "The left side, sir!"

In that first week, I thought about a lot of things that had never seemed worthy of consideration in the past.

CHAPTER 4

Frank Perry and I had requested and received permission to room together. Although we had been friends since third grade, attending different high schools had pulled us apart. Nonetheless, I really looked forward to having someone familiar to share my room. With all the unpleasant surprises of life as a rat, I needed the security of a friend. I knew that something was wrong when my first twenty-four hours on campus passed with no sign of Frank and no word from him. The room got emptier and emptier while I got lonesomer and lonesomer. I knew that he had been assigned to the room. Where in the heck was he?

Finally just before suppertime, Frank and his older brother David stumbled through the door. They were hot, tired, and totally exasperated. They had wandered from barracks to barracks all afternoon trying to find our room. Both of them greeted me with, "How in the *!#! did you manage to find this %#* room?"

It was not an auspicious beginning to Frank's college career. He and David brought his gear up to the room as fast as they could so that David could start for home. David was supposed to be home before dark and there was no way that he was going to make it. David was frustrated and mad. Frank was worried about his brother, upset about his rat haircut, and perturbed with the situation in general and hazing in particular.

Right after David's departure, the supper bell rang. Frank was startled by the bell, but delighted to know that we were going to get something to eat. He was even less prepared for the hassle of the mess hall than I had been. He was famished, but he didn't get to eat much of his supper. What he did eat seemed to stick in his craw. His aggravation was souring his attitude toward everything and everybody. His open face displayed his feelings all too clearly and his handsome dark good looks made him stand out in a crowd. All of this, coupled with a very sensitive nature, spelled trouble.

A rat with an obvious attitude problem attracted harassment like his grey wool uniform attracted lint. Frank got started off wrong with the upper classmen and things rapidly went from bad to awful. Back home his well-built body, black hair, gorgeous blue eyes, and charming personality had made him King of the Hill. He simply was not prepared to live like a rat. Clemson certainly was not prepared to treat a rat like a human being. A witches' cauldron of trouble was mixed and beginning to bubble.

In this situation, having seven brothers was an advantage. Because they had hassled me all my life, I figured that I could survive anything the upper classmen could dish out. Although I had not knuckled under to my brothers, I had learned how to avoid antagonizing them unnecessarily. I had also learned how to bide my time and to get even in subtle ways rather than via frontal assaults. Little brothers learn guerilla tactics as a means of survival. Frank had no idea how to cope with such a situation.

Poor Frank. Nothing suited him. He reacted openly to the taunting and thus attracted more harassment. Everything about our room was wrong. He didn't like having to sleep on the bottom bunk because he didn't want anybody to sleep above him...he was sure that the top bunk was going to fall on him...he didn't like his desk...the rat rules were ridiculous. His list of complaints was endless.   In a desperate effort to keep him from deserting me, I tried to make him feel better. My offer to trade bunks was refused because he might fall off the top bunk and forget to hang onto his parachute. Swapping desks wouldn't solve anything either. Nothing seemed to help.

Like most cadets, he fussed about the food...nothing was prepared the way he liked it. He had never had to face Irish potatoes three times a day. Hash browned potatoes for breakfast, French fried potatoes for lunch, and baked potatoes for supper was just too much. On this point I agreed with him. Every Clemson graduate surely must have consumed at least two tons of potatoes prior to graduation. A few days of calisthenics and drill did improve the flavor of the food, but it didn't help anything else.

Finally I confronted him. "Frank, you've plowed with a hard tail mule as much as I have. What's eating you? Is the drilling getting to you?"

"No, it's not the drilling......it's this whole *!*# rigmarole that's killing me!"

His words had a strangled sound and I knew that Frank was fighting hard to control himself.

"Are you homesick?"

He hesitated before he stammered, "N-no......not exactly."

"Do you miss your girlfriend? I sure do miss Carolyn. Man, I'm telling you—just one little hug would make me feel a heap better."

As he stood up too fast, he blurted, "I just can't stand any more of this d----- treatment! Not even billy goats or mules are abused like we are."

My assurances that things would improve after the first six weeks didn't help. I had found out that the upperclassmen would lighten up and life would be easier for everybody after the novelty of rat rules wore off. Frank was too miserable to plan that far ahead. He just wanted to get out.

Then he hit me with his big news. "I have to work out one more thing...then I'll probably be moving out...I'm really sorry, John...just wait until tomorrow and I'll let you know for sure what I'm going to do."

That hurt. I had been on campus less than a week and I had lost my hair, my rights as a human being, and my roommate. Nobody cared whether I lived or died, not to mention whether I was happy. Why had I thought the farm was so bad? At least there Carolyn, Mama, and Sonny Boy were around to comfort me when things went wrong.

By the next day I was feeling pretty rough. My thoughts kept going back home. I knew their exact routine—who was doing what, when, where, why, and how. They didn't know one thing about what I was going through. If they had known my situation, they would at least have worried about me. Well, Carolyn, Mama, and my sisters, Louise, Blanche, and Adeline, would have worried. My brothers, durn their ornery hides, would have enjoyed my misery! They would have reminded me that I had insisted on being the big shot and going to college. They would have figured that I ought to have stayed home and helped out on the farm. Since they were having to do my share of the work in addition to their own heavy loads, they wouldn't have wasted their sympathies on me. I tried to figure out a way to improve my situation, but I wasn't making much progress.

At lunch, Cadet Colonel Bell announced our first mail call. That afternoon, he and several assistants pulled a dozen mail bags out on the second story porch above the guard house. The whole mob of miserable, bald-headed rats stood on the ground waiting expectantly like chickens waiting for somebody to throw them some corn.

Col. Bell would read out the name on the envelope, the lucky cadet would holler, "Here!" and one of the assistants would sail the letter in his general direction. Eager hands would pass it back until it got to the right man. All of us hoped desperately for a letter and struggled valiantly not to show our feelings.

When my name was called, I thought my heart would burst with excitement. Somebody cared enough to write to me! As soon as I saw that it was from Carolyn, I tucked it quickly into my shirt pocket. That one would be read in private without these goons peering over my shoulder. As my shirt surrounded the letter, thoughts of Carolyn surrounded me. Her pretty face framed in golden brown curls, sparkling blue eyes with more than a hint of mischief, a firm chin that bespoke determination if not outright stubbornness, soft curves belying her awards for physical fitness, and best of all, the knowledge that she loved me...yes, sir, she was my girl.

My name was being called again. Bless my bones! Who else had written to me? Mama! Her third-grade writing was labored and I knew how hard she must have struggled to write a letter. I choked up remembering how she had encouraged me to work hard in school, to go to college, to make something of myself. If Mama could handle letter-writing, I could handle hazing. I would stick it out regardless of what happened.

Mail call took over an hour. I could hardly wait to get back to my room to read my letters. If they had been inscribed on golden tablets, they wouldn't have been any more precious.

Frank wasn't in the room. I enjoyed reading my letters several times each before I began to wonder where he was. Then I noticed that all his gear was gone. It was several days before I discovered that he had arranged to drop out of the military program and to enroll as a non-military student. He would work on the college dairy farm, board with a family, wear civilian clothes, and escape the drilling, hazing, and calisthenics that had made life as a cadet impossible for him. He sure wasn't making life any easier for me. Even though I was alone again, Carolyn and Mama had reinforced my resolve. I was going to make it.

CHAPTER 5

I kept telling myself that there must be a few nice things about starting a college career. Myself surely was having a hard time finding them. Getting uniforms was followed by the choosing of rat slaves and the beginning of drills. Both involved further suffering for all of us rats.

When all the room assignments had been made, we rats were lined up in the halls. The upperclassmen looked us over like cattle at the stock market and chose their slaves for the year. Rat slaves were required to do everything their masters ordered. The only thing that an upperclassman could not order a rat to do was clean a rifle other than his (the rat's) own. We could be given regular duties as well as "do this now" orders. There seemed to be nothing too hard, too ridiculous, or too degrading to require a rat to do. Some of the upperclassmen must have spent hours dreaming up new and creative ways of harassment.

I just thought I was getting away from a slave driver when I left the farm. What I did was swap one slave driver for two full-timers plus almost 1500 part-time slave drivers!

Two juniors, James Herriot and A. O. McCall chose me to be their slave. James was a line sergeant. He had grown up on a farm down in the lower part of South Carolina and was working toward a degree in farm management. He and I had a lot in common. McCall had grown up on the Clemson campus and seemed pretty sissy to me. He was a staff sergeant working toward a degree in civil engineering. Although we didn't have many common interests, we could get along.

As masters, Herriot and McCall were pretty good. I had to make their beds every morning, shine their shoes, and do whatever else they decided they needed to have done. They were not really abusive like some of the upperclassmen. They weren't exactly soft either. I didn't appreciate having to walk half a mile to the post office to mail a letter or to pick up 3-cent stamps, but they could have been a lot worse.

Any upperclassman could order any rat to do anything. If the

25

rat objected, he could be paddled by the offended upperclassman. Rats could also be paddled for infractions of rat rules. There was always somebody watching for the most minor infraction. I avoided a lot of the problems incurred by my brother rats because I followed the advice of my high school teacher. Just keeping my mouth shut and being relatively inconspicuous saved me a lot of grief.

By now all of the upper classmen were back at school and we were settling into a rigorous military routine that would make or break you. I thought that if I went for a hundred years before I heard another bugle or saw another black stripe or another bald head, it would be too soon. I was still determined that I was going to make it in spite of everything and everybody. If thousands of other rats had found their way through the maze, I could do it, too.

After some hard thinking, I realized that military routine is designed to be followed by rote rather than by reason. It is pretty easy to follow if you pay attention to what you are doing and resist the urge to show off or to think for yourself.

The military portion of our day was under the supervision of a regular U.S. Army Colonel. He was assisted by several regular army officers. The majors taught classes in military science. The captains and several first and second lieutenants handled other phases of our training. These men demanded and received full military courtesy at all times and in any place they encountered a cadet. They all carried little black books in which they recorded our sins of omission and commission. Most of them were decent guys, but there were a few who seemed to be direct descendants of the Borgia clan.

The student body members had ranks similar to those in the army. All freshmen were privates. Sophomores could be either privates or corporals. There were about one hundred and eighty corporals. They wore two black stripes on their sleeves. Juniors could achieve the rank of sergeant. They wore three or more stripes on their sleeves to denote whether they were line sergeants, first sergeants, battalion sergeant majors, regimental sergeant majors, or brigade sergeant majors. Seniors could achieve a rank anywhere from private up through second and first lieutenant, captain, battalion major, regimental colonel, or brigade colonel which was the highest student rank.

Those who achieved officer status, lieutenant or higher, wore silver emblems to denote their rank. I went to college to learn how to be a veterinarian, but Clemson seemed to think that I was there to learn how to march and to drill. We went to classes in the mornings and to the drill field in the afternoons. It seemed that we marched everywhere we went except to the latrines and to classes. I kept wondering when they would figure out a way to have us march there, too!

The military organization of the campus worked this way. There were eight men in a squadron. They were chosen roughly by height and ability to perform. Each squad was led by a corporal. Four squads made up a platoon which was led by a platoon sergeant and a platoon leader who was a first lieutenant. Two platoons made up a company which was commanded by a captain and an executive lieutenant. (I always felt that there was about as much need for an executive lieutenant as there was for a dog with three tails. Of course, nobody asked for my opinion, and, as usual, it didn't matter what I thought.) Four companies made up a battalion which was commanded by a lieutenant colonel or a major and six battalion officers. Four battalions made up a regiment which was commanded by a colonel and eight regimental officers. The two regiments formed a brigade which was commanded by the brigade colonel, assisted by ten brigade officers. We learned quickly that rank has its privileges. Most of us worked hard to achieve a higher rank.

Those afternoons on the drill field were a trial to our souls as well as our bodies. There just isn't much inspiration to be found in listening to cadence counts while you keep your eyes fixed on the backside of the cadet in front of you. With nothing to provide shade from a hot sun nor to break the force of a cold wind, there is no place hotter in summer nor colder in winter than a drill field. They seemed to be designed for maximum misery! The only escapes from drill were rain and notes from the infirmary. It's a wonder the Clemson campus didn't look like Death Valley—it never seemed to rain during drill! Notes from the infirmary could be obtained only if your death appeared likely to occur within a few hours. You might as well plan to spend your afternoons drilling. Even Houdini would have had trouble getting out of it.

Our day began at six a.m. when that blasted bugle shattered our dreams with reveille. Then came an hour of calisthenics. After that, we fell into company formation and marched to the mess hall. We ate as fast as we could, rushed to make our rooms ready for inspection, and then we had to make up our upperclassmen's rooms and get to class by eight o'clock. Mornings were filled with classes. All freshmen took pretty much the same basic courses. I took mathematics, English literature, military science, chemistry, and some electives that were required to get into veterinary school.

At noon we had ten minutes to get to our company area, fall into company formation, and march to the mess hall for lunch. After lunch, there was a precious bit of free time.

From one o'clock until four o'clock was freshman drill. We learned what the orders meant and how to execute them precisely. First we got into company formation. Capt. Ruff would call our company to order. Then we counted off as we extended left arms to measure proper distance from the next man. Then came roll call by the first sergeant following the order of the first lieutenant. When the roll was called and every man had been accounted for, the sergeant reported to the first lieutenant who then reported to the captain. Now Capt. Ruff would call the company to attention and order, "Forward, march!" Another long, hot afternoon would be spent pushing one tired foot in front of the other as cadence droned on endlessly, rifles got heavier, and eyes grew weary of watching the rear end of the cadet in front of you.

We also learned the manual of arms. This involved taking a nine-pound Springfield rifle and turning it every way but loose. We were convinced that God Himself forbade that we drop one—they were considered government property and inviolate. Unfortunately, we were not considered to be as valuable as the rifles. With all of our gyrations to avoid dropping our rifles, it seemed that when we were not accidentally hitting ourselves with them, we were hitting or being hit by other cadets. It became almost as tough to maintain self-control as to develop the necessary hand-eye-ear co-ordination to perform the drills. A well-executed rifle drill is a joy to watch, but it's a bruising experience to master.

Misery and drilling became synonymous. Learning the commands, movements, and formations was like learning a new language. To make it worse, the commands got more indistinct as fatigue, heat, and frustration bore down on us. Two hours of drill in full sun on a hot September afternoon should have been sufficient torture for anybody. Just to make sure we were thoroughly miserable, we were required to wear our uniforms. Those 100% wool britches made us itch worse than poison ivy. Our uniform shirts were soon soaked with sweat and clinging to our backs and arms while they scratched our necks. Our shoes seemed to shrink and to find new places to pinch with every step. Why, Lord, why did I ever complain about life on the farm?

At least our squad corporal knew how to handle his men. He gave reasonably clear instructions and soon had us drilling with some semblance of precision. Of course, we had the usual number of collisions, strays marching off in the wrong direction, and assorted other errors, but we were definitely making progress.

After drill there were two hours of free time. We could go to the post office or to the laundry, study, write letters, or get our uniforms ready for the next day. There was always something that needed doing—brass to polish, shoes to polish, or some idiot rat assignment for an upper classman.

At six o'clock we fell into formation for retreat. While the bugler sounded retreat, we stood at attention. We remained in formation while the flag was lowered and folded. Then we marched to the mess hall for supper. Our places were assigned by company and squadron. The brigade commander would ask the blessing and make the announcements. When he finally got around to commanding, "At ease!" we were permitted to eat, but not to relax. Eating must be done by the square, proper respect must be shown to upper classmen, etc. etc. etc. We had plenty of food to eat at the table, but heaven help you if you decided to take any food out of the mess hall. Food in your room was a cardinal sin punishable by a whole bunch of demerits.

Each table had a captain. His duty was to report any misconduct occurring at his table.

When I was appointed captain of our table, I reminded our eight men that we had supposedly been reared as civilized people rather than as heathens and that I did not want to have to report any heathenism. I also made it clear that I had no desire to be gigged for not reporting any heathenism that might occur. Even though I wasn't the biggest man at our table, my country boy strength and no-nonsense attitude established my control in a hurry. We had no trouble at our table.

After supper most evenings the upper classmen would call a rat meeting. They would bring their paddles and do all sorts of things to provoke us into violations of the rat code. Violations earned us the privilege of "assuming the position" (feet on the floor, hands around ankles, head down, and posterior at a most convenient angle for making contact with the paddle) and receiving licks with the paddles. One night James and McCall each laid six hard licks on my defenseless butt. Even though the pain and the injustice and the humiliation burned into my soul, I was determined not to let anyone know how I felt. Outwardly, I displayed only cool indifference to the whole situation. Later they called me into their room and explained that they had been testing me to see how strong I was. Both of them apologized for hitting me and swore that they would never do it again. More importantly, they both assured me that I would have their protection from then on—if anybody dared to give me any trouble, they would handle it. That pledge made my life a lot easier.

Occasionally a senior officer would decide to amuse himself and his friends by hassling a rat. He would order the unfortunate one to his room. The host and his friends would all have paddles, short handled brooms, coat hangers, or sabers with which to paddle the guest if he committed any violation of the rat code. None of these objects felt good, but the brooms hurt least and the coat hangers hurt worst.

My turn came all too soon. I was called to Capt. Ruff's office. As I approached his door, I wondered what on earth I had done. I was fully and properly dressed, my uniform was clean and pressed, I had shaved carefully, my shoes were spit-shined, and I had not broken any rules. Knowing full well that neither defiance nor cowardice would help me, I decided to play the military game to the hilt giving military courtesy prime attention.

My knock was answered with a command to enter. Lord, have mercy! There sat all of the company officers like the lions waiting for Daniel. When I reported, "At your service, sir!" in a voice that sounded much firmer than I felt, the captain informed me that I had been reported for giving trouble in my platoon. Sure that there was a misunderstanding, I looked directly at my platoon lieutenant. Lt. Layless ducked his head. There would obviously be no help from him.

"Well, Rat Riddle, do you affirm or deny the charge?" Capt. Ruff's voice made it clear that there would be no time for meditation.

"I do not care to affirm or to deny the charge. Perhaps Lt. Layless could shed some light on the complaint for me."

Capt. Ruff snapped, "You, Rat Riddle, are a smart a--, and I am going to give you something to remember me by! Will it be with the paddle, the broom, or the saber?''

Some choice! Nonetheless, I responded, "At your pleasure, sir."

Pulling his saber from the scabbard, he snarled, "Assume the position!"

As I bent over, he hit me four hard licks and then asked, "How does that feel?"

Laughing, I asked, "Is that the best you can do?"

Shocked, he blurted, "I pass to Lt. Layless."

Layless hit me four hard licks and then asked how that felt.

Standing up, I looked at both of them for a minute and then said, "If I couldn't do any better than that, I would be d----- if I would pick on a helpless rat!"

Astonished, they stared at each other and then at me before they burst out laughing.

Capt. Ruff recovered first. "Cadet Riddle, you turned the trick on us. Congratulations on being a real cadet! You can be sure that we will see that you are not mistreated by anyone in this company. You may return to your room."

Well, that wasn't so bad. My behind stung a little, but my soul was elated. They had done their worst and I had beaten them at their own game. That session in Capt. Ruff's office smoothed my path for the rest of my time at Clemson.

At eight o'clock was long roll. We would fall into formation in a wide hall of the dormitory for the last roll call of the day. After roll call, we were restricted to our rooms except for trips to the latrine. This was the time to study and to make preparations for the next day. At eleven p.m. the bugler played "Taps" to signal lights out and the end of another long, lonely day. To this day, the playing of "Taps," especially at a funeral, recalls the loneliness, misery, and desperate resolve to make it that characterized those first weeks at Clemson.

Loneliness and discouragement bore down on me like dead weights. It was bad during the day as I struggled to learn a whole new way of life. I had always been part of a big, rowdy family that was exceptionally close-knit. Now I was surrounded by strangers. Life on the farm had been hard and I had been hurt physically and emotionally many times. Animals, equipment, and people had all inflicted accidental or intentional damage at one time or another. The difference was that on the farm there was always something

or somebody to make me feel better when life got tough. A smile from Mama, a friendly tap on the shoulder from a big brother, a soft nuzzle from Sonny Boy, or just having one of the cats or dogs snuggle against my leg would remind me that there was still love and goodness in the world. Now there was nobody to care nor to comfort and nowhere to hide. At night, after "Taps," life became almost unbearable. The mournful notes seemed to bring back all the hurts and frustrations and discouragements of the day. The room became a prison cell, noises and shadows became threats, and life seemed too hard to endure. There had to be an answer, but what was it? I was too big to cry and too little to deal with the agony.

Finally I asked Sgt. Covington if I would ever get another roommate. He assured me that sooner or later some rat would request a transfer and then I would have a replacement for Frank. He warned me that neither of us would have any control over who the man would be nor when a transfer would take place. He also told me that the man would probably be a misfit or an undesirable who had been pushed out of another company. Convinced that nothing could be worse than being alone, I requested that he get me a roommate as soon as possible.

Realizing my loneliness and my need to belong to a group, Sgt. Covington suggested that I try out for the rifle team. That didn't help anything. I was a crack shot, but I was disqualified because I fired from my left shoulder. All of the team members fired from the right shoulder.

Some of my classes weren't working out too well either. I had been warned not to sign up for Dr. Kinard's English classes because he was tough. Unfortunately, by the time I was ready to sign up for English, all the other classes had been filled. After signing up for Dr. Kinard's class, I had gone to visit him. He seemed pleasant as I told him about my academic background and my reasons for transferring from St. Albans to Simpsonville High School. I had not been able to make up all the English I had missed in grammar school. My high school grades had been straight "A's except for English—those had been "B's and "C's. He thanked me for coming and for explaining the situation to him. He also made it clear that he expected me to do my best and not to expect him to go easy on me. I had assured him that I would make every effort to meet his standards. I truly was doing my best, but it didn't seem to be good enough. In desperation, I asked my upper classmen to tutor me. They helped as much as they could, but English classes were like swimming in cold deep waters filled with treacherous currents and sharp rocks. To add to my woes, my class in animal nutrition met down on the dairy farm which was almost a mile from the other classrooms. I had to run as fast as I could to get down there for class and then run all the way back to get to my next class. Mercifully my classes in math, chemistry, and military science presented no problems. The shorthand I had taken in high school made my college work a lot easier. I took down my professors' lectures in shorthand in the classrooms and then transcribed them in longhand in my notebooks at night. Full lecture notes coupled with concentrated study of the textbooks practically guaranteed me "A's in everything except English.

Gradually I was getting some handles on the situation. If I could just hang on long enough to get a new roommate, maybe things would work out.

CHAPTER 6

About two weeks passed before roommate number two arrived. I came in exhausted and disgruntled from a hard hot drill, looking forward to a few minutes of rest. There in the middle of my room stood what I thought must be an apparition. He stood six foot three on those rare occasions when he unfolded completely, his ape-like arms hung down to his knees, his size fourteen shoes pointed north and south when his face pointed east, and he held his head back as though he were trying to peer under the rims of his extra-thick glasses! So help me, he looked like a cross between an idiot and a clown wearing a military uniform. His belongings were strewn all over my bed and desk as well as the empty bed, the desk, and the floor.

As I stood transfixed by awe, disbelief, and pity, he stammered, "My name is Jason....I suppose I should have said, 'Rat Jason,' sir."

Somehow I managed to tell him that my name was John Riddle and that he did not have to address me as "Sir." Then I explained that I was a nut about tidiness and order because I did not want either to live in a mess or to get the demerits that were sure to come from not having the room properly made up. Finally, I asked him to clear me a path across the room and to remove his gear from my bed and desk.

Jason had to be seen to be believed. My reactions to him spun like an emotional kaleidoscope. He seemed to have been put together by the same committee that constructed the camel. He was so loose jointed and gangly that you almost expected him to fall apart when he moved. His movements were anything but graceful or coordinated. He was obviously a nice boy who had been well brought up. He had good manners, but appeared to be utterly lacking in social skills, self-confidence, and common sense. He talked constantly, asked stupid questions about things he should have learned his first day on campus, and was totally naive. He was obviously going to be the victim of a lot of pranks.

As he struggled to get his gear put away properly, we exchanged background information. He was from Spartanburg County; his father was a mail carrier; his mother was a teacher. Well, at least he had not escaped from the zoo even if he did bear a strong resemblance to a gorilla. I swear that he would have been a great exhibit for the Scopes' defense team. It took the rest of the afternoon for him to get his gear into some semblance of order. I dreaded facing Saturday morning inspections with Jason as my roommate.

Saturday morning inspections were rough. When you heard that gang of officers and sergeants coming down the hall, your bed had better be made up by the book, your rifle had better be perfectly cleaned, all of your gear had better be folded properly and be in exactly the right places, and you had better be carefully shaved and groomed and wearing a fresh uniform with all the brass polished to a high gloss and your shoes had better be spit-shined. No dirt, dust, or disorder would pass unnoticed nor escape demerits. When they knocked on your door, you would answer, "Enter." The first sergeant would order, "Attention!" You stood as stiff and straight as a board at the foot of your bed and held your rifle at the order arms position. The officers would check to see that the socks were rolled the right way in the drawer and that all the underwear and shirts were laid out correctly. When ordered to "Present arms!" you handed your rifle to the officer and prayed silently while he squinted down the barrel and rubbed his glove over it to check for a smidgen of dirt or dust. When they finished the inspection, they would leave the room without making any comments. You could check the bulletin board later in the day to see if you had gotten any demerits.

While Jason was putting things away, I went over to see Sgt. Covington. He was expecting me. Jason had been pushed out of another company as an undesirable. Sgt. Covington knew that Jason and I would not have anything in common, but there was nothing that he could do about it. My one consolation was his promise that if I would put up with Jason, he would give me the benefits of all doubts when problems arose. With a heavy heart, I agreed to try to make the best of a bad situation.

With the newness wearing off, we began to feel a little more secure. With a little security, rats reverted to being boys rather than cadets. Coached by the upper classmen, we began to play tricks on each other. Most of them were funny and caused little more than inconvenience and temporary loss of dignity to their victims. The comic relief did a lot to relieve our feelings of helplessness and home-sickness.

As I had feared, Jason became the butt of many jokes and pranks. His naivete made him the perfect fall guy because he never suspected that anybody would do anything other than what he was supposed to do or that any situation could be anything other than what it appeared to be. You could tell that he hadn't grown up in a big family!

James and McCall, my upperclassmen, dared me to short-sheet Jason's bed. I knew how the trick worked, but I had never done it. Since it was almost time for Jason to return from the laundry, James and McCall volunteered to do the work while I kept watch. Those guys were good. Quick as lightning they pulled off the covers, folded the top sheet and put it on the shelf with Jason's other clean linens, folded the bottom sheet up and tucked it in so that there appeared to be two sheets on the bed, replaced and tucked the covers, and tightened everything down so that the bed looked perfectly made. By the time Jason reached our hall, James and McCall were back in their room.

With a lot of effort, I managed to act as though nothing had happened. That night I made sure to finish studying early and to get to bed before Jason did. You wouldn't believe how long it took that guy to get ready for bed. He fooled around for over an hour while I played possum and waited for him to go to bed. Finally he knelt beside the bed as he always did and said his prayers. By the time he finished his prayers and turned off the light, I was fit to be tied.

Jason put on a show that was worth waiting for. He tried to get into bed, but his feet would only go halfway down the bed before they were blocked by the folded sheet. Sure that he had made a mistake, he pulled his feet out and pushed them back under the covers four times before he gave up and got out of bed. He couldn't turn on the lights because "Taps" had already sounded so there he was fumbling around in the dark trying to fix his bed without waking me up. I was about to have convulsions trying to keep from laughing out loud. In desperation, I pulled the pillow over my face to smother my giggles.

By the time I got enough control of myself to peek out, Jason was struggling to make up his bed using the one sheet and talking quietly to himself all the time. It never occurred to the poor guy that the reason he couldn't find the other sheet was that it wasn't there. Finally he muttered to himself, "Well, d--- it to h---, I know I made this bed right this morning and sheets don't just disappear!"

I was in agony trying to suppress my laughter as Jason got madder and more frustrated. At last he got the bottom sheet tucked in right, but there was still no top sheet. He got so enraged that he snatched off the bottom sheet, swore as he threw it into the corner, and explained to himself that he would be all right if he just slept on the mattress.

It took me at least two hours to settle down enough to go to sleep. My sides and face ached with the effort to keep from laughing out loud.

The next morning neither of us mentioned the incident. In the daylight, Jason quickly discovered that he had only one sheet. He got another sheet from the shelf and made his bed properly, apparently without realizing that I had been aware of the whole affair. It never crossed his mind that I could have been responsible for his problem. I felt a little guilty about taking advantage of him, but it was still one of the funniest things I've ever seen. After thinking about it for a little while, I felt sorry for the big hulk and decided not to play any more tricks on him.

Unfortunately, the tricks did not stop. Other people played tricks on him without my knowledge. One night he got ready for bed unusually early. I wondered if he had tricked me and was going to play possum as I had done. Surreptitiously I checked my bed. Everything was okay so I sat down at my desk to write letters to Carolyn and Mama.

That night Jason said his prayers very quietly as though he wanted to make sure that no one other than God heard him. Suddenly I realized just how miserable and desperate he felt. Nothing had gone right for him since he had come to college. Instead of being accepted as a person, he had been pushed around, shoved out of his room and company, and made the victim of all sorts of pranks. Although he was physically big, in many ways he still had the helpless innocence of a child.

As he slid under his covers, he stopped and made a surprised sound as his feet went down to the bottom of the bed.

Looking up from my writing, I saw that he was stretched out full length. Certain that he had not been short-sheeted again, I asked him what was wrong. There was nothing obviously wrong with his bed.

While answering, "Somebody has been messing with my bed again
.... this time they have put a Coke bottle in it!" he was fumbling
under the covers trying to get the bottle. When he got his hands
on it, he pulled it out from under the covers. That was a bad mistake. As the bottle was being pulled out, we heard a distinct pop-
ping sound followed by a gurgling sound. Water poured all over
everything. I did not believe that one Coke bottle could hold enough
water to wet his pajamas, sheets, blankets, and the floor, but I was
watching it happen. This was worse than having a cow kick over
a milk bucket.

Somebody had filled a Coke bottle with water, put a string
through a cork, put the cork in the bottle, and tied the end of the
string around the bottom of the bed. The bottle had been placed
under the covers near the foot of the bed. The string was long enough
that the cork would not pop out until the bottle was pulled about
halfway up the bed. This would make the water pour out on the
victim's pajamas and bed to give the impression that he had wet
himself and the bed. For a jock, this would have been funny; for
Jason, it was a tragedy.

Shocked by the cold water, embarrassed at the obvious implica-
tions, aware of his inability to explain them satisfactorily should
his tormentors appear, and hurt at still another indication that he
was not a part of the crowd, Jason got quietly out of bed. With
an air of resignation, he changed his pajamas.

With a sensation akin to a hard blow to the chest, I watched the
last spark of hope and fight die in Jason's eyes. As I helped him
remake his bed with dry sheets, I told Jason that I was sorry about
the incident because I really was sorry.

He sat quietly on the edge of the freshly made bed for a little
while. The air in the room seemed to grow heavy with his misery.
I stood beside him, wondering what to do. Finally he blurted out
in a voice distorted by despair, "Maybe I just ought to pull out
and go home!"

Tricks and pranks were okay, but there was something very wrong
about destroying a young man's spirit. I knew what happened when
you broke the spirit of an animal .... I just couldn't let that happen to Jason. He could aggravate the life out of a saint sometimes
with his dumb questions and his incessant talking, but he was still
a human being. With all the persuasion I could muster, I fought
to convince Jason that he could make it and that things would get
better if he would just stick with it a little while longer.

Finally he said that he would think about it and pray about it before he made a decision.

I knew that whoever had rigged up the bottle would ask me about it because that would be the only way to find out Jason's reaction. I told Jason this and promised him that when I found out who had done it, I would see that the guilty party at least got his a-- whupped and that if possible, we would do something spectacular to get even. I took great pains to caution Jason not to mention one word about the incident to anybody. He was just to wait as patiently as he could while I played detective.

Well, it took three days, but I solved the mystery. A smart alecky freshman who lived down the hall was the perpetrator. He made the mistake of asking James, my upperclassman, if I had mentioned Jason and the water bottle. James promptly reported the question to me because he felt sorry for Jason and because Jason was my roommate. He knew me well enough to know that I would be looking for vengeance and he was more than willing to help me get it.

After a brief discussion, James agreed to help us cool the offensive gentleman down. This involved grabbing him, fully dressed, when he came in from class and holding him under a cold shower until we were convinced that his passion for playing tricks had been sufficiently cooled. This would require four people. It didn't take us long to recruit another freshman to help us.

When Sir Smart Aleck came in from his last class of the day, we were stripped down to our skivvies and waiting for him. We rushed him and before he knew what was happening, James and I grabbed his legs while Jason and the other freshman grabbed his arms. When we dragged him to the showers, he was still fully dressed in his uniform including his cap. By the time we let him go, he was thoroughly soaked, freezing cold, and as mad as a dozen wet hens.

Jason's parting shot as we released him was, "Now the next time you want somebody's bed wet, go piss in it yourself!"

Everybody cheered and Jason began to laugh. By the time we got back to our room, dried off, changed our wet drawers and hung them up to dry, Jason's eyes were sparkling. He grabbed me in a big bear hug and I thought for a minute that he was going to squeeze me to death.

When he turned me loose, he said fervently, "You know, if it hadn't been for you, I probably would have just given up and gone on back home, but now there ain't nobody on this campus big enough to run me off. I know it's a sin to get revenge, but I think the Lord will forgive me this one time."

He reared back, beat on his chest Tarzan-style, and hollered, "By God, let 'em come on—I think I can take care of myself!"

After a minute, he looked over at me and said, "Well, I can take care of myself if you will be my detective."

I agreed to be his detective on one condition—that he not squeeze me so hard the next time. I put on a big show of thinking that my ribs were broken. Poor Jason! He took me seriously and got very upset. When he came over, patted me softly on the shoulder, and apologized for hurting me, I jumped up, popped him a good lick to the shoulder and burst out laughing before I bellowed, "Give 'em h---, rat!"

Jason turned out to be a pretty good old lady. He wasn't perfect, but neither was I nor anybody else. In spite of everything that had happened, we both knew that we would never be totally alone again and that we could handle whatever and whoever came along.

Nearly everybody on the campus seemed to be smoking cigarettes. When I was at home, I never even considered smoking. Home was a whole different world where there were no drills, no hazing, no marching, no Jason, and no homesickness. It didn't take much to persuade me to try a cigarette just to make me feel better. I remembered that my daddy had asked me to promise him only one thing before he brought me to Clemson—that I would not smoke. I had never broken a promise to him nor to anybody else. I was learning that homesickness, loneliness, and misery play mind games with you. I became convinced that smoking would improve my feelings and that I could handle the explanations one way or another.

That first cigarette tasted terrible. My throat and lungs burned, I choked, my head spun like a yo-yo, and my stomach seemed determined to dispose of my supper. Unfortunately the symptoms were very short-lived and then I felt calm and very grown up. I smoked two cigarettes that first night, three the second night, and suddenly I was a smoker.

My promise to my daddy kept gnawing at me. Finally I sat down and wrote him a long sad letter. I listed all of my trials and tribulations: we were treated like prisoners; I was homesick; I missed my family and my friends; drilling was worse than working in the fields; hazing was terrible; etc. The list was really pathetic. Finally I got around to explaining that I had started to smoke—very lightly!—

as a sedative. The letter ended with a promise to explain further when I got home—if I ever got there again. It's a good thing Papa knew a lot about boys or he would probably have brought a squad of commandos to rescue me.

Jason and the cigarettes helped a little, but they did not solve my problems. I was still pretty miserable. Thoughts of home and visions of going A. W. O. L. haunted me. Finally I went back for another talk with Sgt. Covington. This time he suggested that I try out for the freshman drill team. He had the task of observing the men in our company and making notes on their progress in learning and executing the commands. He would recommend forty men from our company who would try out for the drill team. His little black book indicated that there were only three guys in the company who were better than I was.

The Clemson Drill Team consistently won first place in competitions with other college drill teams. They performed at football games, parades, and special occasions all over the country and were considered to be the most unique drill team in America. To be a part of something that good would really be an accomplishment. Sgt. Covington warned me that the competition would be stiff, that there would be a lot of extra drilling involved, and that I would have to learn a lot of new commands and fancy routines. Well, I never had been one to back down in the face of competition nor hard work. Figuring that anything would be better than sitting around being miserable, I told him to go ahead and turn in my name.

The next Monday afternoon Captain Ruff drilled the whole company for two hours and then dismissed everyone except the forty people Sgt. Covington had recommended. He explained how the process of elimination worked in selecting the members of the drill team and warned us that we would be required to do a lot of extra work. Then he told us that drill team members received a number of privileges not granted to the rest of the student body. With the explanations completed, we got down to work. The next two hours were spent learning the new commands. We had to be able to execute those commands as smoothly as a well-oiled and beautifully designed piece of machinery.

For the next two weeks, we drilled until we were ready to drop. I began to wonder whether practice was going to make me perfect or kill me. When we weren't drilling for practice, we were drilling in competition. First there was competition within the company, then the battalion, then the regiment, and finally the brigade. Those who survived all the levels of elimination would become the freshman drill team. The list would be posted the week before the Carolina-Clemson game. My weary blistered feet were glad when all the competition was over. I had made it all the way up to brigade level. Waiting for the list to come out wasn't easy, but it surely did beat all that extra drilling.

Our first leaves would be issued for the last weekend of the South Carolina State Fair which was traditionally scheduled for the last week in October. The Clemson Tigers and The Carolina Gamecocks would play their annual football game and it seemed that everybody in the whole state took sides. By this time, I didn't give a hoot about football nor anything else that had to do with college. I just wanted to go home.

One of the requirements for getting a leave was that your hair be long enough to hold a part. As mine grew back in, I plastered it down in a part with Octagon soap to be sure that everybody could see that it was parted. I was going to move heaven and earth if that became necessary to get home.

The traditional transportation for cadets in those days was to hitch-hike. Catching a ride was pretty easy because most drivers were willing to pick up cadets in uniform. Like everything else, Clemson had its rules for hitch-hiking. These were unwritten, but, brother, they were observed. My upperclassmen taught me the ins and outs and emphasized that neither rank nor class standing entitled anybody to step in front of another cadet trying to hitch a ride. Once we stepped off that campus, rat rules, seniority, rank, and all that other foolishness was dropped and our human rights were restored.

Excitement mounted as Fair Week approached. The novelty of hazing had worn off and we no longer had to square corners and all of that other idiocy. We had learned what was expected of us and how to do it. Life had settled into a tolerable routine.

The only times we were permitted to be out of uniform were during labs when we wore scroungy civilian clothes and at bedtime when we wore pajamas. Just before Fair Week, I was hurrying from the laboratory to the barracks to change into my uniform for drill. As I passed the Administration Building, I met Major Dumas. He was a regular army officer and one of the most hated men on campus. I saluted him and was saluted in return. At that moment, another freshman in lab clothes came running around the corner of the building. He neither slowed down nor saluted. Major Dumas erupted with a roar, "Come back here, you G-- d----- rat!"

The startled cadet stopped, turned around, and asked, "Do you mean me?"

#*% yes, I meant you! Why in the #*% didn't you salute me? You met me head on!"

The cadet explained that he did not realize that he was supposed to salute when he was wearing civilian clothes.

That just enraged the major further. He was rude, crude, and totally unreasonable even when he was in a good mood. When he was mad, he was terrible. Still at full volume, he hollered, "I don't give a #%* *#% if you are wearing your pajamas or your birthday suit, you had better salute me any time you meet me! Do you understand that?"

The freshman's apology was ignored as Major Dumas pulled out his little black book and bellowed, "Come here and give me your name, your company, and your captain's name! I am giving you fifteen demerits and putting you on probation. If you get another fifteen demerits within the next six weeks, you will be brought before the review board. If they so rule, you can be shipped out!"

I have never forgotten the incident nor the effect it had on me. Major Dumas convinced me that an authority figure is much more impressive when he conducts himself like a gentleman than when he roars and threatens like a beast from the jungle.

Finally the list of men who had made the freshman drill team was posted. I was one of the four from my company who had made the team. Before I could decide whether to be happy that I had made it or to regret all the extra drilling that would be necessary, I walked back to the barracks. The whole crew seemed to be waiting for me. I knew I was in trouble the minute I saw that they were all stripped down to their drawers. Before the door closed behind me, they had grabbed me and were dragging me toward the showers. Those clowns nearly drowned me as well as my uniform before they decided that I was sufficiently cooled off! For retaliation or celebration, the showers were the cadet's ultimate weapon. If I had to have an unplanned shower, I was glad that it was in celebration. If those guys had been mad, I might not have lived to tell about it.

Final inspection was on Thursday night. As soon as I knew that I had passed it, I packed my suitcase and got ready to go. I could snatch my suitcase and run for the Greenville Highway as soon as I got out of classes Friday morning. Man, this leave had been a long time coming.

CHAPTER 7

When my last class ended at eleven o'clock Friday morning, I did my best imitation of greased lightning getting to my room, putting away my books, grabbing my suitcase, and getting out to the Greenville Highway. This was one day that I was not even interested in food. Skipping lunch was a small price to pay for a head start in the hitch-hiking line.

There weren't many guys in front of me and they were being picked up pretty fast. In less than thirty minutes I was in the car with a middle-aged couple from Atlanta. I felt a little uneasy about riding with strangers, but it was a far better option than waiting for the bus.

The Browns were nice people and we had a pleasant trip. I wanted to holler, "Hooray and Hallelujah!" when they said that they were on the way to Charlotte. Since they would go right through Greenville, I wouldn't have to lose time trying to catch another ride.

They asked a lot of questions about my experiences at Clemson. I was too excited about getting home to do much talking, but I answered their questions politely. They had heard a lot of stories about how tough Clemson was. I was tempted to tell them some tales that would prove the point. After I thought about it for a little while, I decided that it would be wiser not to distract him from his driving by telling horror stories. Things that might slow him down were to be avoided as carefully as we avoided dropping rifles. I conceded that things got rough occasionally and then turned the conversation to being excited about getting home. I was very careful to mention that if I got to my father's dairy headquarters in Greenville before two o'clock, I could catch a ride out to the farm on one of the dairy trucks. Mr. Brown sensed how much I wanted to catch that truck and speeded up a little bit.

When we pulled up in front of the dairy headquarters, I could hardly breathe. Now I could dare to believe that I was really going to get home. I thanked the Browns for their kindness and sprinted into the garage. Man, that was the prettiest milk truck I ever saw! In just a minute we were on the way to the farm and I was happier than a cow in fresh clover.

After hugs from Mama and my sisters and handshakes and slaps on the back from my brothers, my daddy and I sat down under the chinaberry tree in the back yard. We talked about all sorts of things. "Mr. Charlie" shook me up by asking if I had a cigarette. I had dreaded having to deal with that subject. Feeling guilty and very uncomfortable, I fumbled in my pocket and slowly handed him my pack of cigarettes. I wondered if I were going to need the running room that surrounded me. "Mr. Charlie" did not think kindly of broken promises. He believed that a man should be as good as his word. Finally he broke the tension by telling me that he was very proud of me for being man enough to write and tell him about my smoking. He knew how hard it had been for me to tell him the truth and he made it quite clear that he understood the situation. He took out a cigarette, lit it, and gave the pack back to me. In that instant, I knew that, as far as he was concerned, I had achieved manhood.

After a few more minutes of conversation, I went to look for my big brother, Bly. Carolyn would be expecting me about dark and I needed to borrow his car. He had anticipated the request and filled the car with gas that morning. He hassled me a little while and then grinned and gave me the keys.

With that settled, I could go up to the kitchen to visit with Mama while she cooked supper. I wanted to get out of that uniform and be John Riddle, family member, rather than a Clemson cadet. Oops! Eating all those potatoes had put some weight on me. Not one pair of my dress pants fitted. I sat there in the kitchen, looking like a bellhop, while Mama and I talked. She knew absolutely nothing about college, but if it concerned me, she wanted to hear about it. I didn't want her to worry so I fixed up my stories enough that she wouldn't guess how hard things had been for me. We never could fool Mama completely, but we could hide some of the more gruesome details of our experiences.

After an hour or so, my brothers called me to come down to the dairy barn. It was milking time and there was no way I was going to get out of helping them. I shucked off that uniform and slid into a pair of overalls and old shoes as I hurried out to the barn.

As soon as I walked through the barn door, I stopped as suddenly as though a big hand had grabbed me by the straps of my overalls. Nothing looked right. The cows were there, and the familiar dairy barn smells were there, and my brothers were there, but every-

thing else had changed radically. Papa had installed electric milking machines while I was gone. After I had milked at least ten
thousand cows by hand, he installed milking machines as soon as
I left! Well, I was going to ask him about that. My brothers teased
me a little and then I went to find Papa.

In a joking tone that hid my feeling that he had done me wrong,
I asked him why he had waited until I left to put in the new equipment. His answer left me speechless.

"Son, when I lost you, I lost one of the best milk hands I've ever
had. I had to do something to keep up with the work."

He broke the silence by asking if I were going off that night. When
I told him that I was going to see Carolyn, he supposed that I would
need a little spending money. I agreed with him and reminded him
that I surely hadn't had enough to hurt anybody in the last two
months. He rummaged around in his pockets and finally pulled out
two five dollar bills. Wow! That was serious money. I thanked him
jubilantly and ran back up to the house to change clothes and to
eat supper.

Mama and the girls had cooked a wonderful meal. I ate my full
share, but I didn't waste any time. Impatience to see Carolyn was
pulling me like a big electro-magnet pulls iron filings. As soon as
I dared, I told them how much I had enjoyed my supper, excused
myself from the table, and lit out for Carr's Creek. Carolyn was
watching for me. She opened the door almost before I finished
knocking. When I saw those shining eyes and wide open arms, I
would have been perfectly content just to stand there and hug her
for the rest of the evening. That kind of "carrying on" was not
allowed. A quick hug was all that we dared to share before we went
back to the kitchen to see "Mr. Paul" and "Miss Jennie." That
hug was much briefer than either of us had planned...those dad-
blamed brass buttons on my uniform produced an instant ricochet
and bruised ribs!

That evening was like so many others that we would share over
the next fifty years. We sat around the kitchen table and talked as
we devoured one of Miss Jennie's special cakes and a pot of coffee.
We discussed my life at Clemson, Mr. Paul's experiences as a cadet
twenty years earlier, Carolyn's adventures as a day student at Furman, and the happenings of the community. It was heavenly to be
a guest of honor instead of a rat!

I really worked to give the impression that all I did at Clemson was strut around in that fancy uniform and attend classes. They never suspected how much I had struggled nor how miserable I had been.

Finally Carolyn and I excused ourselves to go up to the living room. We held hands and talked about everything and nothing. Just being together was enough to make me believe in heaven. Ten-thirty curfew arrived all too soon. We made plans to attend a movie Saturday night, shared a careful kiss—those buttons were impossible!—and I went back to the farm.

I parked Bly's car carefully and tiptoed into the house. There was no such thing as slipping past Mama's bedroom without being noticed. You would be much more likely to slip past the Secret Service Detail at The White House! Mama always heard each of us come into the house. No matter how late it was nor how quiet we were, she recognized each of us by our footsteps. As I got even with her bedroom door, her light came on, and she called, "John, come in and talk to me for a minute."

I sat down beside her bed and we talked quietly for at least an hour. She wanted to know everything that happened at Clemson. I answered her questions about all sorts of things from the numeral "one" pinned on my shirt collar through Jason, homework, classwork, drill, food, and homesickness. I admitted that I had been terribly homesick. We agreed that she could not even imagine what it was like. Never in her life had she been away from everybody and everything she loved for six endless weeks. We discussed my plans to complete two years at Clemson and then to go on to Iowa State or to Auburn for my degree in veterinary medicine.

We also discussed the shortness of breath that bedeviled her occasionally. Although she put on a good show about how unimportant it was, she didn't fool me. Realizing the harshness of her life stung me worse than any paddle at Clemson. Her life was harder than mine would ever be.

As usual, Daddy slept through the whole conversation. He went to bed to sleep—not to listen for boys coming in at all hours of the night. She held on to my hand as though she wanted to keep me beside her. We talked about things at home and in the community until both of us began to nod. At last, we said goodnight and I tiptoed upstairs.

I surely was glad to find an empty bed. It was great to go to sleep without "Taps" and to look forward to waking up without "Reveille."

At three a.m. the dairymen got up to start their day. I declined their invitation to join them. With a stern request that they turn off the lights and leave quietly, I turned over to enjoy a good snooze.

At exactly six o'clock I waked up and lay there listening for that cussed bugler to blast forth with "Reveille." When I realized where I was, I turned right back over and went back to sleep. The smells of country ham and sausage rising from the kitchen waked me the next time. I was out of bed, dressed, and downstairs before you could say, "Scat!"

After a good breakfast—without potatoes!—I spent the morning riding around the farm and the community with Papa. After lunch, I took a nap.

Later in the afternoon, I challenged one of my brothers to a shooting match. We went down to the river and shot at snakes, turtles, frogs, and nearly everything else that moved.

Mama and my sisters cooked a real company supper for me. Good food and good family fun were things I had missed and I enjoyed every bit of it. As we were finishing our meal, I asked Bly what he had done with the photograph of me with my head clipped bald. He laughed and said that he had given it to Carolyn. I knew that he was teasing because I had already asked Carolyn about it. After some spirited discussion, he confessed that he still had it. Since I was going to use his car, I couldn't drive a very hard bargain. We finally agreed that he would give the picture to me on the condition that I show it to Carolyn that night. The family had a grand time guessing what Carolyn would say and do when she saw it.

Finally supper was over and I was on my way to Carr's Creek and Carolyn. This time she respected those blasted buttons! A flanking approach was a lot safer than a frontal one. This time I got a real hug instead of a ricochet. After a quick visit with her parents, we were on the way to the movie. I showed her that miserable picture and she was horrified that her sweetheart had been treated so badly. Enjoying her sympathy, I assured her that she could never imagine all the awful things that I had endured. Before she got too upset, I warned her that the bad guys had made me a mean man. With the proper emphasis on "man," I sounded like a real tough guy. She seemed very impressed and convinced that I could take care of myself.

After the movie, we went back to her house. I stayed a little later since it was Saturday night. We agreed that we would sit with our parents at church the next morning so that people wouldn't talk. I would visit with her for a little while after lunch and then go back to Clemson. With that out of the way, we talked about her experiences as a day student. I gave her a hard time about all the adventures she was missing by not living on campus. After seeing that picture of my bald head, she was just as happy to remain a day student.

We had a friendly debate about whether Furman or Clemson would win the Thanksgiving football game. I assured her that Clemson would stomp Furman real good, but she was just as convinced as ever that Furman would do the stomping.

I hated to leave her that night and the next afternoon was even worse. Standing there on the porch, she looked mighty pretty and I knew perfectly well that the guys at Furman weren't blind. Well, life's hard sometimes. I had to leave her and I still had to find a way to get back to Clemson.

My brother Joe had just bought a new Plymouth. I thought he and his girl would drive me back to school. Joe had made special plans that did not include going to Clemson and he wouldn't even consider changing them.

Finally I talked one of my brothers into driving me to the bus station. For sixty cents I could ride on the Greyhound bus from Greenville to Clemson and get there well before our eight o'clock deadline. I still had some money left from the ten dollars my daddy had given me plus the money that Mama had slipped into my pocket. Goodbyes were quick because everybody seemed to have plans for Sunday night. Before I knew it, I was on the bus and on the way back to college.

CHAPTER 8

The bus ride was short and uneventful. By the time I had finished a quick nap, we were pulling into Clemson. By six p.m. I was back in my room and ready to take on the world.

Most of the other cadets seemed to have gotten a new lease on life during the weekend, too. Like me, they were ready to get on with the program.

I might not have been so enthusiastic if I had known what was coming. I knew that we were going to start practicing for the drill team. Even though that meant extra hours of drill, I didn't mind at all. Practicing the intricate routines or watching the senior drill team was a thrill. It bothered me a little to know that I wasn't going to be on the senior drill team because I would be going to another school by then. I decided to keep that information to myself so that I could at least be on the drill team for two years. A major advantage of being on the drill team was that we got a few extra weekend leaves. Those were worth the extra drills any time.

The other new adventure wasn't nearly as much fun as drill team practice. About the time we thought we had the basic drill routines mastered, we were ordered to show up on the drill field dressed in old clothes. Not one item of our uniforms was to be worn. There was no explanation of what we would be doing, but you could bet it would be rough and dirty—that was the only possible explanation for having us out of uniform.

Having learned that Clemson surprises usually weren't pleasant, I wondered what sort of misery they had conjured up this time. Maybe we were all going to engage in hand to hand combat or participate in a huge wrestling match. Nobody would give us any clues, so we just showed up on the drill field as ordered.

As soon as we formed up into squads, we were marched at a brisk pace down a dirt road. Good golly, Miss Molly! The obstacle course! Now that obstacle course was a man-eater if there ever was one. My heart sank as I listened to the instructions. There were bars, logs, water hazards, and barbed wire fences to jump; fences to crawl through on your belly and fences to climb over; logs and low

52

branches to crawl under; and all sorts of other ungodly obstacles to surmount. The worst thing of all was the wall. We would be given special instructions when we reached it.

Jumping the bars and crawling under fences wasn't too bad. Growing up on the farm had given me lots of practice at both activities. When I reached the wall, I knew that I had to quit playing and get serious.

That wall was twelve feet high and constructed of butted timbers so that there was nothing you could get a hand or foothold on. There were four ropes which hung down four feet from the top. The instructor explained that we were to stand back about fifty feet, run up to the wall at full speed, jump up, grab one of the ropes and pull ourselves over the wall. How in tarnation was I supposed to reach up that extra twenty-seven and a half inches? I was still trying to figure out the answer to that when I heard my name being called. This was really my lucky day—I was going to be one of the first to try to get over the wall! With a little more of this kind of luck, life could get really grubby.

Well, I had never run away from a challenge and I wasn't going to start now. I backed off, ran toward the wall at full speed, and collided with it. I had misjudged the point at which I was supposed to jump for the rope. At least I learned one thing—that wall was solidly constructed. I was a little wobbly when I stood up and I felt like a fool, but otherwise, I was okay.

An upperclassman demonstrated the proper way to run up to the wall, jump, run up the face of the wall, and grab the rope. When he came down the other side, he walked up to me and announced that if I didn't make it this time, he would paddle my b--- with the four foot paddle he had stashed behind a tree.

Maybe it was desperation...or maybe his demonstration was extra good...but somehow I managed to scramble up to the rope and pull myself up and over the wall. The law of gravity made it easy to get down the other side even though it didn't provide any protection against breaking your neck in the process.

After the wall there was a full mile jam-packed with challenges. To get through them, I crawled, ran, climbed, and used muscles I didn't know I had. I was hot, sweaty, dirty, and very tired by the time I finally reached the end. Then I had to wait for the rest of the company to catch up since I was one of the first cadets to reach the end of the course.

Being optimistic, we figured that we would just walk or drag our weary bodies back up the road to the drill field. Wrong! This was Clemson and Clemson was building men. As soon as the last straggler stumbled up to us, the captain ordered, "Fall in and count off!"

The next two orders were, "Right face! Double time march!"

We double-timed all the way back to the drill field. Finally, we halted on the field and stood in formation while somebody read the list of those who had made it over the wall and satisfactorily completed the course. Twenty-five of us had made the list. Finally we were dismissed to stagger back to our rooms and fall into bed.

Everybody whose name was not on the list had to go back and run the course every day until he completed it satisfactorily. The whole company ran the obstacle course once a week until time for end of semester exams. If there were a vote to determine the most hated thing at Clemson, that obstacle course would win for sure. Nothing else would even get close.

Gradually we were permitted to do a few things just for fun. The Y.M.C.A. had a huge swimming pool, a game room, and pool tables. There was a movie theater in town. My favorite athletic events were the boxing matches. When I was invited to join the boxing team, I declined. There were enough things to fight without looking for battles.

I continued to enjoy watching the matches. Occasionally there would be a free-for-all before the regular matches. About twenty young black guys would climb into the ring to compete for the $10.00 or $20.00 prize awarded to the last man left standing in the ring. When the starting bell rang, the melee began. A few of the contestants would jump out of the ring as soon as they were hit once or twice. About fifteen of the guys would get into a real slugging festival. When each one decided that he had had all the licks he could take, he would climb out of the ring. Gradually the numbers would decline until there were only three left inside the ropes. Usually two of those would gang up on the third man and eliminate him fairly quickly. Then the real fight started. Sooner of later, one of them would give up and the other would get the money. Those events were often hilarious although no script writer would dare to write such a scene today.

Finally, Thanksgiving came and with it the long-awaited Clemson-Furman football game. Carolyn and her parents were coming up for the game. Now we would see who stomped whom!

The day of the game dawned grey and bitterly cold. Then the
snow started. After all those weeks of looking forward to a perfect
football afternoon with Carolyn, it just couldn't snow. Oh, but at
Clemson it could. It snowed like the dickens. We had planned to
meet down at the Y about thirty minutes before game time and to
walk down to the stadium. I was there fifteen minutes early, but
there was no sign of the Carrs. The snow came down harder and
harder and the wind whistled around the buildings as I buttoned
my mackinaw up to my neck and paced back and forth.

I could hear the noise from the stadium and most of the play-
by-play on the p.a. system. By the end of the first quarter Clemson
was leading and I was frantic. It just wasn't like the Carrs to stand
me up. My imagination worked overtime creating horrible accidents.
As the second quarter began, I walked on down to the stadium to
squirm and shiver and worry. Even though Clemson won the game,
it was a miserable afternoon for me.

After the game I caught a ride to Greenville. One of my brothers
picked me up and drove me out to the farm. As soon as I could
decently get away, I borrowed Bly's car and drove—or slid—over
to Carr's Creek. Carolyn was as upset as I was. The snow had made
them late getting to Clemson. They had apparently gotten to the
Y about two minutes after I had left. Since I had their tickets in
my pocket, they had listened to the game on the car radio. They
had been as worried about me as I had been about them. After apol-
ogies and explanations all around, we enjoyed cake and coffee with
Mr. Paul and Miss Jennie. Finally we could go up to the parlor
for a few minutes alone. That was the first time I had been really
warm all day. I was so glad that Carolyn was still in one piece, I
couldn't even tease her much about Furman's loss to the mighty
Tigers!

Before we knew it, 10:30 had arrived and I had to leave. The
rest of the weekend was very much like the State Fair Weekend had
been. Mama had delayed her big Thanksgiving meal until I could
enjoy it with them. That was a feed. If it could be grown in the
garden, Mama had grown it, preserved it, and fixed it for dinner.
I felt like a toad with a belly full of buckshot by the time I left the
table. Days were spent with the family and evenings were spent with
Carolyn.

All too soon, it was Sunday evening and I was back at school
and settling back into the routine. Jason had gotten the hang of

college life and was getting along pretty well. He could still be exasperating at times, but all in all, he was a pretty good old lady.

We wore our mackinaws to ward off the cold except during drill. To see how tough we were getting, we were frequently drilled in shirt sleeves in frigid weather. As long as we were marching briskly, we didn't feel the cold. As soon as we stood still for a minute or two, we looked like leaves in a whirlwind. The officers didn't like cold weather drills any better than we did. That contributed strongly to short or cancelled drills. We relished the extra free time and used it to study or to goof off a little bit.

At night when the heat was turned off, I really appreciated the wool Chatham blanket that Mama had splurged to buy for me at J. C. Penney's in Greenville. I had been horrified when she spent twelve dollars for one blanket for me to take to Clemson. She had made a wise choice, though. That blanket kept me warm through two years at Clemson, four years at Auburn, and still keeps me warm today. We have had it rebound a time or two and I still have it on my bed. After nearly fifty years, it remains a cherished reminder of my mother's love. Sometimes I wonder which will give out first—me or the blanket. In any case, we will be together as long as both of us survive.

Except for occasional rat calls when all the freshmen had to line up in the halls for a rat inspection, the upperclassmen had accepted us as a part of the student body. Hazing was rare and mild. One night just after the Thanksgiving holidays, we had a rat call. For the first time in months, the lieutenant ordered me to assume the position. What was this all about? Capt. Ruff and the company officers had promised never to hit me again and I certainly hadn't done anything to deserve any licks.

In response to the question as to which weapon I preferred, I gave the traditional response, "At your pleasure, sir."

As I bent over, I heard Capt. Ruff whisper, "This is the rat we beat the h--- out of and he just laughed and called us sissies!"

The lieutenant's arm dropped to his side as he whispered, "You hit him."

Capt. Ruff replied, "I'm not about to hit him. Let's just admit that we've got the wrong rat."

The lieutenant agreed and Capt. Ruff ordered me back into formation. I have always believed that they didn't hit me because they figured that I would embarrass them again.

After rat call ended, Capt. Ruff called me to his office. He and three lieutenants were waiting for me. One of them said, "Rat Riddle, you almost got your a-- beat tonight!"

Somebody else said, "We didn't recognize you at first. Those hall lights are getting dimmer by the day."

I laughed it off and assured them that I had not forgotten their promise.

That night the rats got together and decided to take Capt. Ruff to the pool at the Y the next afternoon and cool him off a little. Right after lunch, we grabbed him strutting into the barracks in his dress uniform. He yelled, struggled, kicked, promised never to make another rat call, and did everything he could think of to save himself, but it was no use. The rats were under the wheel and we were going to drive this time. We threw him into the pool and cooled him off so thoroughly that he mellowed out unbelievably. He began to come around at night to check on us and to see if there was anything he could do for us. At times he would even sit down and chat with us in our rooms. That was very unusual behavior for a company commander. Eventually he became known as "Mother Ruff!" As a company we worked hard and made him look good. He reciprocated by being nice to us and even praising us occasionally. That didn't happen very often at Clemson in the 1930's.

Jason went home that weekend. I planned to enjoy my private room while he was gone. Shortly after long roll on Friday night, I got terribly sick. Somehow I stumbled into the latrine. Vomiting and diarrhea made me so weak I was sure I was dying. Well, I wasn't going to be found dead in the latrine! Summoning every ounce of strength and will, I made it back to my bunk. I didn't stop in anybody's room nor call anybody because I knew that being caught out of your room after long roll was a serious offense.

I was doubled up with pain and writhing in my bunk, waiting to die, when Sgt. Covington stuck his head in the door. One glance convinced him that something was badly wrong. Approaching my bunk, he asked quietly, "Are you sick or what?"

I blurted out that I was dying. As he felt my forehead, he said, "Boy, you look bad. You're as white as that sheet. We need to get something done for you in a hurry. You stay right where you are and I'll be back shortly."

He called the infirmary. I don't know what he told them, but they told him to get me over there on the double.

When he came back into my room, he was followed by two husky orderlies with a stretcher. As they set the stretcher down, the sergeant told me that they were going to take me to the infirmary. He helped me to get clean pajamas and a towel before he ordered me to lie down on the stretcher and not to get off until the doctor said to get off.

I thought those orderlies were going to have to be mighty strong to carry me the half mile to the infirmary. They were gasping for breath by the time they got out of the building. By the time they got to the top of the steps at the end of the quadrangle, they were completely winded. One of them asked if they could set me down for a minute to rest.

I wasn't used to being carried so I offered to walk. They refused my offer saying that they had been ordered not to let me get up. After a brief pause, they picked up the stretcher and struggled onward. About half way to the infirmary they asked if I could possibly walk just a little way. I walked all the way to the walkway leading into the infirmary. Then I got back on the stretcher so that they wouldn't get into trouble for violating their orders.

Dr. Milford dismissed them after they had helped me to get onto the examining table. As he checked me over, he asked a lot of questions. Finally he told me that he thought I had a very severe type of food poisoning called botulism. He was going to give me a shot to ease my pain and keep me in the infirmary for a few days. I was too sick to care what he did as long as he eased my pain.

Dr. Milford and a nurse got me into one of those gosh-awful hospital gowns and put me to bed. As sick as I was, I was glad my brothers couldn't see me in that rig. After they gave me a shot of painkiller and started intravenous fluids, I fell into a troubled sleep. At eight o'clock the next morning, Sgt. Covington made the first of his twice daily trips to check on me. He assured me that it was okay for me to stay in the infirmary and that I was not to worry about anything but getting well. I was surprised to find out that Dr. Milford had told him that they had almost lost me the previous night. I had been in shock when I arrived at the infirmary.

The infirmary staff ignored all the military rigmarole and just gave me the best possible care for the next four days. They gave me enough shots to cure everything that could possibly infect me for the next four years. I didn't want my folks to know that I was sick because they would worry about me. When I was dismissed,

Dr. Milford gave me a letter for Capt. Ruff. I had a hard time walking back to my room—I had never been so weak in my life.

Shortly after I got into my bunk, Sgt. Covington appeared. He told me that Dr. Milford's letter had excused me from all drills for two weeks and that I was to attend classes only when I felt like it. God bless Sgt. Covington. He was a great guy.

I stumbled through the days until the Christmas holidays gradually regaining my strength. Knowing that there would probably be at least a thousand cadets in the hitch-hiking line, I arranged for one of my brothers to pick me up after my last class before the holidays.

Holiday fever was sweeping the campus. It showed up everywhere. All of us were counting the hours until we could go home. I was as excited about climbing into Bly's car to go home as I had been about coming to Clemson. At least the surprises at home would be happy ones. I still had some scars from some of my Clemson surprises.

CHAPTER 9

Spending the Christmas holidays at home was almost like going to heaven. I could sleep as late as I pleased, I didn't have to listen to a single note from a bugle, there was nobody to salute and no orders to obey, no drill nor obstacle course to conquer, no uniform to wear, and best of all, I was a big man at home and in the community because I was going to college. My bout with botulism had trimmed me down enough to fit into both of my suits and all three pairs of my dress pants. I could traipse around like a gentleman farmer instead of being restricted to wearing either my uniform or my overalls. For two and a half weeks I managed to stay too dressed up to help with the milking or anything else on the farm. Amazingly, my family let me get by with it. Perhaps I was still a bit puny or something, but I wasn't going to look this kind of gift horse in the mouth.

Just once during the holidays I put on my uniform and attended a party for some high school boys who were thinking about going to Clemson. As guest of honor, I was asked to tell them about the wonders of college life. I played the game to the hilt—strutting around in my uniform, I made college life sound like a great adventure full of fun and glamor. Since nobody had prepared me for the harsh side and I had survived, I figured that these guys could handle a few surprises, too. I did emphasize that they should enjoy the advantages of being seniors because going to Clemson could be like diving into cold deep water.

They were so excited about the glamorous aspects, the warning didn't even register. I regaled them with some well-doctored tales that fanned their college fever before I left to visit an old flame.

Mary and I had dated a few times in high school. She had seemed to think that I was pretty impressive. Since I was dressed up anyway and the evening was still young, I decided to surprise Mary by dropping in on her. She may have been a little bit surprised herself, but she sure surprised the heck out of me. Instead of giving me a hug, she stepped back quickly and said, "Well for heaven's sakes, it's John Riddle! Come on in, John, and meet my husband."

61

Whoa! That line wasn't supposed to be in the script. Thinking fast, I said something about having come by to meet her husband and to wish them well in their marriage. This seemed to please her and to get me off the hook. Still feeling a little awkward, we went in to meet Tom.

Well, Tom was certainly nobody's prize catch. He was a meek, scrawny little guy who looked like he was scared half to death. He acknowledged the introductions and then sat there like a wart on a frog while we talked about all that had happened since graduation. When Mary started describing their wedding, I realized that she was winding up for a full length replay. I conveniently "remembered" that I was late for my date and made a hurried departure. So much for that romance.

Carolyn and I spent a lot of time together. Although we saw a few movies and went to a few parties, we spent most of our time at her house. The Carrs made a big to-do about Christmas. I loved their Christmas tree and all the decorations and special activities. They must have wondered sometimes whether I hung around to be with Carolyn or to enjoy the holiday atmosphere in their house. Since Christmas was a very special time for them, they went all out to celebrate it and to share their joy in the season. This was a new experience for me.

Mama and Papa were always too busy dealing with necessary activities to deal with all that folderol. Christmas gifts were limited to very small children. Decorations weren't even considered. Now food was another matter. Mama and my sisters prepared a memorable Christmas dinner that could have fed half of the county. They served everything you could think of putting on a farm family's table except Irish potatoes! They knew how tired I was of those endless platters of potatoes at Clemson. We had fun being together, especially since there were several new sisters-in-law to liven up the family gathering. I wondered if they missed sharing gifts, putting up decorations, etc. as much as I did. Of course, nobody would have thought of mentioning such a thing. Heaven only knows what Papa's reaction to such blatant foolishness would have been and none of us wanted to risk riling him. After dinner I hurried over to Carr's Creek.

Carolyn and I had shopped carefully for gifts for each other. I couldn't wait to see her face when she opened the box with the necklace I had agonized over choosing. All that struggle to decide on the right one was rewarded when her eyes lit up like the lights on the tree. She had chosen a dark wool sweater to keep me warm on those cold lonely days at Clemson. I didn't tell her that just thinking about her was enough to keep me warm any time. Once in a while I would wonder what it would be like to be married to Carolyn, but marriage was a long way down the road. For now, we would just enjoy being sweethearts.

My brothers and I squeezed in a few rabbit hunts and suddenly the holidays were over. Although I hated to leave home and Carolyn, I was anxious to get back to Clemson. I worried a little about what I would do if Carolyn ever surprised me like Mary had done....somehow, I just couldn't picture Carolyn getting serious about anybody but me....on the other hand, I couldn't have guessed that Mary would marry anybody like Tom, either.

The bus ride gave me a chance for a nap and then it was back to the barracks, the camaraderie of the fellows, and the nitty-gritty stuff like studying, drills, and labs.

CHAPTER 10

The first day I was back, I tried to figure out a way to get rid of that blasted bugler without getting caught. There were many things that could have been done, but I never could come up with a workable plan for carrying them out without risking detection and a whole lot of trouble. Oh, well, having to listen to the bugle wasn't going to kill me—I just didn't like it worth a cuss.

The cold winter days weren't fit for much except studying and I did my full share. All of my classroom and lab work was going fine except for English. I dreaded facing Dr. Kinard's English exam. My fears were justified. His exam was a real bugger bear. When semester grades were posted, I had A's in everything but English. Dr. Kinard gave me a conditional grade and permitted me to retake the exam. I prepared myself every way I could think up and then worked like a demon on the exam. Dr. Kinard passed me with a D.

To everybody's surprise, I signed up for Dr. Kinard's class during the second semester. Academically, the second semester went very much like the first one. I did manage to switch my schedule around so that it wasn't necessary to run to my class at the dairy and then run back. That was a relief. For English, there would be no relief. I struggled the whole semester. Dr. Kinard was understanding and he was fair—he was not charitable.

As a member of the drill team and a good student, I got a few extra weekend passes. Many times we didn't know until Saturday morning that we had passes. I learned to keep a little backpack ready so that I could grab it and run for the highway as soon as the list was posted.

One Saturday morning I rushed out to the highway and got a ride very quickly. As the driver started to pick up speed, the car began to weave all over the road. About that time the odor of beer became very strong. While I was trying to decide what to do, the driver reached over into the back seat, picked up another bottle of beer, and began to drink it. I offered to drive so that he could relax and enjoy his beer. That just made him mad.

He bellowed, "!#%* no, I don't want you to drive! This is my car and I'm going to drive it! Don't you like my driving? I can drive just as good as anybody!''

He was staying to the left of the center line at least half of the time and I was getting nervous. My destination was home—not heaven. In desperation, I asked if he would stop and let me out. That was a mistake, too.

His furious response was, "!#* no! I stopped to pick you up because you wanted a ride and you are going to ride until I get to where I'm going. Don't you think I have anything to do but spend the day stopping and starting?''

He was going too fast for me to jump out without getting hurt....at the rate he was going, we were going to crash into the first car that we met on a blind curve if we didn't hit a tree first....what in the heck could I do?

I made a third mistake by asking him where he was going. That steamed him up further and he snarled, "None of your %#* business! You just sit still and be quiet!''

He finished his beer quickly and reached back to get another one. When he couldn't find one, he demanded to know what I had done with his beer. He didn't believe me when I said that I hadn't seen his beer. He called me a %$#! liar and a few other choice names as he continued to weave back and forth across the road. When he got to the next little town, he stopped at the first store with a beer sign. He ordered me to stay in the car while he went inside to get his beer.

As soon as he disappeared into the store, I jumped out of the car and hightailed into the Greyhound Bus Station next door. The station manager listened to my story and called the police for me. The next bus didn't leave for an hour, but that was better than getting killed by a drunken driver. I bought my ticket for forty cents and waited for the police to arrive. Although I felt bad about having the man arrested after he had been good enough to pick me up, I knew that he was a real hazard to himself and to everybody else on the road. When the police got there, I told them the story and asked if they would detain the man until I was safely on the bus. He had threatened to beat me if I got out of the car and I sure didn't want any more trouble. When they agreed to keep him in the "clink" until he sobered up, I pointed him out to them. I watched from the window as they put him into the police car and drove away. That experience cured my desire to hitch-hike.

The rest of the weekend was much better than the beginning. Carolyn and the family all encouraged me to do the rest of my traveling by bus rather than by thumb. I was glad to comply.

On another weekend pass, not many weeks after that, I took the last bus back to Clemson that would get me there before eight o'clock. The weekend had been jam-packed with activities and I was tired so I settled back for a good nap. Just as I dozed off, I heard an awful noise and the bus swayed and screeched to a stop. A cow had run out into the road and the bus had hit her broadside. It took forever to finish the police reports, to settle the cow's owner down, and to get a new bus to finish the trip. There was no way for me to get to Clemson in time for roll call. Mercifully the driver and one of the policemen gave me statements explaining the situation. When I took them to the first sergeant and the captain, those statements kept me from getting into a lot of hot water.

Campus life had settled into a livable routine. Although we were busy, we found time to relax and to play around a little. The desperation of the first few weeks had gradually disappeared along with the hazing. We knew what was expected of us and we had learned how to survive on campus. We began to look forward to spring and its special activities like Parents' Day.

During one of the first warm days of spring, we had a brigade review in honor of a visiting general. He was a cavalryman with the fanciest boots and spurs you ever saw. The reviewing officers stood on a grassy knoll on the right of the drill field. As each company passed in review, the general would take one step forward and return the salutes of the cadet officers. Just as we reached the area in front of the knoll, the captain raised his saber in salute and ordered, "Eyes right!"

As the general took his step forward, his spurs locked together and he fell flat on his face! The whole company was about to burst out laughing when our quick-thinking captain changed his cadence count. "Hut! Two, three, four!" was replaced by, "Straighten your face or ship your a--! Straighten your face or ship your a--!" chanted sternly and in perfect rhythm. Clemson came very close to losing a whole company right there. Seeing that general land on his nose in full view of the whole brigade was enough to break up even the most disciplined cadets.

As soon as we got out of earshot, we all burst out laughing. Even the captain was laughing as he asked, "Wasn't that the funniest !#* sight you've ever seen?"

Spring was also the time we fought mock battles. They were set up on the back portion of the campus and were as realistic as the officers could make them. We fired blank cartridges, stormed machine gun nests, and generally tried to "play army" as enthusiastically as a bunch of kids. The only fun spoiler in the whole operation was having to scrub out the barrels of our rifles with Octagon soap after the battles. The black powder from the blanks was tough to get out. If we left it in the barrels, they would rust and we would catch "Hail Columbia!" for sure.

As we got closer to Easter, the weather got hotter and the drills got longer. Guys who were not in good physical condition frequently passed out. We could not even look at the fallen man. The captain would order two cadets to help the over-heated man into a sitting position. He would sit with his head between his legs like a dog until he felt like standing up again. He would be helped to his feet. If the dizziness went away, he would rejoin the formation. If he fainted a second time, two privates would bring a stretcher and carry him to his room.

Easter Sunday was Parents' Day and the time when we really put on a show for visitors. It was sad that my folks never came to see me at Clemson. They regarded college campuses as a totally alien land. I was delighted when Carolyn and her parents accepted my invitation to visit the campus on Parents' Day. I had a pass for the weekend which stipulated that I be back on campus by noon on Sunday. The Carrs assured me that they would get me back on time. Mr. Carr knew very well the consequences of being late since he had attended Clemson twenty years earlier.

That was a perfect weekend. The weather was lovely and everything worked out just right. The Carrs were as excited as if they had been my parents. They visited our room, attended the parade, and really had a ball. Jason and I had that room in the kind of shape we would have prepared for a visiting general. I drew out the whole brigade's drill formation so that they would know where to look for me. It's a little tough to pick out one cadet when two thousand of them are marching in a moonlight parade, but they tried to spot me.

The moonlight parade was probably one of the most spectacular displays the cadets put on during the year. We wore our white dress uniforms with grey blouses and performed our most intricate drill routines. Even people who didn't have sons or friends at Clemson came to see it.

Carolyn was beautiful and all the excitement stirred her up so that she seemed to sparkle. I was so proud of her. It didn't hurt my feelings a bit when the other guys fell over themselves to be nice to her. I made it clear that this gal was mine just in case anybody had any ideas that she might not be.

After Easter, the school year wound down quickly. A circus atmosphere developed when the seniors finished all their work and had nothing to do for the last few days before graduation. Some of their pranks were masterpieces of mischief and ingenuity. While the rest of us were struggling with term papers and exams, the seniors strove to outdo each other and their predecessors with spectacular shenanigans.

Since their handiwork had to be done under the cover of darkness, waking up became an adventure. Like children at Christmas, we couldn't wait to get up and see what the seniors had done. They knew that it was impossible for the administration to watch all of them all of the time, and they gloried in their freedom.

One morning we found an old model Dodge sedan turned upside-down in the middle of the quadrangle between the four new barracks. We never knew whether they carried it down the twenty steps from the street or down a thirty-foot embankment. Not one scrape mark could be seen on the steps and not a blade of grass was trampled. Of course, nobody knew anything about how it got there. It must have been senior magic!

Another morning there were eleven privies lined up down the exact center of the drill field. Some budding engineers were practicing their skills. I'll bet eleven families from the surrounding area would have liked to practice some mayhem. Can you imagine stumbling out to the privy and finding nothing there but the throne?

Col. Weeks, the commandant, got a jolt one morning when he unlocked his office on the third floor of the administration building. He had been replaced by a large Holstein cow! She was a little perturbed by her surroundings. Every time she moved, she knocked over something. The noise would make her jump back and she would collide with something else which would crash to the floor. Like all cows, she reacted to stress by depositing generous quantities of feces. By the time they got her out of his office, there was enough manure to fertilize a very large garden and Col. Weeks was steamed up enough to run the campus laundry equipment for a week without firing up a single boiler.

The Holstein caper generated a series of meetings. The army officers held meetings with each other while the president held meetings with the professors. With all that brass and all those brains, nobody came up with a workable preventive measure for senior pranks. As usual, the administration handled the clean-up to the tune of about $25,000 a year and the seniors continued to exercise their own brand of magic and mischief.

The manager of the campus laundry and dry cleaning plant was also a magician of sorts. He memorized every student's face, name, and laundry number. This was delightful when you were in a hurry because he would call out your name and number to the workers when you walked through the door to pick up your clothes. It was the downfall of two sophomores who printed notes on their shirt cuffs to aid them on a calculus exam. After the exam, they took the shirts to the laundry to get rid of the evidence of their cheating. The manager noticed the cuffs and preserved his evidence. When they came to pick up the shirts, they were stalled until the guardhouse staff picked them up. After a meeting with the dean of the mathematics department and a faculty committee, they were expelled.

Another sophomore was expelled for wrapping toilet paper around the sprinkler heads. He planned to light the toilet paper and create an uproar by setting off the sprinkler system. He figured that the flame would generate enough heat to activate the system and destroy the evidence of his prank at the same time. Unfortunately for him, he was spotted by a lieutenant who was making secret rounds. After a military trial, he, too, was expelled.

It bothered me that three young men ruined their reputations and their chances to get an education by making one foolish mistake. Life can be hard for those who don't play by the rules.

Like everybody else, I was delighted to see the school year end. I had done well in everything but English. Dr. Kinard had given me a "D." That wasn't great, but at least I had passed the course.

I was jubilant when I headed back to the farm and Carolyn for a whole summer.

CHAPTER 11

Since it was a foregone conclusion that I would work for Papa, I hadn't bothered to make any firm plans for the summer. There was no question that he would see that I stayed plenty busy. The first news at home was that Marshall was getting married; the second was that I was going to take over his milk delivery route in two days. Wow! Papa thought that I could learn the route and all the bookkeeping and collection details that went with it in *two* days! I was pretty confident of my ability to handle almost anything that came along, but this was a big assignment even for a man.

Papa heard me out when I reminded him that I knew nothing about making deliveries except what I had picked up in the three or four times I had ridden the truck the previous summer. At that time, the delivery boy had been sick and I had just run up to the houses with the milk while Marshall drove the truck and told me what to do.

Charlie Riddle had no intention of hiring anybody to drive that truck when he had a boy at home—especially one who was going to college! He assured me that I could handle it and that he was counting on me to do it.

Since he was sending me to college and paying all of my expenses, I had no choice but to give it my best effort. I agreed to take on the delivery route.

The worst part of the whole situation was having to get up at 3:00 a.m. The truck had to be loaded with milk, iced down, and rolling out of the barn by 4:00 a.m. The route was so long that deliveries had to go with drill team precision in order to finish before the ice melted. I rode with Marshall for the next two days and found out just how much there was to learn.

The commercial portion of the route was fairly simple. There were twenty-eight A and P stores and a few independent grocers to which we delivered every day. The independents paid for each delivery when they received it. The A and P stores required that duplicate invoices be made up for each store, each day. The invoices would be signed by the store manager when he received his delivery. At the end of the month, we had to fill out a long form which had each store listed separately and a space to record the amount of each day's delivery to each store. The completed form was mailed to A and P's Charlotte office. They would send us a check for the milk within five days. The biggest challenge was to get the residential route finished in time to start the commercial route at 8:00 a.m. when the stores opened. Although there were a few times that we had to make an extra trip in order to keep the stores supplied, we rarely had problems with the commercial route.

The residential route was a whole different story. Delivering the milk and collecting the money was always an adventure. Between the people and the dogs, we had to be alert for anything. If my training had led me into combat, that route would have prepared me for it at least as well as the standard military training program. I would drive the truck and make the necessary notations in the route book. John, a young black man about twenty years old, rode on the back of the truck. He would swing off the truck, carry the milk up to the porch or to whatever place the customer had designated, exchange the full bottles for the empties, and run back to the truck. He was a good helper and an excellent deliveryman. I watched him swing off that truck many times carrying six glass bottles of milk, make his delivery, and jump back on the truck before it came to a complete stop.

The first morning I drove that big new truck out of the barn without Marshall I felt like a big man and like an apprehensive child. Aided by John, the route book, the grace of God, and a lot of luck, I finished the last delivery within ten minutes of Marshall's regular schedule. Papa was impressed and John and I were relieved and very proud of ourselves.

Not every day went that smoothly. It was standard procedure for dairies to request that their customers confine aggressive dogs during deliveries. It was equally standard for the customers to forget or for the dogs to get out of their restraints. One morning about an hour before daylight on a dimly lighted street, John swung off the truck carrying two bottles of milk. Just as he reached the top step at the Jones' house, Tiger, their big, vicious, mixed-breed dog charged out of the shadows and lunged at him. In a classic one-two punch routine, John broke both bottles of milk across Tiger's head. Tiger made a howling retreat to the end of the porch while John picked up his empties and fled to the safety of the truck.

Great! John was all shook up, the Jones' steps were covered with milk and broken glass, Tiger was howling loud enough to wake up half of the county, and lights were coming on all through the Jones' house. Taking a deep breath, I walked carefully up to the porch and rang the bell. Before I could get my finger off the bell, an absolutely livid Mr. Jones snatched the door open. He raved and ranted until he was breathless. While he caught his breath, I reminded him quietly and firmly that he had promised to keep Tiger confined. Then I asked if I could borrow his broom and a bucket of water to clean up the mess. He brought the broom and the bucket and continued his tirade while I did my cleaning. Then I called John and asked him to bring me two quarts of milk.

John's firm response was, "I'll meet you halfway up the walk, but that is as far as I'm coming."

By the time I handed him the milk, Mr. Jones had cooled down a little. He said that he would continue to get his milk from us only if I would personally deliver his milk. If John so much as set foot on his porch again, he would cancel his order. Knowing that John was less than enthusiastic about encountering Tiger again, I agreed to deliver the milk myself if Mr. Jones kept Tiger confined. "The customer is always right," rang in my head.

We kept the bargain for six weeks before I sent John back to deliver his milk. The next morning there was a cancellation note in a bottle on the Jones' porch. The arrogance of the man made me furious. I stalked up to the front door and held the door bell button down until Mr. Jones jerked the door open. He was mad because I had waked up his family. I was even madder. Before he could say a word, I told him that he was totally unreasonable and demanded that he pay his bill and return all Riddle Dairy bottles at once—six, according to my records! Stunned, he brought me the bottles and the money. Still fuming, I informed him that I planned to report the incident at the next dairymen's meeting. My parting shot as I stormed down the steps was, "That ought to be enough to guarantee that nobody will deliver your milk and you can buy it from the store yourself!"

Another morning John twisted his ankle as he jumped from the truck. We were approaching Capt. Cox's house. He taught military science at Clemson and apparently had chosen the house for its defensive position. It sat on top of a steep hill. There were ten steps, then a slanting walkway, then ten more steps, another walkway, and finally five steps up to the porch. Feeling sorry for John, I told him to put some ice on his ankle while I ran up to the house. I set two quarts of milk down on the porch, picked up two empties, and started down the steps. Whoa! A huge German shepherd lunged at me. I ducked, he sailed over my head, turned three cartwheels before regaining his balance, and charged at me again. Using a bottle as a weapon, I hit him in the head. As the bottle broke, the dog backed off, shook his head, and charged again. I broke the second bottle on his head. This time he got a bad cut and went howling back to the house. Shaking like the proverbial willow in a windstorm, I fled to the truck. That rascal John was laughing fit to kill. It took me a few minutes to calm down enough to drive the rest of the route.

The next morning John refused to deliver Capt. Cox's milk. On the porch, I found a note in a bottle asking me to ring the bell. I did and a very angry Capt. Cox opened the door. He had his mouth open to yell at me when he recognized that I was Cadet Riddle. Although I had been in his class the previous year, he had not known that I was a part of Riddle Dairy. He mumbled something about not having connected me with his milk supply before he asked what had happened the previous morning. He had found his dog howling in pain from a severe cut on the head just as our truck had pulled away. Even though the vet had stitched him up and thought that he would recover nicely. Capt. Cox wasn't happy about having his prized dog injured.

I told him exactly what had happened and offered to pay the vet's bill. He hadn't gotten a bill and he had calmed down enough to acknowledge that he was at fault for not having locked the dog securely in his pen. He warned me that Butch had been trained as an attack dog as he expressed his relief that I had not been seriously hurt. He agreed to keep Butch locked up, we shook hands, and I went back to the truck. No wonder Papa had trouble keeping good delivery people!

Saturday afternoons and evenings were spent in Greenville. I spent part of the afternoon collecting payments from residential customers and then went by the dairymen's bottle exchange. Each dairy would drop off bottles that had been returned to it erroneously and pick up its own bottles which had been dropped off by other dairies. An employee at the exchange sorted the bottles by dairy.

Collections could be a real hassle. I blessed those folks who left their checks in an envelope in the bottles and cursed those who had to be visited six times before they paid us. A typical adventure in collecting started when I stopped by Mrs. Smith's house about two p.m. The maid said that Mrs. Smith wasn't at home. When I told her that I needed to collect for the milk, she said that Mrs. Smith would be back in an hour. At three p.m. the maid said she wasn't sure when Mrs. Smith would be back. I told her that I would come back when I finished my other collections because Mrs. Smith was already more than a month behind in her payments. Mrs. Smith snatched the door open and lit into me with a royal tongue lashing when I got back about five p.m. She finished by saying that she was paying me in full, returning all our bottles, and cancelling her order for Riddle milk.

Well, Papa hadn't sent me out to lose customers so I explained that we had been patient about her slow payments, that Papa had sent me out to do the collecting during the summer, and that I had to do a good job so that he would send me back to Clemson in the fall. Before long peace was restored, I had my money, and she had decided that Riddle milk was the best in town and that we should continue to deliver it to her. Whew!

During the summer, I dated Carolyn every Wednesday night and every Sunday night. We went to the usual wiener roasts, ice cream churnings, church socials, movies, and parties. My getting up at three a.m. didn't help my social life a bit. Although I loved being with Carolyn, her ten-thirty curfew usually found me ready to go home and go to bed. She knew that I worked very hard and she didn't complain about our short evenings or our having just two dates a week. She knew that she was my girl and that was enough for her. If she had known about my Saturday evenings in Greenville, she might not have been so understanding.

When I finished my collections, I would drop by the Brady's house. Mrs. Brady had four delightful daughters, a big house, and a big heart. Mr. Brady had a new car that was always available for the girls to drive. I rarely saw Mr. Brady and I suspected that he had a regular Saturday night date with a whiskey bottle. When I got there, Mrs. Brady would insist that I take a nap in her guest room while she and the girls fixed supper. Bonnie was cute, fun-loving, and affectionate. She didn't go to college and she didn't have any serious goals. Her major interest was having a good time. After a good meal with lots of charming conversation, Bonnie and

I would take her father's car and go to the movies. When the movie ended, we would drive up to Paris Mountain. That was everybody's favorite place to park. We could look down on the lights of the city and look up at the stars and smooch a little. Since I always took Bonnie home by eleven p.m., our folks never objected to our relationship. Even though we had a good time together and I thoroughly enjoyed my Saturday evenings with the Brady family, I knew perfectly well that I could never be seriously involved with Bonnie.

Early in August a letter arrived from Clemson. If Papa would send in a check for my first semester's expenses, I could pre-register and avoid all the long lines. That sounded good to me. Papa gave me a cashier's check made payable to Clemson College. I filled out all the forms that had come with the letter and sent the check and the forms back to Clemson.

A week later a large packet came from Clemson. In it were a letter informing me that I had been promoted to corporal, the numeral two to wear on my collar, and seven pairs of stripes! The letter requested that I return to school three days early to help organize my company. It also gave me my room assignment. I would be living on the third floor of barracks number one. Ouch! That old barracks had gotten a lot of wear and tear. It was livable....after that there wasn't much to be said for it.

Mama carefully followed the instructions for sewing the stripes on my mackinaw, my uniform blouse, and my five uniform shirts. While she sewed, I explained to her that they indicated that I had achieved the lowest ranking non-commissioned officer rating on campus and the highest rank that a sophomore could get. She really didn't understand the whole military rigmarole. She was proud and happy because I was proud and happy. I couldn't have been any prouder of a captain's bars at that time.

Now the question of who would take over my job as truck driver had to be answered. Papa thought that Joe was the best choice for the job. Joe had other ideas. He hadn't even finished high school and I had already had a full year of college. I could just stay home and drive the truck, according to Joe's way of thinking. Well, life with the Riddles was never easy. I got Papa and Joe together and told them firmly that I intended to park that milk truck the day before school started and that it could stay parked until they got another driver.

That statement shocked them into silence. I reminded Joe that I had learned the route in two days and he would have two weeks to learn it. There was no way that he could say that he couldn't do what I had done. Between us, Papa and I convinced him that he was the man for the job. His easy-going manner and warm personality really did enable him to get along with the customers and the dogs. He rode with me for a week and then announced that he was ready to take over the route.

In the week that I had left to get ready for school, I did a lot of thinking. It would be great to be a master rather than a slave and to be a squad leader rather than a rat. Now I could get even for all the frustrations I had endured the previous fall. Then some other thoughts crept into the picture. Animals always responded better to calmness, kindness, and firmness than to anger, mistreatment, and hysteria. Rewards worked better than punishment in training animals. If training broke an animal's spirit, the animal would never be of much value. I had been very successful at training Sonny Boy and many other animals on the farm. If humans are the highest form of animal life, wouldn't the same techniques apply to training cadets? What would happen if I trained my squad the way I had trained animals? I would have done anything to please Sgt. Covington—the first officer who had shown me any kindness. The more I thought about it, the more I became aware that Sgt. Covington had treated me like a human being and that he had motivated me to do my best. The other screaming, swearing, ridiculing, and paddling officers had simply motivated me to avoid them and trouble by staying quiet and by doing as little as possible in order not to draw attention to myself. There was no doubt in my mind that Sgt. Covington had a superior method. If I could improve on Sgt. Covington's techniques, I could have the best squad on campus. Could I manage to apply my theories without getting into a battle with the company officers and the military men? Major Dumas would probably go into apoplexy if anyone dared to suggest that cadets should be treated with kindness and respect! The more I thought about it, the more convinced I became that I could develop a superior squad by using my own methods. Until somebody forced me to do otherwise, I would train my squad the Riddle way.

The only other big problem was how to get myself and my gear moved back to Clemson. I asked Bly if he would take me. He grinned and asked if they were going to cut my hair again. When I said, "!#%, no!," he made it clear that he wasn't about to take me. To add insult to injury, he vowed that he had only taken me last year so that he could admire my bald head.

Bly teased me for two or three days before he decided that it would be such a pleasure to get rid of me, he would be glad to make the trip.

CHAPTER 12

The hardest part of leaving was telling Carolyn and the family goodbye. Carolyn had agreed that Saturday nights would be mine just as they had been the previous year and that made it easier for me.

It didn't take long to drive over to Clemson and to get my gear moved into my room. This time I had a three man room. Like last year, my roommates hadn't shown up. I chose the top bunk, thanked Bly for bringing me, and had most of my gear put away before he had time to reach the city limits.

I wandered around the halls for a little while, watching the freshmen come into the barracks and sizing them up. I was torn between choosing a slave early while the picking was best or waiting to let my roommates share in the choice.

After a while I went down to the captain's office and knocked on the door. When he invited me to enter, I observed all the military courtesies. He introduced himself as Capt. R. L. ('Bud') Knox, introduced his three commissioned officers, shook my hand, and invited me to sit down. Man, this sure was different from last year.

We chatted pleasantly for a little while. He verified my room assignment (331), gave me the names of my roommates, Cpl. William Bussey from Greenville and Cpl. Richard Caughman from Columbia, and asked me to help keep order in the halls.

When I asked on what authority I could keep order, he snapped, "Those #% stripes on your sleeve and your own good judgment!"

As I was leaving, I mentioned that I wanted to get back on the hall so that I could choose a good rat slave. Captain Knox smiled as he rose and said, "I know just the slave for you. Rat Gleason in room 328 is as good a rat as you can find. I know him personally and he is a good boy. Go on down to his room and if he is in there, nail him before somebody else gets him."

I went down to Room 328 and knocked on the door. This was the beginning of my experiment in the Riddle method of training. It wasn't customary to knock on a rat's door despite the fact that it would have been basic courtesy under any other circumstances.

A tall, pleasant-looking young man opened the door. When I asked
if he were Rat Gleason, he acknowledged that he was. I ordered
him to come with me. He asked where we were going. Feeling my
authority, I informed him that rats did not ask questions, they just
obeyed orders.

We went across the hall to my room. I introduced myself, told
him that he would be the slave for Room 331 for the year, and
proceeded to show him how to make up my bunk. Trying to be
tough, I told him that he had better produce because displeasing
Bussey or Caughman would probably get him paddled. I knew perfectly well that I wasn't going to paddle him and that it wouldn't
do for him to find that out yet. Apparently he sensed that I liked
him because he grinned. I ordered him to wipe that smile off his
face and then asked why he was smiling. He said something about
having heard about taking care of a room for upperclassmen. I could
tell that he was pleased to have been chosen by me. After telling
him that he was to inform anybody else who tried to claim him that
he was already taken, I dismissed him.

Rat Gleason hesitated for a moment and then asked if he could
come back after supper to talk some more. Feeling lonesome myself and remembering how miserable I had felt last year, I agreed
that he could come and visit after supper. While I was telling him
that the mess hall would be open from six to seven p.m., I decided
to invite him to join me for supper. He was so delighted that he
asked if his two roommates could come, too. I might as well be
the shepherd for all three lost souls if I were going to be bothered
with one. Hoping that I sounded properly stern, I ordered him to
have himself and his old ladies dressed in their best clothes at my
door promptly at six o'clock. I planned to take a nap and they were
to awaken me in time for dinner.

That three a.m. wake-up time from the dairy business was still
bugging me. I had a good nap and was waked up by Rat Gleason's
knock exactly at six o'clock.

Shocking as it may have been to the other cadets, inviting those
three rats to eat with me was one of the best moves I've ever made.
Even though they kept up a constant stream of questions beginning with, "Where's the mess hall?" I tried to be patient and to
answer every question decently. I didn't want anybody to feel the
way I had felt this time last year. My rats gave every indication of
wanting to please me. Around the mess hall, I could see other rats

being subjected to the kind of treatment I had endured the previous year. The victims were not getting off to any better start than I had. The harassment was making them edgy and miserable and they were making stupid mistakes and getting into more trouble. By contrast, the three rats at my table were following all the rat rules in an alert intelligent manner. During the meal, they asked if they could visit with me after supper. I agreed that they could all come to my room if they would leave when I requested time alone with Rat Gleason. That was the way they all learned to make their beds properly—they practiced on Bussey's bunk and Caughman's bunk while I supervised. Those three rats seemed to be responding to the Riddle method and nobody had raised any objections. Feeling good about the situation, I invited them to have breakfast with me the next morning. Seeming to be both shocked and pleased, they accepted at once. They returned to their rooms while I gave Rat Gleason a little extra instruction on how to keep our room in top shape. I wanted to be sure that my old ladies were pleased with our slave. When he had mastered his lessons, I sent him to his room and settled myself down for a good night's sleep.

Breakfast was pretty much like supper had been. The three rats were properly obedient, yet pleasant company. Shortly after breakfast, my first old lady arrived. William ('Bill') Bussey from Greenville introduced himself. After I introduced myself, he hesitated for a minute before he mentioned that his family got their milk from Riddle's Dairy. We both laughed when I told him exactly where we had been setting the milk on his porch and he told me that his mother wouldn't think of buying milk from any other dairy.

Bill was a happy-go-lucky fellow. He chose the single bed and then inquired as to who had made it up so well. I told him how we had acquired Rat Gleason and why the beds had been made. That suited him fine. We were off to a good start.

The next morning, Dick Caughman stuck his head in the door and inquired as to whether he had any old ladies. I told him that he had one in the room and one out running around. Dick was six feet tall with the erect carriage of a born military man. He was every inch a gentleman and a real pleasure to have around. When I told him about our choices of beds, he said that he preferred the lower bunk so everything was working out fine. He, too, heard the story of how the beds got made and how we had obtained our rat. We discussed our company officers. I liked all of them except one platoon lieutenant who looked sneaky and lazy. Dick laughed and said that he would probably be the lucky one who got the #% as his platoon commander. I laughed and suggested that he at least give him a chance before he condemned him.

Dick thought for a minute before he laughed and said, "Yeah, you're right. Shoot, John, I've known you ten minutes and I'm already trusting your judgment more than my own. We'll do all right."

From the hall came the sort of uproar that could only be created by Bill. I asked Dick if he heard the hyena coming down the hall. He did and he was a little perturbed to find that the hyena was our old lady. About that time Bill charged in with all the grace of King Kong. I introduced them and then left them to get acquainted. After a little while we got around to discussing ourselves and our families. Bill was working toward a degree in textile engineering. Dick's father and older brother were veterinarians and Dick wanted no part of that. He planned to get his degree in mechanical engineering. They laughed when I told them that I was a genuine Southern Redneck who was going to grow up to be a veterinarian. Although our backgrounds and ambitions were different, I thought we were probably going to get along well together.

At my suggestion, we got Rat Gleason to come down to the room so that we could start him off properly. As our slave, he needed to learn our likes and dislikes. I got a little concerned when Bill hassled Gleason a mite too much. Just about the time I decided to say something about it, Bill backed off. I soon discovered that he did a lot more barking than biting.

During lunchtime announcements in the mess hall on Friday, all company commanders were told to organize their companies during the afternoons. All cadets were to remain in their rooms until they received further orders. About two p.m. the lieutenants came around to each room to order us to be in the halls at three p.m. for company formation.

The first formation was a little bit like feeding time at the zoo. Finally we got everyone into his assigned spot and each squad leader and platoon leader was given a roster of his men. Capt. Knox gave firm, clear orders and left no doubt that he was in charge. As I watched the freshmen try desperately to remember what to do and how to do it, I remembered all too well how miserable I had been at this time last year.

The next day I was summoned to the captain's office. To save my neck, I couldn't figure out what I had done to deserve that! I knocked on the door and Bud's deep pleasant voice invited me to come in. Well, he must not be mad, but I wasn't going to take any chances. With carefully correct military courtesy, I reported to him. To my surprise, he told me to forget the military formalities for a few minutes. We chatted amiably about the way things were shaping up and then he delivered his surprise. We had one extra freshman and he wanted to assign him to be a second slave for our room. The only requirement was that I make it clear to Rats Gleason and Farmer that neither was going to be permitted to accuse the other of negligence if their work didn't get done. I agreed and started to leave, but curiosity got the best of me. I asked why I had been assigned the extra slave. Bud laughed and said that it had better not go to my head, but the reason was that I had impressed the company officers. Man, this was really different from last year!

When I got back to the room with my big news, Bill and Dick promptly accused me of brown-nosing the captain. Well, I got that straightened out real fast and then went down the hall to get Rat Farmer. On the way back to our room, I explained to Farmer what had happened in the captain's office and that I wanted him to meet my old ladies. He was a little antsy although Bill and Dick were cordial to him. We talked long enough to feel that we knew each other before I brought Rat Gleason into the room. The two rats already knew each other. It didn't take long to set them straight about their duties. Dick stretched up to his full height and warned them that he would warm their backsides with his paddle if they goofed off or screwed up and that Bill and I would help with the warming. Seeing that they were obviously impressed, we dismissed them.

We had quite a discussion about how we had gotten two rat slaves for our room when there were several juniors with the rank of sergeant living in our barracks. We never did figure it out. We did decide to keep quiet about it. For the whole year we enjoyed having our beds made, our shoes shined, our clothes hung up, our bedding changed, and our laundry and dry cleaning picked up and delivered. We were considerate of our rats and they were loyal to us.

I met with the members of my squad in their rooms, answered their questions, showed them their manuals of arms, and encouraged them to study the manuals before we went out to the drill field.

I made it clear that I expected them to do well and that I was willing to help them. I also told them that since I lived in a three-man room, they were not to come to my room to ask questions. I would answer their questions and explain whatever they didn't understand during the time we were on the drill field or when I dropped by their rooms. I was keeping my resolution to treat them like human beings. I was also protecting myself by not advertising that I was not following the standard operating procedure of brow-beating, threatening, cussing, and paddling them into submission.

The first day on the drill field was a revelation. My squad made very few goofs. They even mastered "To the rear, march!" without stomping each other. The first time I gave that command, two fellows turned the wrong way. I halted the squad immediately and pulled out one man who was executing the commands perfectly. He and I went through a mini drill while the others watched. Then the whole squad went through the same mini drill five times. Every one of those guys did it perfectly! This was unbelievable. Freshmen just don't learn to drill that fast. I had not shouted, threatened, nor cussed a single time. I hadn't even gotten aggravated.

A quick glance around the field showed that I was decidedly the exception. The other squad leaders were sweating, screaming, waving their arms, threatening every punishment they could think up, shoving, and generally acting like madmen. Their poor freshmen were rushing around hysterically and making all the dumb mistakes that frightened, upset boys make.

By the time we got back to the room, Bill and Dick were both acting like enraged bulls. You never heard such descriptions as they gave of how dumb, thick-headed, obnoxious, impossible, and generally awful their squads were. I don't know which descriptions were more outlandish—what the freshman were like or what would have to be done to them to shape them up.

After they had simmered down a little, they both noticed that I was neither upset nor particularly sweaty. As we discussed the afternoon's happenings, it became clear that I had had very few problems. They both immediately swore that I had gotten the pick of the company. When I denied this, they demanded to know why my squad had done so much better than theirs. They got madder by the minute while I asked them if they had met privately with their squads before drill, encouraged them to study the manual of arms, answered their questions, and all that stuff. Of course, they hadn't done any of that !#%#!—even a *#()# rat ought to know enough to study the manual and figure it out for himself.

They got even more perturbed when I reminded them they had made all those same mistakes last year. They denied that they had ever been as stupid as their squads. Very carefully, I suggested that being more patient and less antagonistic worked with training mules and that it might work with freshmen. This annoyed both of them enough to make them stop and think. Both of them sat for a long time, holding a book, but not turning a single page.

After dinner, I went down to Capt. Knox's room. I observed the usual military proprieties until he told me to forget them and sit down. Wording my questions very carefully, I asked if a corporal could use his own methods of training instead of the usual intimidation tactics. Bud acknowledged that I could do anything I wanted to do as long as my squad progressed at least as fast as the other squads.

Apparently his curiosity got the best of him. He asked why I wanted to know such a thing and what I intended to do. I didn't want to create an uproar and I didn't want anybody to torpedo my plan before it had been given a chance to work. Choosing my words carefully, I explained that I felt that the same training techniques that I had used on the farm animals would work on my squad. I had taken the liberty of trying them and at the end of the first day's drill, my squad was three days ahead of schedule in what they had mastered. That really got his attention. We discussed my methods and he agreed to honor my request not to call attention to the fact that I was being different until we could both see if my method continued to work effectively.

Feeling a lot better, I went back to my room. Dick and Bill continued to use the standard methods of training their squads and they continued to come back from the drill field drenched with sweat, as mad and ill-tempered as wet hornets, and totally frustrated. They noticed that I rarely worked up much of a sweat even though the weather was unseasonably hot and that I was never upset. Finally they demanded to know my secret. I was afraid that if I told them too much, they would talk about it enough to bring it to the attention of the military instructors and wreck the whole experiment. They would also have accused me of being soft-headed as well as soft-hearted. I just laughed it off and told them I was killing my rats with kindness.

CHAPTER 13

Chippy, Peter, and Sonny, the three sophomores in the room next door to us, could have won the competition for Clown Princes of Clemson if we had had such a thing. There was nothing that they wouldn't do to each other or to any other convenient body if it would get a laugh. Apparently none of them ever had a serious thought or a serious goal. They were all smart so they didn't have to study very much. They weren't interested in excelling at anything but clowning. This gave them a lot of free time. They proved conclusively the truth of the old adage, "Idle hands are the devil's workshop." The ingenuity and brazenness with which they broke rules—and got away with it!—was awesome.

All of the barracks rooms had a four foot high wainscoting around the walls. Peter found that one of the boards beside his desk was loose. As soon as he mentioned it, all three of those rascals started working like convicts to get the board out. The wainscoting was composed of three inch wide by four foot tall tongue and groove boards. When they got the first board out, they found a two by four inch brace between the studs. It didn't take those engineers long to figure that if they took out some of the boards and shaved off the tongues, they would have a secret cache for food. They could put stuff on the brace and have a perfectly good shelf. No more nine p.m. starvation times for them! Having food in the barracks was a heinous crime according to the authorities. According to Chippy, Peter, and Sonny, the only crime was getting caught breaking a rule. After several hours of secret labor, the wall cache was ready. The boards could be slipped out or replaced in a split second. They started out bringing bread from the mess hall and jam, jelly, and preserves from the store. As time went on and nobody discovered the cache, they got more innovative. Before long they had a toaster, a hot plate, and heaven only knows what else in that wall.

Clemson did not waste money by having more than the absolute minimum amount of wattage in the barracks. If you plugged in anything anywhere in the building at night, all of the lights promptly dimmed. This alerted the officers to the fact that some illicit ac-

tivity was going on. The officers would begin a room-by-room search to find out what was happening. That didn't disturb our neighbors one bit. They would plug in the toaster, make the toast, spread it with butter and jam, devour it, and get everything put away before the officers could get to their room.

As non-commissioned officers, Bill, Dick, and I were supposed to report any illicit activities. We knew perfectly well what was happening next door. Somehow, we never could bring ourselves to report the Clown Princes. They were our friends and we thought it was funny to watch the officers scramble to try to catch them. They might just as well have tried to squeeze a handful of mercury. After debating whether we absolutely had to report them, we decided that they weren't doing any real harm. Eventually we made a three-way vow not squeal on them.

One of their stunts made me uncomfortable for several hours before it happened and for weeks afterward. Sonny and I were walking through the woods near the campus on a beautiful Sunday afternoon in late September. We were discussing John C. Calhoun when Sonny stopped suddenly and demanded, "Wait a minute. I see just what I need!"

Heaven help us. That rascal had seen a huge black snake sunning himself. The snake was already getting sluggish. Sonny ordered me to watch the snake and to keep its attention until he could kill it. He found a big stick and then carefully circled around behind the snake. He looked like an Indian in the movies making a sneak attack. He hit the snake on the head and created instant chaos. The stunned snake started slithering toward me and Sonny started yelling, "Catch him, J.T.!"

With a quick sidestep, I gave the snake the whole path. Fear wasn't the problem—I knew that he wasn't poisonous. Being a country boy, I knew that if I touched him, I would smell like a snake and that isn't exactly a pleasant odor. Sonny wasn't going to lose that snake. He finally caught it and they had a real battle. Sonny would hit the snake and think it was dead. When he would try to pick it up, the snake would coil around him. Sonny would struggle until he could throw it off and then he would hit it again. When the snake finally died, Sonny started trying to figure out a way to take it back to the barracks.

This was too much for me. "What in the #% are you going to do with a seven foot long black snake?"

Sonny just laughed and told me to wait and see. Finally the crawling reflex subsided and Sonny stuffed the snake into the pocket of his mackinaw. You can believe that he had a pocket plumb full of snake! I never did know how he managed to hold it in there until he got back to his room.

As we walked back, Sonny planned his trick. Thinking out loud, he said, "That turkey Chippy is scared to death of snakes....If I put this baby way down at the foot of his bed, he'll find it first with his feet....Then he'll pull it up with his hands to see what it is....When he fastens his eyeballs on Blackie, baby, it will be diaper-changing time for sure!......Now, J.T., you and I are the only ones who are going to know about this. You had ****** sure better not breathe one word about it, do you hear? .... When anybody says anything about it to me, I'm going to act as innocent as a new-born babe and lie like a carnival barker in front of the girlie show!....You had better do the same thing, ole buddy!"

Chippy was as high-strung and nervous as a race horse. This trick might be funny, but it could be serious. I suggested quietly that Chippy might get hysterical or even have a heart attack if he were truly terrified of snakes.

Sonny was too busy laughing and anticipating the uproar to think straight. He snapped, "I don't give a **** what it does to him. Now you just keep your mouth shut and don't screw this up. This is the best gig I've ever pulled."

Sonny would walk along quietly and then burst out laughing again. I got tickled just watching him.

Feeling very uncomfortable, but not knowing what to do, I agreed to get Chippy and Peter out of the room and to stand guard while Sonny fixed Chippy's bedtime surprise.

After I got back to my room, worries kept nagging at me. Finally I went next door and called Sonny out of the room. I made a final effort to persuade him to get rid of the snake. Nothing doing. Reluctantly agreeing to keep my mouth shut, I went back to my room.

Somehow I went through the familiar motions of retreat, supper, study hour, long roll, and another period of study before "Taps." I felt like I was sitting on a time bomb. Nothing could keep my mind off Chippy and the snake. Instinctively I knew that all sorts of bad things were going to happen as soon as Chippy went to bed. Bill and Dick were both trying to study for a major math test. My edginess was getting to them, too. I decided to get ready for bed since I wasn't getting any studying done. Dick slammed his book shut as he swore at his own inability to concentrate.

I climbed into my top bunk, Dick knelt to say his prayers, and Bill continued to mutter and to struggle with his math. When Dick got into his bunk, I pretended to go to sleep. The barracks seemed unusually quiet. Suddenly a series of blood-curdling screams erupted from next door. As their intensity mounted, the sound became more like a wild animal than a human. Occasionally the screams would be interrupted by a horrible retching noise as though someone were trying to throw up the calluses on his feet.

As the pounding of running feet came from all directions and converged outside our door, Dick opened it. Stepping back, he said, "Something is bad wrong next door. The captain, two lieutenants, and the first sergeant just ran in there! Visiting rules be *%! I'm going to see what's happening over there!"

The heaviness in the pit of my stomach felt like Stone Mountain. Bill grumbled about the uproar and went back to his studying. When Dick came back, he was half-laughing and half-crying.

Trying to sound innocent, I asked what was happening. "You would have to see it to believe it, J.T. Some bastard put a big ole snake in Chippy's bed. The poor boy is having fits. It's awful ....but it's funny, too. He thought it was a hose until he reached down there and pulled it up. When he saw what he had in his hands, he went wild. The captain and all the brass are over there now. I don't believe they can handle this."

I jumped down and started putting on my robe and slippers. When Dick suggested that they weren't going to let me in, I asked if he wanted to bet on it.

When I opened the door to the room, I felt like somebody had slugged me in the stomach. Chippy was alternately screaming and retching and obviously in a state of total hysteria. Blood from the snake and the contents of Chippy's stomach were everywhere. Capt. Knox stepped over and asked me if I had any suggestions. When I told him to call the infirmary right quick, he ordered me to stay in the room and he left to make the call.

Bud came back with two freshmen and a stretcher. Chippy was still screaming as they carried him out. After ordering somebody to get rid of the snake, he ordered Peter and Sonny to clean up the mess. The rest of us were ordered to return to our rooms and to settle down.

I went back to my room ....I didn't settle down. I spent most of the night wondering how I could have handled the situation more effectively and whether I could have prevented Chippy's disaster.

When Chippy came back from the infirmary about noon the next day, he looked like a bunch of Halloween goblins and ghouls had worked him over. I felt awful just looking at him. This was too much like a replay of Jason's agonies.

At long roll Monday night, Capt. Knox ordered us to parade rest. He chewed our tails thoroughly because he believed that somebody in the company was guilty. He stated that whoever was the perpetrator should come by his office before noon Wednesday and be man enough to acknowledge his guilt. If that did not occur, the company officers would talk privately with each man in the company until they found the scoundrel.

Well, the scoundrel was never caught. Sonny told me later that Chippy had vowed to kill whoever put that snake in his bed as soon as he found out who did it. Fearful that he would carry out his threat, we kept quiet about it.*

*(Now, after more than forty years and the deaths of all three of my clown princes, I can finally get it off my chest. It still isn't funny to me.)

CHAPTER 14

My academic schedule had been set up so that I would have plenty of time to drill my squad. Mathematics, chemistry, and military science were a breeze. Although I had a little trepidation about having Capt. Cox as my professor after having slugged his dog with the milk bottles during the summer, I needn't have worried. We got along well inside and outside of the classroom. English under Dr. Kinard was still a bugger bear to be wrestled on a daily basis. German was just as bad as English when it came to making life miserable for me. Since one year of a foreign language was required for admission to veterinary school, I had to take it and pass it. Like chopping cotton or cleaning out the barns, English and German were necessary evils. I had handled the first two and I was going to handle the last two.

My squad was making good progress. Nobody had questioned my method except my roommates. They thought I must be goofing off since I continued to come in from drill in a good mood and wearing relatively dry clothes. They continued to come back from drill soaked with sweat and swearing like mule skinners. I still felt that they would only ridicule my method if we discussed it. It made me uncomfortable when they asked questions and I gave them evasive answers, but what else was there to do?

On one of those nights when sleep was elusive, I thought for a long time about the changes that were taking place. My temper was definitely under better control. I had become more patient with myself and with other people. My tolerance level was also rising. Situations and people that would have fired me up to the boiling point last year were being viewed from a calmer, more analytical perspective that led to solutions rather than to explosions. Calamities that panicked others just strengthened my resolve to do what had to be done. I had learned to try my own methods rather than blindly accepting "the way we've always done it." The freshmen and upper classmen seemed to like and respect me. Nobody thought I was soft even though I had never paddled nor otherwise abused a single rat. It could be that adhering to the Golden Rule was practical even in a military school. Growing, changing, learning, trying new things, taking responsibility for my own life, helping other people...maybe this was what becoming a man was all about.

My love life wasn't going as well as my school life. Carolyn had agreed that Saturday nights were mine whenever I got home. I was getting home almost every weekend although I rarely knew before Saturday morning whether I had earned a pass. The first weekend in October I got a ride home late on Saturday afternoon. After a quick supper, Joe dropped me off at Carolyn's house on his way to see his girl.

As soon as I walked up to the porch, I knew something was wrong. There was a strange car in the driveway. Miss Jennie answered the door almost before I knocked. She greeted me awkwardly and said that Carolyn had another date. "Carolyn has a what? She said herself that Saturday nights were mine!" "I'm sorry, John. We don't have anything to do with who dates Carolyn when. I think it would be best if you didn't come in the house tonight."

Whoa! I wasn't going to let Miss Carolyn Carr off that easily. Did they think she was just going to enjoy her date while I walked back to the farm? Thinking fast, I asked if I could use the telephone. She reluctantly consented and let me in the door. As I passed the living room, I caught a glimpse of a Clemson uniform and noticed a tense silence. Well, I would fix Miss Carolyn Carr's evening as royally as she had fixed mine.

Going straight to the telephone, I called the Brady's house and asked for Bonnie. When Bonnie answered, I put on an act that could have won an Academy Award. Speaking very distinctly so that Carolyn would hear every word, I sweet-talked Bonnie into coming over to pick me up. It wasn't hard to convince Bonnie that I was absolutely wild to see her. Her enthusiastic assurance that she would be right over made me feel better. I thanked Miss Jennie for the use of her phone and walked out of the house through the kind of tense silence that precedes a violent storm. I closed the door with unnecessary firmness and went out to the sidewalk.

Bonnie whizzed up in her father's car, slid over just enough to let me get under the steering wheel, and then wrapped those loving arms around me. I hugged her so tight, it's a wonder she didn't break. I was too mad to be gentle about anything. Good ole Bonnie just assumed that I was enthusiastic about seeing her and didn't ask any probing questions. At the movies I held Bonnie's hand and fumed about Carolyn. The combat scenes in the movie made a convenient cover for my hostility. Between a big moon and an affectionate Bonnie, I had calmed down by the end of the evening. I arranged to spend Sunday afternoon with Bonnie before she took me home.

Although Bonnie and I had a good time Sunday afternoon, I hated to go back to school. This was my first major spat with Carolyn and it was really sticking in my craw.

The sporadic letters between Clemson and Carr's Creek were awkward. Both of us were angry, confused, and hurt and we swung back and forth between being vindictive and conciliatory. It was weeks before things settled back down into a comfortable relationship. Carolyn had given me a shock that rattled my toenails. For the first time in six years, I had serious doubts about the future of our relationship. Bonnie reveled in the extra attention I lavished on her as I struggled to resolve my feelings about Carolyn. Carolyn was worse than a Chinese puzzle. I loved her and hated her.... she was wonderful and awful.... she was loyal and fickle.... she was smart and just plain dumb....she was sweet and considerate and she was as stubborn as a billy goat and as balky as a donkey.... she was ambitious and she was working hard to reach her goals, but she wasn't going to let me or anybody else take her for granted....she was prettier and smarter than Bonnie but not nearly as anxious to keep me happy.... she was my girl and she was two-timing me! Buzzing like a hive of angry bees, my thoughts produced both honey and venom.

I threw my extra energy into training my squad. They would be the best *#*# squad on campus. I taught them the manual of arms in their rooms, tutored them on the meanings of the commands, encouraged them, and sympathized with them until they would have knocked themselves out to please me any time and any place.

A big surprise hit us on the drill field just before State Fair Week. Without warning, it was announced that all squad leaders would sit out drill while the captains and platoon lieutenants led the freshman squads through competitive drills. The judges were the regular army officers and they would grade each squad on a point system. Feeling as antsy as though we were waiting for a pop quiz, the squad leaders sat near the judges.

As our squads drilled, we watched, prayed, laughed, cursed, and sweated. Some of the squads were awful and some of the mistakes could have come straight out a script for the Keystone Cops. Each squad leader suffered agonies as he watched the goofs of his own squad and laughed with gusto at the mistakes of the other squads.

Lord, have mercy! Captain Knox was drilling my squad. Breathing became a little easier as I realized that my guys were really looking good. They had studied their manuals, practiced their moves, and learned the commands. Best of all, they kept their heads, listened carefully, and responded confidently and well. I had warned them that when the surprise drill competition came, they would probably get some unfamiliar commands and that it would be wise for them to study all of the commands in the manual. Obviously they had done just that. Capt. Knox really put them through their paces and they responded as though they had been born and reared on a drill field. Out of the corner of my eye, I saw that many of the other squads were still having problems.

After the squad drills we returned to company formation. Capt. Knox explained that it would be three or four days before the results would be posted. Finally we were dismissed. I praised my guys for a job well done as we left the field. Most of the other squad leaders were doing their mule skinner routines.

That night Bill, Dick, and I discussed the drills. Dick was enraged because one of his squad members had continued to go forward when they were given the command, "To the rear, march." "That dumb buzzard was all by himself before he realized what he had done! Then he ran like a headless chicken to catch up with the squad! These rats get dumber every day!"

Bill was beside himself with fury at his squad. The rat who forgot the manual of arms and nearly dropped his rifle had really gotten his goat. "They are all stupid *#*%, but that turkey is impossible!"

When the conversation turned to my squad, they marvelled that my guys hadn't missed a single command and had executed the manual of arms perfectly. About that time there was a knock on the door. We expected an officer since this was a no visiting period. We stared like owls at Capt. Knox's rat slave. He had come to tell me that Capt. Knox wanted me to report to his room at once.

Well, what was this all about? Dick recovered first and said, "Go on, J.T., and let him tell you how wonderful you are."

Bill made a similar, more colorful comment as I went out the door.

Good grief! All the company officers were in Capt. Knox's room.

As soon as I reported to him, Bud dropped the military formalities and we spent the next fifteen minutes discussing the Riddle way of training a squad. They acknowledged that I must be doing something special because my squad had looked so good. Finally Bud laughed and said that we would have to wait a few days to see how good they had looked to the brass. He dismissed me, thanked me for doing a good job, and we exchanged good nights.

Bill and Dick were bursting with questions when I got back. Feeling impudent, I swore that Bud had chewed my tail for goofing off, for having a poorly trained squad, and for producing insufficient quantities of sweat and profanity among other things.

Their response was unprintable.

When the judges' sheets were posted, the Riddle method was vindicated. My squad's total score was far ahead of all the others. Man, that was some thrill.

I was still riding high when Dick and I tried out for the special drill team. Bill had declined because just marching to the mess hall was more than enough drilling to suit his taste. We were all shocked when I was eliminated. We figured that try-outs for me were just a formality. Capt. Knox told me later that my height had kept me off the team. They had decided to keep all the heights within the range of five feet, ten inches to an even six feet. My five feet, eight inches didn't fit. Dick made the team and I was the first of six alternates. Well, I could be happy for Dick and I could be feel better knowing that at least I wasn't keeping somebody off the team who could stay on it after I transferred to vet school. I still hated losing!

In many ways things were pretty much like my freshman year. That *** bugler still blasted us awake every morning and made shivers run down my spine every night. The days were filled with calisthenics, classes, labs, drills, meals, errands, and studying. The evenings passed with a little recreation and a lot of study. There were some vast improvements—I wasn't a rat nor a slave, I had two slaves to do my bidding, Dick was the table captain, I got along well with my old ladies, and I went home almost every weekend.

There were two jokers in my deck. One was Carolyn and the other was Rat Coleman.

Carolyn and I had each seen the other with dates on Saturday night and that was supposed to be our night. Usually those encounters were accidental. Occasionally one of us would deliberately take a date where the other was likely to see us. We were both too proud and too stubborn and too hurt to deal rationally with the problem. There were fireworks and hurt feelings every time it happened. Both of us had some serious doubts about our future together and neither of us was willing to end the relationship.

Rat Coleman was an arrogant braggart from Charleston who was always spouting off about the superiority of Charleston and Charlestonians. According to him, the cadets from Charleston ran Clemson the way they wanted it to be run. That didn't set very well with anybody. It riled me worse every time I heard it. I spoke to him privately several times and told him that rats didn't come to Clemson to brag about anything. He was warned that he had better keep his mouth shut about the glories of the Charleston contingent. When that didn't make him stop, I promised to beat the + ¿*@ of him the next time he made such a statement in my presence.

A few days later at lunch, Rat Coleman sat at our table and spouted off again. I asked him if he remembered my promise. He said that he remembered it and that he didn't believe a word of it. While he added a few other smart comments, I reached the boiling point. I ordered him to repeat for the benefit of the whole table what he had been promised. On the second try, he got it right—until he added that he wasn't afraid of me nor my threats.

In a flash, Dick was on his feet and unscrewing the cap on a pitcher of syrup. As he emptied the whole pitcher on Coleman's head, he snapped, "Now, Mr. Smart A--, you can bet your sweet a-- that you will be Cpl. Riddle's guest in our room promptly at 7:30 tonight. You can come yourself, or we'll find you and bring you there!"

All of us gaped at the rivers of syrup running down Coleman's face and uniform. It was an incredible mess that was drawing stares from all over the mess hall. Still fuming, Dick growled, "Now get your sweet a-- out of here!"

We finished our lunch and I went on with the scheduled activities of the afternoon. I put Rat Coleman pretty much out of my mind until supper time. He did not sit at our table but he was the central topic of discussion. Dick assured me that if I didn't beat the +*#% out of Coleman, he would.

If I was going to paddle a rat, I was going to do a creditable job of it. Bill, Dick, and I got out our paddles and put them so that they would be handy before we settled down to study.

At 7:30, Rat Coleman knocked on our door. Apparently the boy didn't learn very fast. The first thing he did was attempt to lie his way out of the situation. I cut him short and ordered him to assume the position. As he bent over, I noticed that his pants were already getting tight across his rear—a sure sign of city-boy softness. My first lick shattered the paddle into a dozen pieces. That surprised all of us. Coleman started to straighten up and Dick snapped, "Just stay where you are, rat!" as he handed me his paddle.

I hit him five additional licks, being careful to make a convincing noise without doing any real damage to anything but his pride. Then I ordered him to straighten up and promise me that he would never brag again about how the Charleston boys ran Clemson. He made the promise and I dismissed him. The whole incident left a sour taste although the shattered paddle tales grew to legendary proportions.

The next day Coleman requested and was granted a transfer to another company. All of us were relieved to be rid of him. He had affected the whole company like a cockle burr—always irritating and never helping anything.

After long roll, Bud Knox came by our room. He needed some information in order to make his report on the reasons for Coleman's transfer. We told him the whole story including the syrup and the paddle. He laughed with us and agreed that Coleman hadn't left us much choice if we were to maintain our positions of command. He had figured that Coleman had created the problems. Before he left, he assured us that we had nothing to worry about.

Thanksgiving and Christmas came and went much as they had the previous year. Nothing spectacular happened as we plodded through the dreary cold of January and the end of the semester. Life had settled into a routine that was almost dull.

CHAPTER 15

In January when the flu epidemic hit the campus, chaos followed. The campus was quarantined—sick cadets couldn't be sent home and families couldn't enter the campus to take care of them. With more than five hundred cadets sick with influenza, the infirmary's twelve beds and limited staff were swamped. When the quarantine was announced, the cadet colonel asked for twenty volunteers from the pre-med students to help with nursing duties. Volunteers would meet in the mess hall immediately following lunch. I thought about the advice about not volunteering for anything and decided that this was an emergency and that I should do what I could to help.

Close to one hundred and fifty cadets met with Dr. Milford and Col. Weekes. They explained the seriousness of the situation, told us what we could do to help, and asked us to fill out a form. (You couldn't legally spit without a form if you were choking! Well, what was one more form?) They told us that they would announce at lunch the next day the names of the twenty most qualified to help, thanked us all for coming, and dismissed us.

When I told Bill and Dick about volunteering, they warned me that this was a risky thing to do. I disagreed since we had all been exposed anyway. Then I suggested that we probably wouldn't hear any more about my volunteering because there were so many others to choose from.

During lunch the next day, the list was read and it included John T. Riddle. Those rascals at our table started their razzing immediately. "Well, you won't have to worry about the flu anymore. Ole John will lay his healing hands on the brows of the infirm and they'll get up and walk out healed of all their diseases!"

When I had finished eating, I asked them if they were willing to help me with my healing. When they agreed, I suggested that they could start by kissing my south side when I headed north to the temporary barracks. That startled them into a brief silence.

The temporary barracks were like one of those terrible scenes in a war movie. The male nurses who had been brought in were hopelessly outnumbered by their coughing, gagging, retching, groaning

98

patients. Dr. Milford held a quick meeting with us. He told us the seriousness of the situation, ordered us to wear our white uniform pants and shirts, to glue red crosses on our shirt sleeves at the level the stripes would be, and to forget classes and drills until the epidemic was under control. He thanked us for our willingness to help and dismissed us to return to our rooms, change into the whites and get back pronto.

The red crosses on our sleeves obtained some unusual privileges for us. They permitted us to go anywhere on campus at any hour. Since we would have four hours on duty and four hours off, the mess hall was being kept open around the clock for our convenience. Those red crosses entitled us to order what we wanted when we wanted it in the mess hall. We would not have to choose between getting to meals on time or missing them altogether. At least the administration was creating enough slack in the usual rules to permit us to do what we had to do. We soon learned that privilege has its price.

With over five hundred sick cadets in the temporary barracks and more getting sick by the hour, we had our work cut out for us. Being sick is rough any time. Being sick away from home in a mob scene situation with inadequate care and facilities was creating panic among the cadets. That flu was severe enough to make you think you were going to die under the best of conditions. Under the conditions we had, it was understandable that many of the patients suffered as much from their fears as from the disease. I hurried to my room, changed into my whites, and rushed back to the temporary sick bay.

Each volunteer on our shift was given a clipboard with the names and room numbers of his patients. We checked temperatures, breathing rates, and blood pressures, recorded them on the patient charts, noted any drastic changes, dispensed medicines, and did whatever else we could do to calm them down and make them comfortable. My experiences handling sick and hurt animals with Papa and Dr. Grear had been good preparation for this. Just being calm and confident and treating them kindly seemed to help as much as anything else. At times I wondered whether it was a convenience or a nuisance to have patients who could talk. I didn't have to guess what they wanted or needed; I did have to answer millions of questions and listen to at least twice that many complaints!

Since I was off-duty at supper time, I ate at my regular table.

They were curious about what I was doing and bombarded me with questions. I enjoyed being with cadets who were healthy enough to take care of themselves. I told Dick that I would try to get back to our room during the night if things were under control enough for me to leave sick bay. They hassled me a little about my healing abilities and I made sure they got as much ribbing as they gave.

In my letters to Mama and to Carolyn, I explained that the whole campus was under quarantine and not to expect me to come home for awhile. They would have worried if they had known about my volunteer work, so that wasn't mentioned. They sent me all sorts of clippings about the flu outbreak and how to avoid catching the flu. Heaven knows what they would have sent if they had known that I was working in the middle of the situation.

Things got worse before they got better. There were so many patients it took almost four hours to make our rounds once. Sitting down or resting during the shift was impossible. After a couple of days, our schedules were changed to let us spend every third night in our own rooms. That way we got one full night's sleep for every two nights of working for four hours and being off for four hours. The pace was brutal, the work was physically and emotionally hard, and still the epidemic went on. The male nurses checked our charts and called Dr. Milford's attention to drastic changes in a patient's condition. Dr. Milford made rounds twice a day. We wondered how on earth he could stay on his feet, let alone practice medicine.

After ten days the number of new cases began to drop and the number of patients well enough to be dismissed finally started to climb. After fourteen days Dr. Milford thanked us for our help and dismissed us. Miraculously not one of the student volunteers contracted the flu nor showed any sign of illness.

At the first chapel service after the epidemic, all of the volunteers were summoned to the stage. Dr. Milford praised us for our help and presented each of us with a certificate of appreciation describing our services. The student body gave us a standing ovation—the first one I had seen in that auditorium. We had done a hard job well, we had helped our fellow men, and we had gone the extra mile. Each of us had taken a major step toward manhood.

CHAPTER 16

With the approach of spring came the traditional outbreak of craziness that seems to afflict every college campus. You could bet that our clown princes would come up with a spectacular stunt. Peter was the rascal this time. Unfortunately, I found out what he was going to do before he did it. As usual, I couldn't talk him out of it. This would leave me to wrestle with the misery of knowing who did it and being dishonest with the company officers because I couldn't tell the truth without being disloyal to my friend. Why did I always have to be around when they did something major?

It started out so innocently—I just walked down to the latrine to brush my teeth before "Taps." Peter was busily wrapping toilet tissue around a sprinkler head. When I asked what he was doing, he replied, "Just rigging up a little excitement to break the monotony of this place. There's more life in the morgue than there is around here!"

As I tried to dissuade him, he finished his wrapping and began draping a strip of tissue to serve as a fuse. He had figured out how long it had to be to give him enough time to get back to his room and into his bed before the water show. He was obviously going to do his thing. If I stayed around to brush my teeth, I was going to share the credit for his stunt. A strategic retreat at top speed was the only intelligent move. Running like a startled deer, I hightailed it back to my room and into my bunk. I told Bill and Dick to turn off the lights and to get into their bunks immediately. We could discuss the reasons after they did it. They were puzzled, but they did what I said.

As we lay in the darkness, talking quietly, I explained what Peter had done. All of us knew that a temperature of 160 degrees Fahrenheit would melt the lead plug in a sprinkler head. This would turn on the sprinkler in the latrine and set off the fire alarms all over the campus. It would also set off an alarm in the fire station and bring out the fire department. This would create a major uproar. Getting caught setting off a sprinkler was a shipping offense.

We all heard Peter run quietly down the hall, enter his room, and close the door. He had rigged the sprinkler carefully and we knew him well enough to know that the trick would work and that he would not get caught. All we could do was wait for the performance to begin.

It didn't take long. The plug blew with a noise like a shotgun being fired. Then came the hiss of water and the clanging of the fire alarms. All through the barracks feet hit the floor, lights came on, and boys rushed to their doors to see where the fire was. The company officers had found enough charred, soaked tissue to know what had happened. They were racing up and down the hall yelling at everybody, "Stay in your room and keep your door closed! Stay in your room and keep your door closed!"

It was tough to close the door and to shut off our view of the madhouse. It was the circus, the Keystone Cops, and the Marx Brothers all rolled into one giant show.

When we closed the door, Dick and Bill started laughing like a pair of idiots. The harder they tried to stop, the more tickled they got. I warned them that they had better quit laughing before the officer stampede reached our door. They just laughed harder. When the inquisitors came around, Bill and Dick somehow managed to get instantly serious. I never did figure out how they did it.

The firemen cleaned up the mess and announced that they would be back the next day to conduct their investigation. Capt. Knox immediately ordered the whole company to fall into formation. That was the most ridiculous looking company of ragamuffins you can imagine. I had no idea that a bunch of boys could come up with such a wide and wild assortment of sleepwear. We wore uniforms during the day—night clothes were anything but uniform! We all started to laugh at our ludicrous appearance. One look at Capt. Knox as he called us to attention stifled any thought of laughing. He was absolutely furious. He left us at attention as he stormed about taking this episode as a personal affront to himself and to his officers—particularly after the snake incident. He preached about responsibility and honesty, threatened to deal personally with the culprit, ad infinitum. I knew that he was just blowing smoke. He wasn't going to find the culprit and he wasn't going to do anything but frustrate himself and everybody else with his investigation. I was right, too. He, the firemen, and the company officers tried everything in the book and still found out nothing. The clown princes had won another round.

A few days later, we had the formal freshman drill competition. Capt. Knox drilled my squad. Those guys were perfect. They did even better than they had done in the surprise drill. While other squads panicked and screwed up, my squad looked like professional soldiers. I could tell that Capt. Knox was thoroughly enjoying showing them off and that they were proud of themselves. Man, it was a thrill to watch them and to know that my training method had worked so well.

Nobody was surprised when my squad won first place in the whole brigade. The after effects surprised the heck out of me. First, I was dunked in the pool at the Y—a privilege usually reserved for seniors. Then I was given a citation by the regular army officers. Third, I was ordered to meet with Col. Bell, the brigade commander, in his room. That was enough to make my heart race. As usual, there was no explanation for the order—just do it without asking any questions.

I changed into a fresh uniform, shined my shoes, and appeared in Col. Bell's room exactly at seven o'clock as ordered. I didn't know whether he would decorate me or hang me, but I was going to be dressed for the occasion. I took a deep breath before saying, "Cpl. Riddle reporting, sir."

His first order was, "At ease!"

Well, he wasn't mad because he invited me to sit down and to light up if I wanted a cigarette. I had left them in my room so that I wouldn't smoke on such an auspicious occasion. As nervous as I was, they would have been comforting, but I survived without them.

Col. Bell's next words were a real shock, "Your company commander tells me that with his consent you have initiated a new method of training your squad and that they won the brigade championship as a direct result of that training. I want you to explain exactly what you did, how you did it, and why you did it. We may adopt it to replace the traditional training method for freshmen!"

Whoa, hoss! A corporal doesn't tell the brigade commander how to do anything! On the other hand, a corporal surely doesn't disregard a direct order from the brigade commander. With my heart perched on my vocal cords, I explained the whys and wherefores, beginning with my own miserable experiences as a frightened rat and my success in training animals on the farm. Realizing that people and animals often respond in similar ways had led me to try those methods which had worked best on the animals. He listened with interest and respect and asked a number of questions. Finally, he smiled, assured me that I would hear more about this later, thanked me, and dismissed me. Whew!

I wondered exactly what I was going to hear...and when I was going to hear it...but I knew perfectly well that asking questions after he had dismissed me wasn't a good idea. "Keep your britches on, John, and just be patient!" rang in my ears from all the times I had heard it as a boy. Resolutely, I kept my mouth shut.

There was too much going on for me to spend time worrying. I had noticed that Dick rarely mentioned his family and that he seldom went home for the weekend. Impulsively, I invited him to spend a weekend with me on the farm. He accepted with alacrity. We agreed to wait for two weeks so that I could make all the necessary arrangements with Mama, the family, and Carolyn to really show him a country good time.

I went home that weekend and we planned all the details. Dick and I would hitch-hike to the dairy office in Greenville and ride home on the truck, Mama would fix up the guest room for Dick and me, Bly would let us use his car Friday night and Saturday might, Carolyn would get dates for him on Friday night and Saturday night, and finally Joe would drive us back to Clemson on Sunday afternoon. I knew better than to mention planning the food. Mama and my sisters would feed us like royalty—starving royalty. They loved to "put on a big feed." With all that settled, I went back to Clemson to anticipate the next weekend.

It was a full week. On Wednesday afternoon we were to have a full-dress brigade review honoring Congressman James F. Byrnes. Those white uniforms looked sharp and our brass gleamed like gold when we marched to lunch. Unfortunately Rat Watson decided that some catsup would improve the flavor of our "mystery meat" patties. I watched with mounting amusement as he struggled to get the catsup out of the bottle and on to the patty. When frustration overcame judgment, he smacked the bottom of the bottle hard. Oh, *%#! The world turned red as catsup erupted from the bottle and hit me squarely in the face. In a heartbeat, I was covered with catsup from my hair to my shoes. The table exploded with laughter. The expression on Watson's face as I wiped the catsup out of my eyes was beyond description. He literally flew around the table and began frantically trying to clean off my uniform as he apologized profusely. It was a futile effort. About the time the laughter died down, I felt a hand on my shoulder. Capt. Knox had seen the whole thing. Battling manfully to keep from laughing, he told me to finish my lunch and then just to ease on back to the barracks and to stay out of sight until after the festivities. He would cover my absence.

After the parade, Rat Watson came by my room and took my uniform to the laundry for me. He was still apologetic and I didn't tell him that I had thoroughly enjoyed my unexpected nap while they sweated out their performance.

Dick and I were ready to go to Greenville the minute we got out of classes on Friday. We were first in the line of hitch-hikers. The third car that came along stopped and picked us up. The couple was from Georgia and they were going to visit friends in Greenville. The conversation was lively and pleasant right up to the moment they dropped us off at Papa's office. The timing was perfect. We got a ride home on the milk truck and by the middle of the afternoon we were sitting in the kitchen enjoying one of Mama's fabulous cakes.

Dick was at his charming best and Mama was in her glory feeding a boy who really appreciated her cooking. Papa came in, visited with us for a little while, and told us that we could use the vehicles in the yard if we needed transportation.

After a little while, we changed into overalls and went down to the dairy barn. Dick met my brothers and stared in awe at the cows and the milking machines. I told him about milking eighteen cows twice a day before I went to Clemson only to have Papa put in milking machines the day I left. He thought that was much funnier than I did.

I picked up two rifles and four boxes of cartridges as we headed out to one of the trucks. We rode down to the river and then hiked along it as I showed Dick the creek, the fishing holes, the swimming holes, the muskrat slides, and other points of interest. We acted like two farm boys playing hooky as we rambled along, talking and shooting at all sorts of things. Dick was fascinated by my shooting ability and by my tales of trapping muskrats for their pelts. He seemed to think that I was Tom Sawyer, II.

By the time we got back to the house, Mama and my sisters had supper ready. They had fixed a meal that would have won "Best in Show" at the State Fair. Papa said the blessing and we settled down to some serious eating—without an Irish potato in sight! Dick charmed everybody with his conversation and with his obvious enjoyment of the food, the family, and the farm.

After supper, we got cleaned up and dressed fit to kill in our uniforms. (We had learned our lesson about eating in those whites!) The family was impressed with our appearance although they weren't sure they would enjoy living with two thousand people all dressed alike. Papa vowed that he never would learn to tell one from another.

By the time we were ready to leave for Carr's Creek, Papa had slipped me twenty dollars, Mama had slipped me ten dollars, and Bly had washed and polished his car and filled it with gas for us. He asked if I needed any money when he handed me the keys and I told him that Papa had fixed that. With a round of good wishes for a fine evening, we set off to Carolyn's house.

Carolyn would have been a perfect cover girl for any magazine. She looked wonderful and excitement made her sparkle. Dick was impressed with her and pulled out all the stops on his charm. She called her parents in to meet Dick. We chatted for a few minutes and then left to pick up Dick's date.

Carolyn's cousin was pretty and she knew how to turn on the charm. She and Dick hit it off just fine. The four of us had a great time going to a movie and getting a hamburger at the drive-in afterward. Eleven o'clock and goodnights came all too early. On our way back to the farm, Dick turned to me and said, "Old lady, you are the luckiest guy I know. Your family is wonderful and Carolyn is an absolute jewel. Don't you ever let that little gal get away!"

I assured him that I had no intention of losing her and that he had better not get any ideas about girl-snatching.

We relished going to bed without "Taps" and waking up about nine o'clock without "Reveille." Mama stuffed us with coffee, country ham, grits, eggs, and her famous biscuits. As we ate, Dick remarked, "Old lady, it's no wonder you come home every weekend!"

Oops! Mama had never heard us use that expression to each other and she thought he was calling her an old lady. After a thorough explanation, she understood what it meant. Dick apologized at least half a dozen times—he was terribly embarrassed and worried that he had hurt her feelings. If he had had any idea how hard Mama's life had been, he would have known how much time she would spend worrying about a little thing like that!

We spent the morning riding around seeing the sights of the community and the afternoon playing Tom Sawyer. He was impressed with my tales of riding Sonny Boy to catch the school bus and other tales of my high school days. I taught him how to shoot pennies in the air, to strike matches by shooting them, and a few other tricks. He hadn't realized that when you wanted to hit a rising target, you followed it up with your sights until it reached the apex of its trajectory and then fired in that split second before it started to fall. He learned quickly and was soon duplicating many of my stunts. Amazed at my shooting skills, he asked why I wasn't on the Clemson rifle team. He was genuinely surprised to learn that I had been disqualified for firing from the left shoulder.

Mama stuffed us with a huge array of food at lunch and at supper. She revelled in Dick's compliments and in his enjoyment of her meals.

That night Carolyn had gotten Dick a date with Jane Campbell. She, too, was a doll. None of us wanted to see a movie so we drove up to the top of Paris Mountain. With stars overhead and the lights of Greenville below, Dick agreed that it was a great place to spend an evening. Life was sweet until at least half of the county showed up to park beside us.

By the time we decided where to go to get something to eat and actually got the food, it was curfew. Reluctantly we took Carolyn and Jane home and returned to the farm for a good night's sleep.

On Sunday, Mama stuffed us with more of her good food before and after church. Shortly after dinner, (it would be heresy to call a meal of that size "lunch!") Joe and his girl drove us back to Clemson in his new red Plymouth. Dick had to study for a calculus test and I had to do a book report. We settled down to study in a hurry, but Dick talked for weeks about his weekend with the Riddles and about my prowess with a rifle. Before long, half the company was calling me "Crack Shot." That was one nickname I didn't like—it was too close to "crackpot!"

CHAPTER 17

Easter came along with the annual Moonlight Parade. Those parades were the highlight of spring at Clemson. It gave me a real thrill to march in the cool evening breeze under a full moon with two thousand cadets resplendent in sparkling white uniforms set off by gleaming black shoes. The long hours on the drill field seemed worthwhile when the whole brigade moved like one magnificent machine. I was disappointed that Mama didn't come to see the parade this year either. She would have loved it if her shy country ways had permitted her to leave the farm and to come to college. Unfortunately she never overcame her fear of embarrassing herself and her family and she never attended any of the special events of my college years.

Wednesday afternoon there was a letter lying on my desk. It was addressed to me and marked, "Company Business—Personal." Now what? I sat on the edge of Dick's bed for a minute to get up my courage to open it. There was a summons to Capt. Knox's office for a private discussion. Lord, I wish these guys would explain what they want instead of making me sweat trying to guess! Well, wishes don't accomplish much. Quickly I changed into a fresh uniform, gave my shoes a fast shine, and went down to see Bud.

He invited me into his room and then let me stand there forever while he shuffled papers. I thought he would never get around to saying, "At ease!" Finally the order came and was quickly followed by the statement that we were going to cut out the formalities and talk man-to-man. At least he wasn't planning to chew my *#.

The subject of the discussion was my future. He had heard that I was going to leave Clemson at the end of the year. I agreed that this was my plan. He reviewed my accomplishments at Clemson. Then he told me that he was offering me a promotion next year that could lead to my achieving the rank of major my senior year. That would lead directly to my receiving an officer's commission in the U.S. Army after graduation. He praised everything from my posture through my academic achievements as well as the accomplishments I had made with my squad. Well, this was something that had never crossed my mind. I had come to Clemson in order to prepare to go to veterinary school. A military career hadn't even been considered and yet here was a fantastic offer dropping right into my lap. Now, what was I supposed to do?

Bud sensed that I was wrestling with my decision and, being Bud, he suggested that I take a couple of weeks to think things over before I answered him. I thanked him for his compliments, for the wonderful offer he was making, and for the chance to think about it. I walked out of his room with a million questions swarming around inside my head.

Still stunned, I went back to my room. This was a tough decision and the answer would affect the course of the rest of my life. Maybe I had better go home where I could weigh the pros and cons privately. I knew that none of the family could help me. They didn't have the knowledge nor the sophistication to judge the offer. At seventeen—well, almost eighteen,—I wasn't sure that I was prepared to make the decision either. Ready or not, I was going to have to make a decision and it had better be the right one.

Friday I went home. I asked Mama if I could take a card table and a chair into the guest room to do some work in private. She agreed to see that no one disturbed me. As she turned back to her work, I saw that she was upset by my request. Finally, she asked quietly, "John, are you in trouble?"

'No, ma'am. I am not in trouble except that I don't know what to do about a wonderful offer that I have received. If I stay at Clemson, I will become one of the highest ranking students on the campus. The problem is that it will delay my becoming a veterinarian. I'm going to sit here and figure out the best thing to do."

Relief showed clearly as she said, "Well, I don't know about ranking, but you have always done good in whatever you've undertaken."

In my mind's eye, I could see Dr. Kinard bristle, but I wasn't going to hurt Mama by seeming to correct her English. Giving her a big hug, I laughed and said, "I'm gonna do good on this, too!"

Unfolding the rumpled yellow sheet of paper on which I had listed my goals when I was twelve years old, I showed her the ones that had been checked off and the ones that remained to be achieved. Assuring me again that she was confident that I would choose wisely, she left me to my struggle. After making a copy of my original goals, I added a few new ones. Then I set up two sheets of paper with headings. One had "Reasons to go back to Clemson;" the other had "Reasons to stick to my original plans."

Reasons for both lists seemed to come out of the very walls. If I went to Auburn, I could get a job and pay for more than half of my expenses. (This would ease my parents' burden.) If I went back to Clemson, I could be a big dog in a big yard. (I had enjoyed being the big dog in the little yard in high school. This was mighty tempting!) If I went back to Clemson, I could get home nearly every weekend and Carolyn wouldn't get lonesome enough to date anybody else. (She had better not even think of dating anybody else!) If I went to Auburn, I could finish my education two years earlier and then I could marry Carolyn. Back and forth, round and round, my mind spun first one way and then another. I prayed for God's guidance in making the right decision. After two hours, I had made up my mind. Getting a veterinary practice established was more important than building a military career; getting married was more important than being prominent on campus; and I was going on to Auburn and to stick to my original plans. Just in case Auburn didn't accept my application, I would apply to the veterinary school in Ames, Iowa, too.

After I had made my decision, I wrote a letter to Capt. Knox thanking him for his leadership, for his personal concern for me, and for his generous offer. I told him that I had weighed all the factors and had decided to go on to Auburn. As a courtesy, I listed my pros and cons and suggested that after he had read them, he could point out anything that he thought I had missed. I put the letter in my backpack so that I could personally deliver it to Bud.

The rest of the weekend passed in a sort of haze. Sunday night I decided to wait until Monday to deliver the letter. Finally, just before Monday's long roll, I took it down to Bud and told him that I had spent a tough weekend and I had come to a decision. After handing him the letter, I excused myself and left.

After long roll, Bud called me by name, "John Riddle," a most unusual occurrence, and told me to come by his room before ten o'clock. I nodded and went to my room to study. I couldn't keep my eyes on the page nor my mind on the material. Finally, I slammed the book shut and got up to go to Bud's room. This startled Bill and Dick. Both of them asked what was wrong, stared when I told them I was going visiting, and warned me that I would get demerits for sure for visiting after long roll. With the comment that I could stand a few demerits, I left them in a state of shock and walked down to Bud's room.

I went through the whole military routine until Bud ordered me to drop it. We went through my letter and my reasons and even looked at that old crumpled yellow list of goals. Bud was amazed that I had set my goals so early and had followed them with such determination and consistency. He assured me that I would be admitted to veterinary school and that I would be a good doctor although he hated for Clemson to lose such a good man. From there we got into a bull session about our families, our childhoods, and our futures. After more than an hour, we shook hands and said good night. There was a tension in that room that brought tears to both our eyes and kept our hands together for long extra seconds. We both knew that our lives would go separate ways and that we were approaching the end of a wonderful friendship.*

When I got back to the room, Bill and Dick demanded to know where in the #%! I had been for so long. I really didn't want to talk about it—that premonition that I wasn't going to see Bud after Clemson was tearing me up. Finally I said that I had gone visiting to get rid of a problem that had tormented me for two weeks....that I had killed my chance for a military career....and that I didn't want to talk....I just wanted to hit the sack. Bill and Dick respected my feelings enough to let me deal with my troubled thoughts in supportive silence. They were there in the room, but they didn't ask any more questions.

There was another first for me that week. After long roll one night, I discovered that I was out of matches. I eased our door open, checked the hall, and slipped across to Private Boozer's room. Just as I asked him for a match, Lt. Jones opened the door and demanded, "Cpl. Riddle, what in #*# are you doing in here?"

I explained that I was getting a match. He explained that I was getting ten demerits. We discussed it briefly and I pointed out that I hadn't gotten a single demerit in my entire Clemson career. He decided to impress the captain by giving me the ten demerits. I thought he must be kidding.

The next day my name and demerits were on the bulletin board. Well, if he could be funny, I could be funnier. Having devised a fool-proof stratagem, I selected ten freshmen to handle the situa-

---

*I went on to become a veterinarian; Bud went on to a military career in World War II.

tion. This was the plan: when Lt. Jones came in from class on Thursday, they were to be stripped down to their skivvies; they would grab him before he even got his cap off and give him a thorough dunking in the shower; then they would run like the dickens back to their rooms before he got the water out of his eyes to see who they were. Dunking a lieutenant was a big deal and some of them were a little skittish. I assured them of two things: (1) they would not get into trouble for dunking Lt. Jones; (2) they would get a whale of a whipping from me if they didn't dunk him. With a final warning that under no circumstances was my name to be mentioned, I left them to finish working out the details. It worked beautifully. When Jones got over being mad and started laughing, he asked why they were drowning him and who had instigated it. They all yelled, "Nobody!" and ran out before he could see who they were.

Three or four days later he came to our room to ask me how I had rounded up that bunch of freshmen who had almost drowned him. Playing dumb and innocent, I told him that if I had wanted him to have a shower, I would have joined them. He said that I had surely put the fear of God—or somebody—into them because none of them would talk. We declared a truce and were good friends for the rest of the year.

The seniors had finished their exams and had begun to work their special brand of magic. Their first trick was to visit the hog pens on the experimental farm and to steal a whole litter of pigs. By some magic, those little pigs managed to make their way into the president's office where they spent the night. By morning, the office had a most unpresidential atmosphere.

Via the grapevine, word got around the campus that senior magic was going to fire the cannon beside the administration building about nine o'clock at night. A relic of World War I, that cannon weighed several tons. It had been mounted on a concrete ramp with about a third of each wheel sunk into the concrete. There was no way to move it so they elected to fire it where it stood. Persons unknown went to Anderson and bought several pounds of blasting powder which somehow got into the cannon. Other magicians used a ramrod to pack the barrel with rolls of toilet tissue. The last touch of magic was to prime it and to drop in a lighted match.

All of us knew that we were not supposed to leave our rooms after long roll at eight o'clock. Rules or no rules, we had no intention of missing this show. We even set up a count-down. Precisely

at nine o'clock there was a monstrous boom and the cadet corps stampeded out to see the magic. It was incredible. The cannon had pulled out of the concrete and turned half-way around. Every tree and building in sight was draped in long flowing streamers of tissue. Even the dairy building, fully half a mile away, was decked out like a Maypole. We were all milling around when Major Dumas appeared. He was steamed up like an over-heated boiler. With his moustache twitching, he pulled out his little black book and began writing. Two cadet captains weighing at least two hundred pounds each approached him and I got close enough to hear one of them say, "Major, in the interest of your personal safety, we suggest that you put that book back in your pocket and get out of this crowd. Things are already out of control and you have made more than your share of enemies. We are not going to be responsible for your safety if you remain." With his Adolf Hitler moustache twitching faster than the nose of a spastic rabbit, Major Dumas assessed the situation for a full minute before he stuffed that *#%! book into his pocket and disappeared. That was my last encounter with the hateful rascal. I didn't even miss him a little bit!

The next morning the campus was a spectacle. Tissue was hanging everywhere. In daylight, the extent of the decorating project was even more unbelievable than it had been at night. The next week in chapel, it was announced that the clean-up and repair costs would exceed twelve thousand dollars!

Exams for the rest of us arrived. I wasn't worried about anything except German. That stuff was even worse than English. Having gotten a "C" at the end of first semester, I convinced myself that an "F" was inevitable. I didn't bother to study for the exam and had no intention of taking it.

When time arrived for the examination to begin, John Riddle was pacing around his room in the barracks. Like a thunder clap, one of his Papa's sayings roared through my head, "A wise man sometimes changes his mind; a fool never does." I grabbed my pencil and raced down to the classroom. The others had a twenty minute head-start on me, but I asked Dr. Rhine's permission to take the exam. He granted it, handed me a set of questions, and told me to find a seat in the back of the room. The first questions were surprisingly easy. The others got progressively harder and I struggled desperately through them. I finished about twenty minutes after my classmates. Dr. Rhine had waited patiently. When I handed him my paper, he asked how I had done. When I replied, "Much better than I expected to do," he dropped my paper into the trash can!

Oh, Lord! This was too much! The room swayed and I thought I was going to faint. After all that struggle, he was going to flunk me without even looking at my work! Then I realized that he was saying something. "Riddle, your grade is posted on the door. Check it as you go out!"

Merciful God! He had given me a "C"! Now I really felt faint. I gasped out, "Donkel, herr doctor! Donkel!" and fled into the fresh air as he wished me good luck.

In my room was a note to see Capt. Knox as soon as possible. I went straight to his office. We had another brief discussion of the advantages of staying at Clemson. Again, I reiterated my decision to get on with my career plans. This time we both knew that further discussion was futile. Bud was still thoughtful—he told me to let him know if I changed my mind by Friday. With mutual good wishes for health and happiness and a firm handshake, we parted for the last time.

I went back to the barracks to pack my gear and to wait for Bly. When he came to take me home, there were sad farewells with many of my friends. In the back of my mind, I seemed to hear a bugler playing "Taps"—a part of my life was ending and I was leaving a rich treasure of friends.*

*Thank God, none of us knew what lay ahead. When I received my first postwar Alumni News in 1946, I counted the names of one hundred and sixty-five of my Clemson friends who been killed in action. The loss was almost unbearable, especially since Sgt. Covington's name was the first one I saw.

CHAPTER 18

The summer of 1939 was a restless time. The world hovered on the brink of war and the feelings of uncertainty trickled down to all of us. I had not been able to decide whether to go to school in Ames, Iowa as Dr. Grear had done, or to go to Auburn. Finally, I sent duplicate applications with the idea that I would go wherever my application was accepted. While admissions committees were deciding my fate, I just drifted with the currents. I spent some time visiting Dr. Grear and some time helping with the farm work. Occasionally I helped out with the milk deliveries. I dated Carolyn regularly and dated Bonnie occasionally. Carolyn was definitely number one in my little black book and I was careful to keep from seriously riling her. Bonnie was a lot of fun, her family spoiled me, and I wasn't ready to give her up if a little attention would keep her on the string.

In mid-summer the ball dropped right back into my lap. My acceptance from Ames arrived on Tuesday and my acceptance from Auburn arrived on Wednesday. I took both acceptances over to Carolyn's house to discuss the pros and cons. Carolyn favored Auburn when she realized that Ames was almost a thousand miles from Greenville County. She knew there was no way for us to see each other regularly with that kind of distance. I was still undecided when I left Carr's Creek to go to see Dr. Grear. Knowing that a firm decision had to be made quickly, I promised Carolyn I would have a decision by evening when we had our regular date. Dr. Grear didn't hesitate to tell me that I would freeze my lips off in an Iowa winter and that his alma mater was just too far from Riddle's Dairy and Carr's Creek. By the time I left Dr. Grear's, I had made up my mind to attend Auburn.

I went back out to the farm to tell my folks that I decided to go to Auburn. Since Mama had never been outside the state of South Carolina, her concepts of geography were sketchy at best. Until I mentioned the approximate distances to Ames and to Auburn, she hadn't given much thought to which I should choose. Distance settled the matter for her—she was all in favor of Auburn.

The news was joyfully accepted at Carr's Creek. Carolyn was ecstatic until I stated that I would be studying too hard to come home very often. That put a definite chill on the evening. Carolyn and I had both gotten spoiled by my coming home almost every weekend from Clemson. She was stunned by my suggestion that she could come to Auburn to visit me. Her eyes snapped as she said, "Sure, I can. I can just see Mother bouncing off the ceiling at the very thought of such a thing!"

The evening was spent making plans and dreaming big dreams.

If I were going to Auburn, I needed to make some arrangements.

I planned to live off campus since that would cost less than living in the dormitory. I needed to get a job so that I could pay some of my expenses. Finding a job and a place to live required a trip to Auburn. Fortunately my older sister Blanche and her husband Jack developed an urge to take a little trip. It wasn't very hard to talk them into taking me to Auburn. We decided that it would be fun to take Carolyn, too. It took some tall promising and persuading before we convinced Mr. Paul and Miss Jennie to let Carolyn go.

They finally decided that Blanche and Jack would be good chaperones although they were not thrilled that we would be away overnight. We had a grand time making plans for the trip.

We left for Auburn early on the first Friday morning in August. In spite of three hundred miles of rough roads, we had a wonderful trip. The day was clear and hot and we were flying high, anticipating the future and thoroughly enjoying the present. When we pulled into the Auburn city limits about 2:30 in the afternoon, we were hot, thirsty, and starving as only the very young can be. While we were having lunch at a little cafe, the owner came over to chat. When I told him why I had come to Auburn, he suggested that I go to the Sheppard Chateau on East Thatch Street and talk to Mrs. Sheppard. He thought she might get both my problems solved at once. That sounded like a good idea to us. By the time we had finished drinking our tea, he had given us directions and wished us well.

At the time, Auburn was a beautiful little village built around an enormous campus. The Sheppard Chateau was easy to find. A pleasant looking lady was sitting on the front porch when we drove up. I walked up to the porch and asked if she was Mrs. Sheppard. She acknowledged that she was as she invited me to come in. When

I introduced myself and told her the reason for my visit, she asked two questions and got two affirmative replies. First, "Can you milk a cow?" and second, "Can you milk two cows?"

My "Yes," was what she wanted to hear. She invited Blanche, Jack, and Carolyn to get out of that hot car and to come up on the porch so that they could be more comfortable. As soon as I finished the introductions, she offered us something cool to drink. We declined with the explanation that we had just come from the cafe. I liked this lady already and she apparently liked me. She told the others to make themselves at home and asked them to excuse us while we talked business. The two of us walked out to the back porch. She pointed to her two beautiful Jersey cows, Daisy and Mae, and stated that if I would take care of them, she would provide room and board for me. We got the details straight right away—I would milk them twice a day, feed and water them, keep the stalls clean, and strain and refrigerate the milk. This was an unbelievable stroke of luck. She really frosted the cake when she added that I could choose my room while I was here. None of the other students had arrived so I would have first choice.

I thought this opportunity was too good to risk losing. As we went upstairs, I asked how many students lived at her house. She said that fifteen actually lived in the house and that she fed thirty-five at mealtime. The rooms were small but pleasant. I agreed to her conditions and chose my room before we went back downstairs. She stipulated that I would have a roommate and I agreed on the condition that I have a say in choosing him. That was fine and the deal was settled. I couldn't believe that things had worked out so easily and so well. I had never dreamed that I could get so much for so little work. She said that she was delighted to hear that my field was Veterinary Medicine because vet students never gave her any trouble—they spent all their time studying! I was having trouble concealing my happiness by the time we got back to the porch. With a quick assurance that I would be back in September, we said goodbye to Mrs. Sheppard and got back into the car.

As we rode away, I laughed out loud at the "hard bargain" Mrs. Sheppard had driven. My traveling companions were as surprised and happy as I was. Life was looking good. We drove past the Veterinary School and then headed north toward home.

The afternoon drive was relaxed and happy. All of us were relieved that I had made such good arrangements. By the time we got to

Gainesville, Georgia, the heat, the roads, the distance, and the excitement had taken their toll. Jack declared that he could not drive another mile. We stopped at The Dixie Hotel to spend the night. Blanche and Jack made sure to take care of both our money and our morals. We all slept in the same room because that was less expensive, and Blanche slept with Carolyn to make sure that I didn't get any improper notions! Well, our parents would have approved and I knew better than to object. We were all so tired, we went to sleep without even talking about our big day.

We showed our farm family background by waking up bright and early the next morning and having a big breakfast in the hotel dining room. Soon we were on the road to Greenville. In another two hours, we were pulling up to Carolyn's house. The Carrs were mighty glad to see their little girl safely back at home. They were pleased to hear my good news and understanding of my haste to tell my family about it.

When we got home, Mama and Papa thought we were teasing them. Room and board for taking care of two cows! That was too much! We agreed that I had certainly been in the right place at the right time to get such a good deal.

With only three weeks left before school started, we had to do some hustling. Mama started worrying about clothes right away. When she found out I wouldn't be wearing a uniform, she insisted that we go into Greenville and get me a new wardrobe. At my request, she took the stripes off my Clemson shirts. They were still good and fitted better than any shirts I had ever had. Everything was bought and packed in my Clemson trunk in plenty of time to ship it to Auburn.

Papa took care of the finances. He gave me enough cash to get by and then set up a checking account in my name. He was still cautious though—the account said John T. but the statements were to be sent to Mr. Charlie! "That way," he explained, "both of us will know where the money is going!"

The three weeks went by so fast that it seemed like we had hardly gotten back from our visit to Auburn before I was leaving to move into The Sheppard Chateau. By the night before my departure, everything had been done but the crying. Telling Bonnie goodbye and having her cry a little wasn't bad. I could handle that and I could handle the fond farewells to Mr. Paul and Miss Jennie. Carolyn was another story. When she started to cry, I got a lump as

big as one of Mama's cat head biscuits in my throat. I had gotten
through Clemson and I wasn't going to squall now—if it killed me!
I held her tight and told her this was necessary if we were going
to be able to share the lives we had planned. She cried and I choked.
Finally there was nothing left to do but to kiss her goodbye and
to leave. Man, it hurt to turn loose when we both knew how long
it is from September until Thanksgiving.

CHAPTER 19

With my trunk en route to Auburn via Railway Express, Mama and Papa got me and my suitcase and headed for the Greyhound Bus Station on Friday morning. Mama had no concept of where I was going and was puzzled when I mentioned the time difference between Auburn and Greenville. If even the times were different, I must be going far away. That realization turned on her tears and they were toughest of all to handle. Trying to comfort her, I promised to write to her often. She tried gamely to smile through her tears as she acknowledged that she wasn't much of a hand at writing. When she said that she would try her best to write to me, it brought home to me afresh how hard her life was and how bravely she shouldered her burdens. I came pretty close to losing the control switch on my tear ducts about that time. Papa started talking about how excited everybody was about having a vet in the family and there we were in front of the bus station. I had time to give Mama a hug and to shake Papa's hand and then I was rolling south toward Auburn.

I spent most of the trip sorting out my thoughts and feelings. By four o'clock that afternoon, I was in Auburn and ten minutes later I was walking up the front steps of my new home. Mrs. Sheppard's greeting was, "There comes my milk boy!"

From Papa's best milk hand to cock of the walk in high school to rat at Clemson to big man on the milk truck to Cpl. Riddle to "milk boy"—life sure ran in funny circles!

Mrs. Sheppard welcomed me and said that several of her other student boarders had arrived. She assured me that she had saved my chosen room and that I could go right on up and get settled. It didn't take long to unpack and put away my things, change into some old clothes, and get back downstairs to see what time Daisy and May were to be milked.

Mrs. Sheppard said that it was still a little early for milking, but I might as well go on and see how I came out. She seemed surprised when I requested some warm water and an old towel to clean the udders. She was definitely shocked to see me back in the kitchen with two pails of milk in less then ten minutes. Since Daisy and May had been more interested in the feed I had given them than in the milking process, I had had an easy time. As she showed me how she wanted the milk strained, we discussed my conviction that sanitation was important. None of her other "milk boys" had ever cleaned udders. When she asked me how I learned to milk so fast, I just laughed and told her that farm boys knew how to do everything. We agreed that the morning milking would be finished before breakfast was served at seven o'clock, that the evening milking would be finished before supper, and that she should order some feed for the cows. I wasn't about to tell her about Riddle's Dairy nor hint that this was the easiest room and board job I could have imagined.

I spent the weekend getting acquainted with my housemates. Mrs. Sheppard asked me to take Sabert Oglesby, her sister's grandson, as my roommate. He was a pleasant young man who was just beginning his college career. Mrs. Sheppard asked me to help him to get his college work off to a good start. He thought I was really something special when he found out that I had attended Clemson for two years. Like all male freshmen and sophomores at Auburn, he had to enroll in R.O.T.C., drill two hours per week, and take one hour per week of military science.

He was flabbergasted at the differences between the military programs at Clemson and Auburn. With my coaching, he breezed through his military training. When necessary, I helped him with his studies. In return, he voluntarily kept the room as straight as though he were my rat slave and was careful not to disturb my studies.

There were eleven other male students taking various engineering courses and two adult boarders. "Doc" Parrish, an Agricultural Extension Service agent assigned to the college, was about thirty years old. We gathered in his room for bull sessions when we were not studying. The other adult was "Red" Robinson, a furniture salesman who was about twenty-five years old. All of us were congenial and I felt that I had really found a good set-up.

Matriculation began on Monday morning. This time I knew the differences between "matriculation" and "castration"! On Tuesday morning, all first year veterinary students met in the auditorium of the administration building. The dean and several professors were on the stage. They welcomed us warmly and then the dean explained the new procedure that they were instituting. They had accepted three hundred students to the program because they estimated that one hundred and fifty of those would drop out after the first semester, ninety more would drop out by the end of the year, and approximately forty-five would still be there for graduation. They usually had about forty-five graduates so they had figured out the attrition rate and then decided how many freshman to accept. This sounded like a challenge to me. I made up my mind that John T. Riddle would be one of those graduates. We were instructed to come up to Vet Hill on Wednesday morning to get our schedules and then we were dismissed.

I walked out with a boy I had known slightly at Clemson. Bob commented that it sure sounded like these guys planned to flunk a whole bunch of people right quick.

By the time I had bought my books, dissecting kits, and other materials, I had made a real hole in my funds. This further convinced me to do well in order to protect my investment. My vocabulary acquired some strange words like anatomy, histology, physiology, and biochemistry, but at least the atmosphere was less threatening than it had been at Clemson.

My first afternoon in the anatomy laboratory reminded me of the obstacle course at Clemson. Both were thoroughly feared, despised, and cursed as places that would separate the men from the boys. The odor of formaldehyde was overwhelming. My eyes burned, my tears flowed, my lunch was doing cartwheels in my esophagus, and I was sure that I was suffocating. When my vision cleared enough to see my surroundings, I saw twenty horses and mules, each with hooks through its shoulders and its rump, suspended from the ceiling in such a manner that they appeared to be just standing there waiting for us. Rigor mortis held their heads erect and all of them faced the same direction. My body was commanding, "Retreat!" while my mind insisted that if hundreds of other vets had survived that outpost of Hell, I could handle it, too.

There was a loud knock and we turned toward the sound. There stood a small man who twitched his moustache and made an absolutely maddening noise clearing his throat with the regularity of a metronome. He said in a heavy German accent, "I am Dr. Mudhenck. I will teach you anatomy and histology. If you become a doctor of veterinary medicine, you will most certainly know who I am and you will master the material in my courses. You may also hate my guts—that will be up to you. You may withdraw from my classes at any time you choose. If you remain, you can be sure that you will know as much as you are able to learn about anatomy and histology. This will not be, as you say, 'a crip course!' "

That last statement was the understatement of the year. He was an absolute demon as an instructor. The lab itself had all the appeal of Hell and he was its worse torment. If he were a typical German Jew, (he wasn't!) most of us could have understood how The Holocaust came to be. He alphabetically divided us into groups of five. My group didn't look very promising. He required that we buy an anatomy textbook which cost twenty-five dollars, a tremendous expense in those days when a week's groceries for a family cost between five and ten dollars. We called it the "Freshman Bible," because a freshman was rarely seen without it no matter where he was nor what he was doing. We also had a manual which he had written in order to guide our dissections. After the first week of anatomy labs, we had lost twenty-five members of the class.

Anatomy lab was scheduled to last from one o'clock until five o'clock on weekday afternoons and from eight o'clock until noon on Saturdays. Schedules didn't disturb Dr. Mudhenck one bit as we soon discovered. He did things as he chose and the schedule could just go to #%*! At five o'clock one afternoon, he ordered us to clean up our areas of the lab and to meet in room 102 of the main building as soon as we had finished. Surprise! Surprise!

When we got to Room 102, that turkey had "a few questions" for us to answer. His *%#! pop quiz consisted of thirty-five discussion questions! When I finished at seven-thirty, everybody else in the class was still struggling, I had writer's cramp, Daisy and May were miserable because they hadn't been milked, Mrs. Sheppard was provoked, and I had missed my supper. The last poor student got out of 102 at nine o'clock!

Dr. Mudhenck never ran out of surprises. When we weren't blinded and choking on formaldehyde, we were blinded and choking on rage at him. My group started on the head and the other groups who shared our horse each had a different quarter.

As we dissected each part, we read the appropriate section in the manual, learned the names, and tagged each part we removed.

We had learned all two hundred and four bones in the horse, which bone was connected to what and by which muscle, before we could begin the dissection. You can believe he gave some wonderful pop quizzes on that.

To add to our misery, Dr. Mudhenck insisted that we each purchase a specific microscope which had a price tag of one hundred and fifty dollars! Well, that sealed my fate. With that much money tied up in books and equipment, I had to stick it out. Mr. Charlie Riddle would have had apoplexy for sure and there's no telling what ailments he would have inflicted on me if I had decided to quit!

When the schedules were finally worked out, I was taking six courses including histology, physiology, and medical terminology three times per week. That medical terminology course was tough since I had never had any Latin. It was another of those courses that thinned the ranks of our class quickly, but it turned out to be one of the most useful courses I had. My study time was divided so that I spent about half of my time on anatomy and the rest on my five other courses. Mercifully, all of my other professors scheduled their quizzes in advance. That gave us time to prepare for them.

By the end of the first six weeks, I had settled into a regular routine—well, as regular as you could be with Dr. Mudhenck! I spent long hours studying, but I made a lot of new friends. It's a good thing that I had learned that people tease you if they like you. When I got home late from anatomy lab, I had to milk while the others ate supper. When I came in the back door carrying my milk pails, they ribbed me endlessly about being a farm boy and having to milk for a living. I just retorted that I would rather milk and make my own way than sponge off somebody else.

My hard work paid off. When grades were posted I had all "A's!" There were three guys with five "A's" and one "B." I came to two conclusions as I looked at the list—I was definitely going to graduate and those three guys would not get ahead of me.

One night I finished studying early and joined the bull session in "Doc's" room. They were discussing me and my profession. "Doc" reared back and said, "Just think, about ten years down the road, I'll be sitting in my office with my feet propped up on my desk just like this. Dr. John will be running from one farm to another ramming his hands and arms up the rear ends of a bunch of cows!"

That brought a big laugh until I asked if he knew what else I would be doing with my hands. He hesitated and then asked, "What else will you do?"

"I'll pull in those five and ten dollar bills by the handful, that's what!"

That broke up the bull session.

CHAPTER 20

On the Saturday morning of the Clemson-Auburn football game, I was picking up some supplies at the bookstore. When I walked back out to the street, I heard a familiar bass voice bellow, "Riddle! Riddle!" There coming up the sidewalk was Dr. Kinard! After a hearty greeting, we went into The City Cafe for a cup of coffee and a long chat. We discussed our four semesters of English when I had progressed from two "D's" up to a "C" and finally to a "B." He told me how surprised he had been to see me come back for more after having such a hard time my first two semesters. Outside that classroom, he was really a nice guy. We sat together at the game, had a very pleasant day, and agreed to keep in touch by letter. I didn't dream that this correspondence would continue until his death many years later.

After a few weeks, I got tired of being teased about being the milk boy. I had also begun to worry about how I was going to get home for Thanksgiving. My money was getting low and there was no telling what else Dr. Mudhenck would require us to purchase. I could either find a way to earn some money or try to hitchhike home since I didn't dare to deplete my funds any further. Knowing that most of my housemates had grown up on farms, I decided to make bets with anybody who dared challenge me, that I could milk twice as fast as he could. If I won, he would pay me ten dollars; if he won, I would pay him ten dollars. There were only two problems: I didn't have ten dollars to cover my bet and I wasn't sure whether Mrs. Sheppard would permit us to gamble in her house. When I talked to her about it, she thought it would be a great way to stop the teasing and to finance my trip. She even agreed to hold the money and to cover my bets (on a loan basis, of course,) if I lost!

The next time the teasing started, I challenged everybody in the room to a milking contest. Four of the guys took the challenge. Believing that Mrs. Sheppard already had my money, each of them put ten dollars into the hat and drew out a numbered slip of paper to determine the time of his contest with me. Mrs. Sheppard kept the money as she had agreed to do. The competition wasn't even close. I won the forty dollars and the bragging rights.

Two of those guys just couldn't stand losing. They wanted a chance to win their money back. I warned them that they just didn't know when to quit. Each of them weighed about two hundred pounds. I weighed one hundred and forty pounds which meant that I had to be careful in choosing things to bet. This time, I challenged them to bend a forty penny nail into a horseshoe shape with their hands. Pride convinced that they could beat me at anything that required brute strength. Figuring that they didn't know how much easier it is to bend a forty penny nail than the shorter, thinner twenty penny nail, I made them a generous offer. I would bet them ten dollars each and let them choose either size nail for themselves while I would agree to bend a forty penny nail. Both of them jumped at the chance to bend the smaller nails and a third boy bet his ten dollars, too.

We agreed to have the contest after supper the next night. One of the boys would pick up the nails at the hardware store the next afternoon to be sure that we each had the right size. Mrs. Sheppard would again hold the money. I went up to my room to study with a big smile—sure as formaldehyde stinks, I was going to be another thirty dollars richer.

The next afternoon I hurried home and finished milking in time to eat with the others. After supper, I picked up a twenty penny nail and a forty penny nail and made a big to-do over the difference in size until everybody began to holler for me to get on with the bending. With my handkerchief, I wrapped the point of the big nail so that it wouldn't cut into my hands and then spiraled the fabric up the shank and wrapped the head.

I showed them all what I had done and suggested that they do the same with their nails. We agreed that this was within the conditions of the bet. I put pressure on the ends of my nail. As it began to bend, the eyes of the onlookers widened. To increase the drama, I put the nail down on my knee to finish making the bend. The room exploded in applause as I held up the horseshoe-shaped nail.

Each of the challengers chose a twenty penny nail. I wrapped their nails as I had wrapped my own and then sat down to watch the fun. Those big guys strained, moaned, cussed, and complained for thirty minutes. While their nails stayed straight, their tempers grew shorter and their vocabularies became increasingly colorful. Finally, they gave up and told Mrs. Sheppard to give me the money.

As I thanked them for their generosity, they asked if I had any more challenges. I laughed and told them that we would not discuss my other challenges because I couldn't afford to make too many enemies at once. They were all good sports and assured me that I had not made any enemies because I had just beaten them fair and square.

Now the Thanksgiving Holidays couldn't come soon enough for me. With seventy dollars, I could afford to go home. That old competitive spirit and the ability to size up a situation and to devise a solution had stood me in good stead.

Before winning the bets, I had told my folks that they would probably not see me until Christmas. Carolyn's letters were getting sadder and I knew she missed me as much as I missed her. Now that the money problem was solved, I sent her a letter telling her to expect me and to keep it a secret.

Now I could almost enjoy anatomy labs because each hour that passed brought me closer to the time when Carolyn and I would be together again. This Thanksgiving there wouldn't be any *** brass buttons to produce a ricochet when I hugged her!

One of my new friends was Walten Glazner from Brevard, N.C. He had graduated form high school in 1929 and had gone into the dairy business with his brother. They had prospered and Walter had decided to become a veterinarian. Like me, he was a freshman and he was working hard to achieve his goal. He invited me to ride home in his new Chevy coupe. We agreed that I would pay for the gas. This was a good deal for both of us. We had a fine trip home and he agreed to pick me up for the return trip. My worries about Thanksgiving were over!

Those five days were wonderful. Carolyn and my folks just smothered me with love and all the things that make coming home such a joy. All of them were amazed that I could earn my room and board by working thirty minutes a day taking care of two cows. Mama would have been totally upset with my method of earning money for the trip home, so that wasn't brought up. The days were spent with my folks and the evenings with Carolyn.

Papa and my brothers took me on several hunting trips. We enjoyed both the hunting and the eating because Mama and my sisters cooked everything we brought in.

Carolyn and I spent a lot of time just talking about our college experiences and our dreams for the future. She was enjoying the prestige of being a junior while I was back to being a freshman. She was doing well at Furman and was very proud that I was leading my class academically. She was sure that I exaggerated my stories of Dr. Mudhenck. Nobody could believe what a monster he was without living through his labs and classes. Her perfume smelled a lot better than his formaldehyde—I didn't even want to imagine her eyes red and her lungs burning and her hair reeking of that stuff. No, I wouldn't even dare her to check out my stories. I just enjoyed being with her and tolerated her doubts. Of all the girls I knew, not one could come close to being as perfect as Carolyn. She was everything I wanted and then some, and she loved me. Life was perfect except that the five days ended way too soon.

CHAPTER 21

The trip back to Auburn was pleasant and uneventful. Life settled back into its groove and sped along toward Christmas. Even Dr. Mudhenck mellowed out enough to start one of his infamous quizzes at four-thirty rather than at his usual five-thirty.

One Saturday afternoon nearly all of the residents of The Sheppard Chateau happened to be at home. The day was mild and most of us had congregated on the upstairs porch to shoot the bull and to unwind from the grind. Somehow we began comparing Clemson and Auburn and the conversation got around to hazing and paddling. After I described the paddlings we had gotten as rats, Jack declared that nobody could hurt him with a paddle. Jack was big and as tough as nails. He weighed about two hundred and twenty-five pounds, he had grown up in a mill town down the river, and he was an athlete who aspired to become a major league pitcher. "Doc" asked me if I would trade licks with a freshman. Before I could answer, Jack hollered, "#%*!, yes! We'll trade licks!"

Since there was no gracious way out, I agreed to trade licks with him. To make it more interesting, I suggested that since Jack and I were each going to suffer a lick, the others could each put a dollar into a hat. While we were collecting the money, somebody went down to the woodshed, picked out a rough board about an inch thick and trimmed one end down to a handle about the size of a baseball bat. We drew straws to see who would hit first. Jack won the draw, grabbed the paddle, and said, "Give me that #%* paddle and I'll show you who is going to get his butt busted! The winner takes the whole pot. Now bend over there, Dr. Riddle!"

Pow! That rascal hit hard and my tail sizzled. This wasn't the first time I had been hurt and it probably wasn't going to be the last. I took a deep breath, straightened up and said, "I think it's time for Mr. Biggus von Assus to bend over right here."

I lined him up carefully so that I could get a running start and shove off the wall with one foot as I hit him. That was an old Clemson technique and it was brutal. He bent over laughing that there was no way I could hurt him. When that paddle connected with

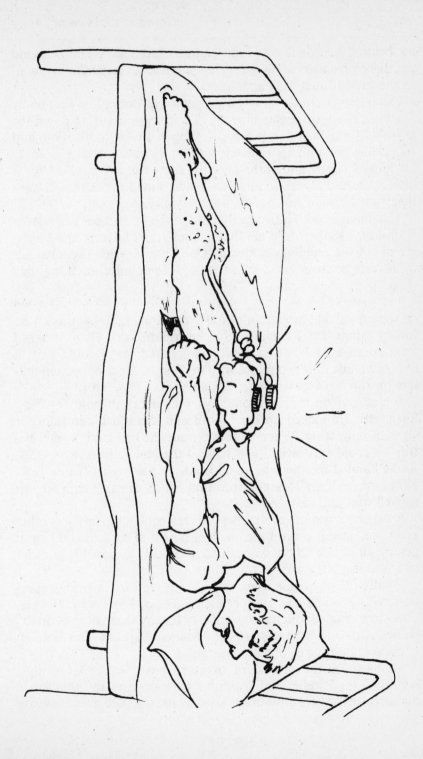

his behind, he fell flat and the paddle shattered. When he stood up, there were tears in his eyes. He made a hasty retreat to his room as the group burst into applause.

I won the sixteen dollars—I didn't enjoy it. Both of us were badly bruised. My bottom was blue and I had trouble sitting down for a week. When Jack didn't come to supper, I went to his room and found him lying on his stomach with an ice pack on each buttock. He looked funny and pathetic at the same time. We talked for a little while and agreed to remain friends. I made up my mind right then that I would not paddle anybody else.

The milking was a little late that afternoon and supper had started without me. Sabert told me that as they started eating and laughing about the paddling contest, "Doc" had advised them to quit testing me because I was smart enough to counter anything they tried.

Just to make life exciting, I challenged "Doc" Parrish that I could do something that he couldn't do. He promptly said that there were lots of things that I could do that he couldn't do. Then he asked what specifically I had in mind. I suggested that I could twist a broom handle into two pieces with my hands. He dropped ten dollars on the table as he said, "This ten says you can't."

We agreed on the ten dollar bet plus a new broom for Mrs. Shephard. He picked up her broom and checked it carefully for signs of tampering. When he found none, he handed it to me. Before he could sit down, I had twisted the handle into two pieces. As he handed me the ten, he allowed, "Challenging 'Little Doc' ain't nothing but a losing proposition for all of us. We might just as well quit and save our money."

I had about run out of sure bets. Since I couldn't afford any other kind, we agreed to drop the challenges. All of us settled down to getting all of our school work done as quickly as possible in order to avoid any delays in getting home for Christmas.

Finally the day came when we could leave for Christmas vacation. Walter and I had another pleasant trip. Thanks to my bets, I had more than enough money to pay for my share of the trip expenses and for Christmas gifts for Mama, Carolyn, and Bonnie. I was working hard, but life was good.

Mama loved the soft warm sweater I gave her for Christmas. Adults in the Riddle family didn't exchange gifts and this was a big surprise for her. She almost cried as she thanked me for always being so thoughtful of her. When I thanked her for the nice things she had done for me, Papa said, "You are welcome," and stuck out his hand. When I shook his hand, I found a twenty dollar bill in my own. There was no predicting Mr. Charlie!

The holidays were glorious. Most of my dates were with Carolyn. My brothers were generous about lending me their cars. Occasionally they even slipped me a little cash. I managed to slip away for one date with Bonnie. I gave her a pretty little pin to wear on her sweaters and she gave me a nice pair of gloves to keep my hands warm when she wasn't there to hold them. Bonnie was a character. I loved her and her whole family and enjoyed being with them even though I knew perfectly well that her name was never going to be Bonnie Riddle. I knew, too, that Bonnie and her mother were both figuring on me as husband material.

Christmas at Carr's Creek was more delightful than ever. Mr. Paul and Miss Jennie accepted me as a part of the family. Carolyn was their only child and I revelled in the luxury of being one of a pair. At my house, I was one of the crowd! Carolyn was happy to have me at home and absolutely ecstatic over the gold locket I had chosen for her. For me she had found a handsome tie pin that really looked sharp. Only three and a half more years and we could be together all the time instead of counting the days until holidays and then watching them melt away.

Papa and my brothers and I did a little hunting and then Walter and I were on our way back to school. Leaving got harder every time, but it had to be done. I told my family and Carolyn not to expect to see me before Easter. That seemed a long way in the future and all of us felt a twinge of sadness. At least the trips with Walter were more pleasant than hitch-hiking or riding on the bus. We enjoyed each other's company and the little car was a dream machine.

CHAPTER 22

When we got back to Auburn this time, the post holiday blues jumped on me with a vengeance. I was almost as miserable as I had been during those first weeks at Clemson. Letters from Mama and Carolyn helped to ease the pain and gradually the misery faded.

We had finished dissecting the head and neck of our horse. Now Dr. Mudhenck rotated each team to a different section of the cadaver. He explained that we could shift members between teams if we so desired. Our team had two boys who just didn't fit. Hobart could not keep pace with the rest of us and George drove us up the wall with his constant chatter about his father's veterinary practice. Hobart wanted to join another group and we requested that George do likewise. We were joined by Jim Green, a serious student, and Tom Talker, a clown. Tom would have fitted in perfectly with my clown princes from Clemson except that he never got me into trouble. I found out much later that he had paid Hobart to trade places with him.

Before long, semester exams were upon us. We struggled through them and waited anxiously for our grades and our new schedules. Things worked out well for me. All of my grades were "A's" and my new schedule suited me fine except that I still had to deal with Dr. Mudhenck. The man knew his subject and he made certain that his students knew it, regardless of the pain involved in mastering it. He was very fair and he had absolutely no mercy on anyone. We were learning anatomy and histology whether we liked it or not.

Between semesters, Sabert decided that he wanted to move into the house next door so that he could room with a classmate who was taking the same courses he had. The classmate's roommate would become my roommate. Mrs. Sheppard had agreed to the swap and the new guy would take over Sabert's job of waiting on tables and washing dishes. That sounded okay until I found out that my new roommate was Tom Talker. There had to be some sort of hocus pocus going on. A little investigation revealed that Tom had paid Sabert fifty dollars to swap rooms with him! I was mad as hell, but the deal had been made and that was that.

Tom was six years older that I was, he had stayed out of college for five years before he settled down enough to pursue a degree, and he had a reputation as a gambler and a clown. He obviously wanted something other than my companionship the way he was spending money to be close to me. Well, the first thing was to find out what he wanted and then I could decide how to handle him.

We did a lot of talking the first night after he moved into the room. I explained my belief in studying every day as though I were preparing for an exam the next day. Then I made it clear that nothing was permitted to interfere with my studies.

Tom asked if I ever gambled. My negative response prompted him to ask me what I had been doing when I bet on the milking contest and all the other contests for which my housemates had paid me money. I thought for a minute and then explained that those things weren't gambles because I knew that I could win.

Tom mulled that over before he confessed that he liked to shoot a little dice and to play a little poker. Being Tom, he had to decorate the story a little by swearing that his daddy had sent him a pair of dice with instructions to use them well enough to send home a hundred dollars a month.

We agreed that his gambling was his business as long as he didn't use our room for his games. He assured me that his regular games with the guys next door would continue to be played in their rooms rather than in ours. Finally, Tom got around to his real reason for becoming my roommate. He wanted me to help him with his studies. A little discussion revealed that he wanted to use my notes since he had trouble keeping up during lectures. Both of us knew shorthand; I was a lot more proficient than Tom. He had a new Remington typewriter and I wondered out loud why he never used it.

The reply was typical of Tom. "*%#! I can't type. My sister gave me that thing because she thought it would help me. All it does is catch dust and take up space!"

With his permission, I rolled a sheet of paper into the typewriter and began typing out the notes I had taken that morning. When the first page was finished, he read it and blurted out, "*%#! This is the first part of old Muddyduddy's lecture this morning! You almost have it word for word!"

We discussed my study methods—take down the lectures in shorthand, transcribe them in longhand, read through them once that evening, and then read through them again just before a test or an exam. He was dumbfounded at my thoroughness. After a little cogitation, he offered to furnish me with carbons and paper and typewriter as well as a salary if I would transcribe my notes on the typewriter and provide him with a complete set every day.

Quickly evaluating the pros and cons of this proposal, I decided that Tom was probably on the level and that his personality and humor would liven things up for me. Just to be sure that we kept this arrangement honest, I agreed to provide him the notes without taking any money since his typewriter would speed up my transcription. He was not to share the notes with anyone nor to discuss the arrangement with anyone. We would try it for a while and see how it worked. If it were a satisfactory arrangement for both of us, we could discuss money later.

With that agreement reached, Tom settled back and started asking questions about the contests I had won. We discussed my milking for Papa, my experiences at Clemson, and lots of other things. Tom laughed and said that if the two of us put our minds to it, we could get rich gambling. He seemed shocked when I insisted that I was going to make my money as a vet. I planned to be both a top-notch student and a top-notch vet and I didn't plan ever to be poor again.

Tom studied conscientiously for the first four days of the new semester. When Friday night came around, he rattled his dice a few times, requested that I leave his copy of my notes on his pillow, announced that he was going next door for his regular Friday night game, and told me not to wait up for him.

I had figured that studying would never interfere very seriously with his gambling. I wished him luck and settled down to my studies. After a few weeks, I realized that Tom was really serious about his studies and that his gambling was simply a profitable recreation.

Once after Tom had a particularly lucky streak, he insisted on taking me with him to the village men's shop. Each of us walked out wearing a handsome pair of riding boots, new pants, and new Western shirts. Tom had paid for everything and he had ordered me to tell anybody who asked that I had paid for my own outfit. Then he confessed that his family knew nothing of his gambling and that he wanted to keep it that way. Apparently his mama was like mine in her attitude toward gambling.

To show my appreciation and to encourage Tom to keep up his good work in the classroom, I went down to the bookstore and bought a set of looseleaf notebooks for each of us. I labeled each notebook carefully and put the notes in them after Tom had gone to bed. When he got up the next morning, he rubbed his eyes and blurted, "*%#! it, John, you and I are really getting uptown and educated at the same time with all this new stuff!"

We enjoyed each other's company and we worked well together in lab, in our jobs at The Sheppard Chateau, and in our studies. At the end of the next six weeks I was still making all "A's" and Tom was doing well. With a song in my heart, I climbed into Walter's coupe and we headed home for spring break.

Those had to be the fastest five days on record. Somehow I spent the evenings with Carolyn, arranged to work with Dr. Grear during summer vacation, spent some time with my family and a little time with Bonnie and the Brady family, and then Walter and I were on our way back to Auburn.

Papa had told me that he was very pleased with the reports the dean was sending him and I had assured him that I intended to see that he continued to be pleased with my progress. Carolyn and Mama had both made it clear that they got mighty lonesome between my visits home. I had promised to make it up to them during the summer. By the time I had my thoughts sorted out, we were back at The Sheppard Chateau.

Social life on the campus heated up in the spring. Some of the girls taught me ballroom dancing and I found that activity very rewarding. The sororities had a lot of dances, the Auburn Knights were a great band (Mrs. Sheppard's daughter sang with the Knights), a friend loaned me his tuxedo as often as I needed one, and there were a number of girls who took it upon themselves to see that I had plenty of opportunities to show off my dancing prowess. All of this got worked into my schedule without damaging my grades or my work for Mrs. Sheppard. Somehow I never quite got around to telling Carolyn about these extracurricular activities and she was too far away to find out about them for herself. I had a good thing going and I enjoyed it to the fullest!

One afternoon during lab, the president of Alpha Psi, the professional fraternity, invited me to join the next pledge class. Wow! From milk boy to fraternity man! This country boy was moving up. He showed me the fraternity's bid list and said that he would probably ask me to help him to persuade some of them to pledge Alpha Psi. I was disappointed that Tom's name was not on the list.

Typically, Tom declared that he didn't give a *%#! whether they
invited him to pledge or not. Since he was my buddy, I managed
to remedy the omission. When initiation time came the next fall,
we suffered together.

Final exams were upon us and then final grades for the year were
posted. I was still in the top four. The others were a bookworm,
an older married man whose wife helped him with his assignments,
and the last was one of my best friends. Papa would get another
good letter from the dean. I was proud of myself. I was the only
one in the top four who worked regularly and I was one of the two
who enjoyed an active social life. My methodical way of handling
things and my businesslike approach to life were paying handsome
dividends.

It didn't take long to make arrangements to keep my job and
my room for the next fall, to ship my trunk, to pack my suitcase,
and to join Walter for the trip home. It was going to be a great
summer. I had earned it and I was planning to savor every minute
of it.

CHAPTER 23

Carolyn, Bonnie, and my family were so glad to see me, they made me feel like "King John" for sure. Before long I had a schedule worked out. My days were spent working with Dr. Grear and my evenings were spent with Carolyn. Between the times spent with those two, I squeezed in time for my family and an occasional date with Bonnie. By the time we threw in some church activities and a few parties, I had a full summer.

I had thought that most of my time with Dr. Grear would be spent observing and providing an extra pair of hands and some extra muscle power when he needed it. Boy, was I wrong! Dr. Grear had a small clinic and one helper, Charlie. Now Charlie was a middle-aged black man who had worked with Dr. Grear for many years. Officially Charlie bathed and clipped dogs and did the unskilled work around the clinic. In practice, Charlie was an amazingly good veterinarian despite his lack of formal training. He had learned by observation and by doing as he helped Dr. Grear. His experience plus his intelligence and his innate sensitivity to animals made him an excellent assistant. I soon discovered that Charlie did a lot of the things usually done by a licensed vet. Overwork and fatigue were chronic problems for Dr. Grear. He had developed a serious drinking problem which further complicated the situation. Charlie had learned to do much of what had to be done to keep things going when Dr. Grear was incapacitated. I learned quickly that Dr. Grear was frequently less than sober and was occasionally too inebriated to function at all. Like Charlie, I learned to keep my mouth shut and to do what had to be done.

Charlie was a master at clipping dogs in various show patterns. Greenville had a great many dog shows and Charlie's services were much in demand. He was very patient about teaching me the various patterns used for specific breeds. In return, I did many of Charlie's chores when I had time on my hands. This surprised Charlie. He hadn't expected "Little Doc" to do any menial labor. I figured that if I helped Charlie with his chores, he would have more time to help me to learn the things that I needed to know.

By the end of the summer, Charlie had taught me at least as much about diagnosing and treating animals as Dr. Grear had.

Charlie was exceptionally discreet in advising and teaching me. When Dr. Grear was out on a call, Charlie would help me to diagnose and treat animals in the clinic. When Dr. Grear or the owners asked questions, Charlie always gave me credit for whatever had been done. Everybody, including Dr. Grear, thought that I was some kind of whiz kid. If it hadn't been for Charlie, I would have been a lot closer to a dud.

Early one morning in mid-summer, a traveling salesman brought in a beautiful English Setter and the remains of a leather shoe. The setter had eaten the shoe during the night and had become ill. The salesman wanted to leave the dog with us for treatment during the day. That afternoon he would pick up the dog and continue his trip to Toledo, Ohio. Dr. Grear assured him that we could handle the situation.

Dr. Grear thought there was nothing wrong with the setter except that her stomach was full of shoe leather. He instructed Charlie and me to stuff empty one ounce capsules with cotton and to put them down the setter's throat. This involved putting our hands way back into the dog's mouth so that the capsules would slide down her esophagus rather than being spat out. He told us to administer two of these capsules per hour for four hours and then to give her an injection to induce vomiting. He verified that we understood what was to be done and then he left to make calls.

Since all of the cages were full and we wanted to observe the dog carefully, we put down newspapers on the floor of the treatment room and kept the setter on a leash in there. The treatment was very effective. That poor dog threw up a mountain of cotton and leather. After she stopped vomiting, she seemed to be doing fine.

Dr. Grear had to make calls to a number of farms and was gone for most of the day. About the middle of the afternoon, I walked through the treatment room and the dog lunged at me with the obvious intent of biting my arm. Charlie saw the whole episode. His comment was, "Oh, *#! You better stay 'way from that dog, Little Doc. I know what's wrong with her now."

I asked if he thought she was tired of having us medicate her all day. His answer sent a chill down my spine and made my belly start hurting.

"Tired ain't got nothing to do with this dog's devilment. She's got rabies for sure. Hold out your hands and let me check them over. You and me have both been putting those capsules down her throat. If we've got any cuts or scratches on our hands, we're in a heap of trouble. And that's not all—Dr. Grear ain't going to want to believe that she has rabies because he didn't notice it. We're going to have one *# of a time convincing him, too. You tell him first and then I'll back you up."

That was a fine kettle of fish. I had already had one series of twenty-one anti-rabies shots when I was about twelve. Dr. Grear had diagnosed rabies in one of our hounds. As a precaution, all of us children who had played with the puppies had been given the shots. Those things hurt. They were administered in the abdomen which meant that you had a sore belly for a month. I hoped passionately that Charlie was wrong.

As the afternoon went on, the dog got increasingly agitated. She tore up the newspapers and tried to eat them. Then she urinated and lapped up her own urine. She was showing classic signs of rabies.

When Dr. Grear got back about five o'clock, I told him about the day's events and our diagnosis. Just as Charlie had predicted, he pooh-poohed everything. According to Dr. Grear, she was playing when she tried to bite me, she was bored when she tore the papers, etc. We were still discussing it when the salesman came back. Charlie and I cringed inwardly as Dr. Grear told him that the dog would be fine because she had gotten rid of all that shoe leather. The doctor gave him some bismuth preparations in case the vomiting continued, collected his rather large fee, and told the owner to go into the next room and get the dog. That dog was as happy as a puppy to see her owner. She pranced out the door looking like she was ready for a show.

When they left, Dr. Grear told Charlie and me that we could forget our notion that she had rabies. We found that a little upsetting even though we knew there was nothing more we could do.

Two days later Dr. Grear received a stunning telegram from a veterinarian in Ohio. The setter had died from rabies and the diagnosis had been confirmed by the state health department's laboratory! Dr. Grear apologized for not listening to us. Then he asked who had been the first to suspect the rabies. Before I could open my mouth, Charlie said, "Little Doc."

At the first opportunity, I told Dr. Grear that Charlie had made the diagnosis. Although I appreciated his trying to make me look good, I couldn't take credit for Charlie's wisdom. Dr. Grear just smiled and said that Charlie and I made a good team. Then he called the health department and arranged for us to get those miserable anti-rabies vaccines. He was terribly upset because he had had seven series of those injections himself. A reaction had necessitated his hospitalization after the last series. He felt guilty about missing the diagnosis and about not listening to Charlie and me. He just couldn't deal with the possibility that he had endangered both our lives.

Charlie and I had no ill effects from the shots except for very sore bellies. With Carolyn, Bonnie, Mama, and the family to comfort me, I didn't suffer a whole lot. Tender loving care in those quantities worked miracles.

The days sped by. The more I worked in the clinic, the more I itched to get back to school to find the answers to my questions. Dr. Grear had a big practice composed of both large and small animals. We handled all sorts of major and minor problems in all kinds of animals. We also dealt with all types of people. I was learning that the owners could be as big a challenge as the animals. The animals couldn't talk and some of the owners couldn't shut up!

When summer ended, we went through the bittersweet rituals of tears, goodbyes, promises to write often, hugs, and handshakes. That was always the part of being at home that tore me up. It seemed that it ought to get easier with practice....it just got harder....especially with Carolyn and Mama.

CHAPTER 24

Three days before registration began, I was back at The Sheppard Chateau. Mrs. Sheppard, Daisy, and May were glad to see me. Tom showed up while I was milking. He still had his job waiting on tables and we had our old room back. Mrs. Sheppard teased us about being her children.

When we compared summers, Tom declared that he hadn't done a thing except loaf and spend his daddy's money. He was ready to get back to his cards and dice. That rascal just couldn't get serious about life.

Registration went smoothly and we got pretty good schedules. We would have anatomy, embryology, physiology, bacteriology, animal nutrition, and medical vocabulary.

That first afternoon back in anatomy lab was rough. The formaldehyde seemed to have gotten stronger over the summer. Our eyes burned and watered, our lunch did gymnastics, and that old sensation of asphyxiation was overwhelming. Since quite a few members of our class did not return, we were told to choose our own dissecting teams. My team was a real mixed bag of backgrounds. Tom was from Alabama, Harry Morgan was from Tennessee, Bill Spence was from Delaware, Joe Stafford was from Florida, and I was from South Carolina. All of us were good students and pretty evenly matched in skills, goals, and personalities. We agreed to get the job done right since so much of our knowledge and our grade came from our lab work. It was beginning to look like a pretty good set-up. When five thirty rolled around, Dr. Mudhenck yelled for attention. We thought he was going to dismiss us. Instead he announced, "Gentlemen, clean up your area and meet me in Room 102 in the main building."

That lousy turkey zapped us with a two and a half hour quiz made up entirely of discussion questions! He wanted to see how much anatomy we had managed to forget over the summer! Welcome back to anatomy lab!

As usual, we began the year cussing Dr. Mudhenck. We finished it the same way and we didn't slow down in the middle. I have never

143

known anybody before nor since who was cussed more frequently nor more enthusiastically than Dr. Mudhenck.

He was surprised at how much anatomy I remembered. I hoped that my classmates had also surprised him.

The sixty-seven members of our class who came back that fall managed to stick it out until graduation except for one boy from Florida. He developed Hodgkin's disease. We watched in horror as all of his visible lymph glands swelled noticeably. He fought valiantly to keep up with his work. Despite constant pain, he never complained. Although we all liked him and tried to help as much as we could, the disease took its toll. When he had to go home, all of us ached for him and for ourselves. If we could have seen into the future, we would have been even more crushed. When he achieved a state of remission the next year, he came back to try again for his Doctorate in Veterinary Medicine. Achieving that degree meant more to him than life itself. He made it most of the way through his senior year. When death came, a delegation of Alpha Psi members served as his pall bearers. In recognition of his courageous effort, Auburn awarded his degree posthumously.

As soon as we settled down to the routine of classes and labs, we had our first meeting of the pledge class of Alpha Psi. We heard all the advantages of membership and got really excited about the wonders of being a part of the brotherhood. Close to the end of the meeting, we were told that initiation would take place during Hell Week in October. We were blissfully unaware that the name of the week was a very accurate description of its events.

September faded into October as we enjoyed football games, dances, and bull sessions and suffered through classes, quizzes, and labs. Letters from Mama and Carolyn arrived regularly, Tom and I continued to share my typed notes, and I enjoyed the company of a number of girls for dances and movies. I didn't write to Mama or to Carolyn nearly as often as I had done in the past. My life was full to the brim and it was beautiful.

On Monday night of Hell Week, the pledge class met and received instructions for initiation. Each of us would carry at least four brands of cigarettes at all times during the week. That would give members of the fraternity a choice when they "bummed" cigarettes from us. There were all sorts of other requirements of that type. Members carried around little black books in which they recorded the sins of the pledges. Those sins would be punished by licks with the paddle on the last night of the week. This was beginning to sound like rat rules at Clemson.

Each of us was given a different list of things to bring to the meeting on the last night of the week. Any item not presented would earn fifty licks on the rear of the offending pledge. I read my list with awe. Among other things, I had to visit the cemetery in Opelika, Alabama, and record the dates of birth and death and the epitaph of each person who had died between 1900 and 1940. Any omission or inaccuracy would earn ten licks. Then I had to count the railroad ties in the seven miles of track between the Opelika and Auburn railroad stations. I had to have three live English sparrows and two live bullfrogs with legs at least eight inches long. The list went on and on.

I had done a little politicking and Tom had been invited to join Alpha Psi, too. We decided to help each other with those *#! lists.

Mrs. Sheppard helped, too. She let us borrow a bucket and a fish net and then got permission for us to catch frogs at a private pond. Tom held the flashlight while I caught my frogs. It required a little struggle, a little ingenuity, and a little cussing before I finally caught two that were big enough. Back at the house, Tom held the ladder while I climbed up to the eaves carrying an old birdcage I had found in the barn and the fishnet from the frog-catching operation. He aimed a bright light to blind the sleeping sparrows while I swung the net. We were jubilant when I caught three sparrows on the first try. Daisy and May had some noisy company in the barn because I sure wasn't going to keep frogs and sparrows in our room.

In order to get all of this stuff, I had to get permission from Dr. Mudhenck to miss two anatomy labs. He let me miss them with the condition that I would make them up on Saturday afternoons. That old rascal would make you finish his labs before your own funeral if he could keep you alive long enough! Celia, one of the sorority girls who frequently invited me to dances, had a car. She agreed to drive me to the cemetery on Tuesday afternoon and to the railroad station on Wednesday afternoon. She surprised the heck out of me by saying that she was delighted that we were finally alone in the graveyard. When I recovered my speech, I asked, "What kind of freak are you to enjoy being in a graveyard?"

With a mischievous grin, she answered, "Well, none of the deceased folks are going to watch us or talk about us either! We might as well have a little fun while we're here!"

That wasn't a bad idea. We got those dates and epitaphs copied in record time and then we had a little fun. After all, it was only fair to Celia to show her my appreciation for her help.

On Wednesday, she drove me to the railroad station. Since the tracks ran right beside the road, I told her to drive to the first mile post and wait for me there. I counted the crossties in that first mile and then multiplied the count by seven. That saved us enough time to have a little more fun and to show a little more appreciation. Celia was cute as well as sweet. We always had a good time together. As long as she and Carolyn didn't know about each other, I could believe that "Ignorance is bliss!"

Tom's list was pretty gruesome. He had to have a pair of buzzard's wings and a dozen screwworm larvae. We borrowed a pair of cavalry horses and rode out into a large pasture behind the Auburn Dairy. We were jumping logs and other obstacles when we found the ignominious remains of some dead animal. As we approached it, a flock of buzzards flew up. In a flash, we figured out what to do. I rode back and borrowed a .22 rifle while Tom rounded up a pair of autopsy gloves, a scalpel, and a cigar. By the time I had gotten back and shot one of the buzzards, Tom was ready to do the amputation. There was some question as to what smelled worse, the cigar or the buzzard. Tom swore that the cigar smoke kept the stench of the buzzard away from his nose. I retreated to a safe distance from both—ascertained by my own nose.

Tom persuaded some of his gambling buddies to get the screwworm larvae from the large animal clinic. He rounded up the other stuff himself. We thought we had pretty well completed our initiation. Well, friend, just let me tell you that we were in for a big surprise when Friday night rolled around.

CHAPTER 25

All pledges had been instructed to report to the basement of the Alpha Psi House at seven o'clock sharp wearing old clothes and carrying all the stuff on our lists. You never saw such a spectacle. As the plunder was displayed and checked, the room began to look like a scene from a horror movie. I had never seen such a collection of ghoulish paraphernalia. We would have made a fortune if we could have filmed the next few hours. For obvious reasons, no pictures were allowed.

Tom and I both satisfied the accountant with our collections. Some of the other pledges had been less successful. They got their britches warmed pretty thoroughly. One of the seniors pretended to be crazy-drunk. Since he weighed about two hundred and fifty pounds, he scared the daylights out of us. One pledge panicked, jumped through a plate glass window, and fled into the night. That created a problem for the officers of Alpha Psi. They ordered all initiation activities to stop until they captured the escapee.

After about an hour, they returned with their prisoner. All pledges were ordered to strip down to their birthday suits and to pile their clothes in such a way that they could put them back on in a hurry. The next surprises were nasty, sweet, and crunchy. Each of us had to drink a huge glassful of a strong solution of Epsom salts. As I forced it down, my old high school teacher's advice ran through my head, "Keep your mouth shut and your bowels open." This drink was certainly going to accomplish the latter. The next order was to lie down on a big sheet of canvas. Each of us was thoroughly doused with buckets of syrup. Then boxes of corn flakes were poured over us and the canvas. Finally we had to roll over and over until we were thoroughly coated in syrup and corn flakes. Talk about being sweet and flakey! We were awesome.

The situation really got interesting when we were ordered to put on our clothes. Can you imagine trying to pull on clothes that stuck firmly to every place they touched? When I got my underwear on, my denim shirt, overalls, and shoes weren't too bad. Those guys who had brought pants and shirts that fitted closely were having a terrific struggle. As soon as I was dressed, somebody put a blindfold on me, led me outside, and put me into the back seat of a car. They had covered the seat with an old blanket to protect it. Shades of Clemson—protect the equipment, the man can be replaced!

We rode for what seemed like an hour before they put me out of the car and laughed, "We'll see you back at the house in a couple of days!" as they sped away.

Getting the blindfold off wasn't easy since it was thoroughly glued to my face and hair by the syrup. When I got it off, the car was out of sight. I assessed the situation as I tried to decide what to do. The temperature was cool but comfortable. The quietness was frightening. There were no lights nor noises to hint which way I should start walking. If anybody saw me, there was no telling what they would do. I could only guess what my appearance would suggest to anybody I met. Well, standing there wasn't going to solve anything. I started walking in the direction in which the car had left.

After about fifteen minutes, I trespassed on the territory of a huge screech owl. His vocal protests scared me nearly out of my wits. When I stopped shaking, I looked around and listened again. There were no visible nor audible clues as to which way to go. I just kept walking.

After about a mile, I heard some dogs barking. The sound led me to a decrepit old shack. I hated to disturb anybody in the middle of the night, but those dogs were raising enough ruckus to awaken the dead anyway. The closer I got to the porch, the more racket those scrawny dogs made. I figured that they had been kicked around enough that they wouldn't get close enough to bite me. They backed off enough to allow me to bang on the door.

At last a sleepy voice inquired uneasily, "Who is dat?"

Blacks in Alabama in those days were frightened by knocks on their isolated shanties late at night. They would have been terrified if they had opened the door and looked at me. They wouldn't have known whether I was a "hant," or a lunatic!

Carefully I explained that I was lost and needed directions to get back to Auburn. He hesitated a minute and then asked, "Which way you come from, suh?"

I described my route as accurately as I could. After some discussion through the closed door, he told me to go back about a mile in the direction I had come. At the crossroad there, I should turn right and follow the road until I reached the "Lokahpokah" highway and then, "You'll for sho' know where you is."

Lord, have mercy! The last thing on earth I wanted was to be seen on the highway like this. Still groping for a solution to my dilemma, I asked how far it was to Opelika.

My adviser stammered for a little while before he said, "Wal, suh, near as I can reckon, it's 'bout eight, or mebbe ten, miles."

This was going to be worse than the obstacle course at Clemson. At least it didn't have dogs. I thanked the man for his help and apologized for waking him up. If I had had anything to give him, I would gladly have done so. As it was, my "brothers-to-be" had left me without a penny or anything else of value. As I stepped down from the porch, the dogs started their ruckus again. Reflexively, I asked, "Do your dogs bite?"

The answer was, "Naw, sah. Dey jus' all bark an' no bite."

With another round of thanks and a fervent prayer that his directions were accurate, I set off down the road. When I got back to the owl's territory, he voiced his displeasure at being disturbed again. This time he didn't scare me. I smiled at the idea that we would be a perfect pair for Halloween.

Walking with my clothes stuck to every hair on my body was miserable. I had never realized how hairy I was until I reached the road, turned right, and realized that those Epsom salts were creating their predictable reaction. I retreated hastily into the bushes and tried to get my britches down. Pulling my skin down would have been just as easy. Epsom salts will not be controlled even with a desperate effort. Very soon, I was filthy and stinking as well as flakey and sticky. Fighting panic, I reminded myself that I had been dirty and uncomfortable a few other times in my life. Resolutely, I set out to find some water to undo the damage.

Pretty soon the welcome sound of running water floated through the night. Instinctively I assumed that the road would cross the stream sooner or later. Sure enough there was a bridge a little way down the road and just below the bridge was a waterfall. Being a country boy, I knew there would be a pool below the falls. Now I could get rid of the flakes, the filth, the stickiness, and the stench. The water in the pool was about four feet deep. It didn't take long to soften the syrup enough to squirm out of my clothes. Like many a woodsman before me, I used sand from the edge of the pool to scrub myself and my clothes. When I was satisfied with my scrubbing, I made my way back to the bank, wrung out my clothes as tightly as I could, and put them back on. Even wet and cold, I at least looked and felt like a decent human being.

Moving down the road at a good steady pace warmed me and my clothes. After about thirty minutes, the night breeze carried the sound of someone whistling nervously. It reminded me of Papa's advice to whistle when the darkness frightened me. The sound was getting closer and clearer as I approached another crossroad. There was something familiar about the way it sounded....for heaven's sakes, it sounded just like Tom! I reached the crossroad ahead of the whistler and hid in the bushes until he got there.

Sure enough, it was Tom. This time, I would be the joker. When he got about five feet past me, I leaped out of the bushes growling and barking like some creature in a nightmare, and grabbed him from behind. Tom was six feet two inches tall as compared to my five feet eight inches. Nonetheless, I scared him almost as badly as Sonny had scared Chippy with the snake. As he stood there speechless and trembling with terror, I felt bad about scaring him.

His first words were, "#♯%! you, John Riddle! I'm going to kill you just as soon as we get back to Auburn!"

I apologized and we both laughed at the evidence that I had literally scared the sh-- out of him. At my suggestion, we set off in search of a stream. When we found a small creek, he soaked himself enough to get out of his clothes. He scrubbed himself while I scrubbed his clothes. We wrung them out as dry as we could, he pulled them back on, and we set out again. We were both getting weak from the action of the salts plus fear and fatigue by the time we heard the sounds of traffic in the distance.

As we got within sight of the highway, Tom perked up. "All right, we're cooking with gas now! One more mile and we'll be back!"

About two a.m., we reached the Alpha Psi House. A few of the others had gotten back and were showering. From the backyard came a shout, "Whoa, mule! Whoa!"

I walked out to see what was happening. There sat Joe Stearns from Kentucky astride a poor old half-starved, swaybacked mule. Still covered with syrup and corn flakes and giving definite olfactory evidence of having taken his dose of Epsom salts, he was the most ridiculous sight I have ever beheld. Doubling over with laughter, I heard him holler, "Come here, Johnny, and help me get my britches unglued from this sharp-backed son of a %*#! If I don't get off soon, more than my personality is going to be split!" Whooping with laughter, I ran back to the door and called the others to see this incredible sight. Before long, we had an absolute circus.

I asked Joe where his saddle was and he replied, "It's all this poor ole mule can do to tote me. A saddle would have broken his back for sure! Now quit your *%! laughing long enough to get my britches loose from this walking sawhorse!"

It took four of us to pull Joe loose. The seat of his pants had more hair stuck on it than was left on the mule's back by the time we set him unsteadily on his feet on the ground. As usual, Joe had quite a tale to tell. He had seen the mule standing beside a rickety pasture fence. When the mule responded in a friendly fashion to being patted on the head, Joe had climbed through the fence and approached the mule cautiously. He had made friends with the mule and finally had climbed on his back. When the mule didn't buck him off, Joe had rigged a make-shift bridle, kicked down a section of the fence, led the mule down to the road, and then remounted his version of an all-terrain vehicle for the ride back to Auburn. Once his britches bonded to the mule's back, there was no way for him to dismount without help. He was literally stuck with his mount until he got back to the Alpha Psi House. Thinking that the mule would find his way back home, we left him standing in the yard. The next morning, the mule was still standing there. Joe led him down to the large animal clinic and slipped him into a stall. It was days before Dr. Wolfe found out how the mule got there and we never did find out where the mule came from.

Getting back to the Alpha Psi House after being dumped on a country road finished the physical rough stuff. We were ready for some sleep as soon as we got cleaned up and heard each other's tales of adventure.

We discovered that the formal ritual on Sunday night was as tough mentally as the physical initiation had been. Several of the pledges threatened to resign from school and to leave town before they got through Sunday night. All of us were sworn to secrecy for life about the formal ritual. When it was finally over, we were given our Alpha Psi pins which were attached to the Greek letter Theta with tiny gold chains. We were now official members of the Theta chapter of the brotherhood of Alpha Psi.

It didn't take long for us to find out that the chapter house was far too small to accommodate its members. Building a new house became the chapter's primary goal. The college could not help us financially; they did give us a beautiful corner lot. Getting the money to build the house was a major obstacle. With a war raging in Europe and the memories of the crash of 1929 still fresh in their minds, nobody was willing to lend $80,000 to a bunch of fraternity boys. Finally our president found a man who owned a little back-alley grocery store in Montgomery who was willing and able to give us a long-term, low-interest loan of $80,000. I always suspected that our benefactor was a little shady although I would never give voice to such a thought. The lender insisted that each member sign a promissory note as collateral and we complied. The money was ours.

We located an architect who drew up the plans for a gorgeous house. It had two stories, enough bedrooms for all of our members plus a few extras, a beautiful living room which would provide ample space for parties, a dining room, and a large kitchen. When the college had approved the plans, we hired a contractor and construction began almost immediately. It was estimated that the house would be ready for occupancy the next fall when school started. We set up our budget and dreamed of the day we could move into the house.

CHAPTER 26

When we reached the end of the first six week grading period, I was still in first place. The same three contenders were still right behind me. I might be a fraternity man, but that didn't change my other responsibilities a bit. Study and work were still number one on my list of priorities. Whenever I could squeeze in the time, I attended dances, bull sessions, football games, and other activities.

One Saturday morning just before Thanksgiving, Dr. Mudhenck informed me that he expected me to meet him at one o'clock at the lab. He needed some help and I had two labs to make up. Those were the only two considerations, as far as he was concerned. Whatever else I had planned could just be postponed or scrapped. Oh, that man was impossible!

One o'clock found us both in the lab as scheduled. He sent me down to the large animal clinic to get the horse in stall one and the box of anesthesia beside the stall. He had made all the arrangements with Dr. Wolfe in the clinic. If I could just get back to the lab without losing the horse or dropping the anesthesia, we could prepare the new horse cadaver he needed.

What a way to spend Saturday afternoon! Knowing that if it had to be done, I might as well get on with it, I hurried down to the clinic, got the horse and the box, and brought them back to the lab. Dr. Mudhenck was clearly surprised to see me back so quickly. When I had explained that I didn't believe in fooling around, he told me to tie the horse to a post while he checked the contents of the box. Apparently he was satisfied with the contents. He cleared his throat and said, "Well, Riddle, let's get to work."

Following his instructions, I climbed a ladder to the roof and located a large stainless steel tank connected to a pipe which ran down the outside of the building to a point about five feet from the ground. At that point, the pipe went through the wall and into the lab. Next I came down the ladder and got the water hose which I pulled up to the roof and stuck into the top of the tank. When the water reached the twelve gallon mark, I turned off the water and yelled to Dr. Mudhenck. He brought two opened gallon jugs of formaldehyde to the foot of the ladder. Gasping and choking, I made two trips up the ladder carrying those jugs. Despite my conviction that I would go blind and fall off the ladder, I got the jugs poured into the tank. That ogre ordered me to stay up there and stir the mixture for ten minutes! By the time I reached the ground, I was staggering.

It took several minutes for my head and eyes to clear. Dr. Mudhenck cleared his throat—didn't he ever turn off that hideous noise?—and asked, "Formaldehyde is rough stuff, eh, Doc?"

Noting my annoyance, he pointed to his throat and said, "I was gassed in World War I. It destroyed my pseudo-stratified columnar, ciliated epithelium cells thus depriving me of the normal mechanism for clearing the mucous from my throat."

I sympathized with him and acknowledged that I understood what he had said. As we worked and he continued clearing his throat with the regularity of a metronome, he insisted that I repeat his names for the cells in the lining of the throat and explain the physiological reason for his problem. Didn't he ever stop teaching?

I repeated the names of the cells and explained that since he had no cilia to create wave-like motions to expel the mucous, he had to force air up through his nasal passages to do the job.

Smiling his approval, he said, "You are a good student, Riddle, a good student!"

Compliments from the monster? I thanked him and told him that I certainly tried to be a good student.

His response was, "Do you think I haven't noticed that?"

Being more interested in getting the job done than in talking, I asked what the next step was. Clearing his throat, he asked, "Can you hit the jugular vein of this horse with a needle?"

When I said, "Yes," he handed me a large needle and led the horse over to the point where the pipe came through the wall. His eyes widened as I hit the vein on the first thrust and a stream of blood spurted about two feet.

Handing me the insertion tube, he told me to connect it to the needle. As I made the connection, I asked him if we were using chloral hydrate as the anesthetic. His affirmative answer led to a discussion of how I knew about chloral hydrate and then to the work I had done with Dr. Grear and Charlie.

He commented that I surely must be interested in veterinary medicine since I worked at it all year. About that time the horse began to weave from side to side. Clearing his throat, he told me to try to get her to lie down on her right side. As she started down, I pulled her tail to the right with every ounce of my strength. It worked. She lay on her right side. When the anesthesia had done its work, Dr. Mudhenck made an incision which exposed the jugular vein and the carotid artery. He slipped a tube running from the pipe containing formaldehyde into the jugular vein and sutured it in place. Then he opened the carotid artery and slipped a long glass tube into the artery and sutured it. The horse's heart pumped some of the formaldehyde into the body as it pumped blood out through the tube and into a drain. When the heart stopped beating, the pressure created by the formaldehyde flowing down from the roof finished replacing the blood with formaldehyde. It took most of the afternoon to get fourteen gallons of the preservative into the horse. Still clearing his throat, Dr. Mudhenck explained that the horse's body contained much less than fourteen gallons of blood and that the extra fluid was necessary to fill all the body cavities.

Finally we propped the front feet so that they were about two feet apart. We repeated the process with the rear feet. Clearing his throat extra loudly and thoroughly, Dr. Mudhenck told me that my work had been excellent, that he was going to count this afternoon as double credit which would wipe out both my make-up days, and that I was dismissed.

Stunned by this miracle, I wished him a pleasant weekend and left quickly before he could change his mind. I almost scrubbed my skin off in the shower at Mrs. Sheppard's trying to get rid of the persistent odor of formaldehyde. Mrs. Sheppard let me wash my clothes in her washing machine before the odor ran off all her boarders. Learning to embalm a horse was not one of my reasons for going to college. Maybe it could be counted as a fringe benefit.

All these extra activities had seriously depleted my funds. There was no time to earn any money to buy a ticket when I learned that Walter was going to visit his girl instead of driving to Brevard for Thanksgiving. Well, I would just have to hitchhike and hope that I didn't get picked up by another drunk.

CHAPTER 27

Figuring that looking nice would help me to get rides, I put on the outfit that Tom had bought for me, added a warm jacket, and walked down to the corner. In a few minutes a fellow student gave me a ride to Opelika. It took a good while to catch another ride. The man who stopped said that he was going to Columbus, Georgia, and that he thought it would be easy for me to catch rides from Columbus to Atlanta and from Atlanta to Greenville. Well, that sounded better than standing on the corner in Opelika. I climbed into his car and we had a pleasant trip to Columbus. He introduced himself as Jess Mulkey of Marietta, Georgia. If I had been able to see three years into the future, I would have known that Jess and his brother would become my clients.

When we got to Columbus, Jess wished me good luck and put me out at the corner of Highway 85 which led to Atlanta. It took me two hours to get another ride. By then it was getting dark and a cold wind was blowing. The driver's pleasant conversation was nice, but I would have preferred a car heater that worked.

I was still cold when he put me out in Atlanta. By the time I had walked almost across the city to get to Highway 29, I had warmed up. Unfortunately my luck had not improved. With just sixty cents in my pocket, I had to catch another ride. After what seemed like an eternity, a man stopped and said that he was going to Central, South Carolina. I got into his car. He was surprised that I knew where Central was until I told him about attending Clemson. We talked all the way from Atlanta to Central. He wished me well as he put me out. Central had a population of about three hundred people and there was absolutely no traffic at 1:30 a.m. Tired, freezing cold, and hungry, I walked to the Greyhound station and asked how much a ticket to Greenville would cost. The station master said that the ticket would be forty cents and the bus would be along in fifteen minutes. Well, I didn't hesitate about buying a ticket and getting on that bus.

As the bus rolled along, I made up my mind that I would not ever try to get from Auburn to Greenville hitchhiking again. That

Clemson uniform was a lot better for catching rides than civilian clothes. Since I had given up the uniform, I had better give up the hitchhiking, too. As much as I loved being at home, it just wasn't worth the misery and frustration of the last fourteen hours.

When the bus got to Greenville at two p.m., I walked from the station down to Pete's No. 1, a drive-in restaurant that was on the Riddle Dairy delivery route. My plan was to get something to eat and to wait for the truck to come by. When it came, I would just ride until it got to the farm. With my last twenty cents, I ordered two hot dogs and a cup of coffee.

One of the waiters asked what I was doing there at that time of night. The whole story of my trip poured out. A gentleman overheard my story and asked how long it would be before the truck came and how long it would take to get to the farm. When I told him that the truck would be along about seven o'clock and would get to the farm after lunch, he shook his head. "Finish your coffee, son, and I'll take you home. You need some rest."

He dropped me off at the crossroads a few hundred yards from our house. I walked quietly across the yard and tip-toed through the back door. As I passed her bedroom, Mama called, "Joe, is that you?"

Not wanting to spoil her rest, I answered, "Yes, ma'am," and went on upstairs.

Gertrude Riddle wasn't easily fooled even at 2:30 a.m. By the time I sat down to take off my boots, I heard the stairs creaking. In another minute, Mama stuck her head through the door. "John Riddle, you rascal! I had an idea that was you slipping in!"

She hugged me like a child and insisted that I come down to the kitchen. She made coffee and sliced one of her ever-present cakes. We ate and talked about the things that had happened at school and about whether Carolyn was expecting me. I told her about the boys in my fraternity although I left out most of the details of initiation. She was amused that Carolyn knew that I was coming and that I had tried to surprise the family. Gradually she realized that fourteen hours in the cold had nearly done me in. I promised her that I would never hitchhike home again. We discussed the flattering letters from the dean that still arrived regularly. She was pleased to learn that after this year, I would be spending most of my time working under supervision in the clinics rather than sitting in classrooms. Then she told me that she had inherited some money from her father. She planned to use most of it to send my younger brother, Herbert, to school. She hoped that he would do as well as I had done. She assured me, however, that she would see that I never had to hitchhike again. With that settled, we shared a hug, and I went upstairs and slept until noon.

Just before dinner was ready, Mama came upstairs to wake me up. By the time I got downstairs, the whole family had gathered in the dining room. The Riddle family knew how to make me feel good about coming home. My brothers and brothers-in-law shook my hand and patted me on the shoulder; my sisters and sisters-in-law hugged me; and everybody talked at once. Mama and the girls had cooked a real "hound dog meal"—by the time you finished eating, you weren't good for anything except to curl up in a comfortable spot and go to sleep, just like a hound dog. They had fresh produce from their fall gardens and all sorts of goodies that had been preserved from their spring and summer gardens. All of them were good cooks and they had prepared all of their specialties. Conversation was lively—especially our discussion of the Alpha Psi initiation. My sisters thought I was terrible to scare poor Tom. Even though he was six inches taller than I, they accused me of picking on him! Papa and the fellows almost choked laughing at my description of the mule riding affair. The conversation got a lot more serious when it turned to my hitchhiking home. They could understand my wanting to surprise them; they didn't sympathize with my desire to be independent. Papa closed the discussion by stating that he didn't want me exposed to that kind of risk any more and that I was to write to him when I needed money to come home.

After dinner, we just sat around and talked until milking time. Bly insisted that I help with the milking if I planned to use his car. As soon as we got down to the barn, he laughed and said, "Get out of this barn, boy! I was just teasing you about milking to see if you had gotten too big for your britches. You can use my car every night while you're home. Just come by the house when you're ready to go and I'll give you the keys."

Apparently everybody was upset about my hitchhiking because I was broke. Mama slipped me some money before supper. After supper Papa gave me enough cash to start a business. When I got to Bly's house, he laid the keys on the table and asked me how much money I needed. With a grin, I asked him how much he wanted me to have.

With a sigh, he said, "¿*@!, boy, you get more expensive every time you come home."

After being reminded that I still had two and a half years to go, he moaned, "I'll never live through it." All the time he was fussing, he was laying a twenty dollar bill down beside the keys. His parting shot was, "You had better enjoy this now. I'm not sure whether the dairy business can support you later!"

Bly got enthusiastic thanks and his wife and little daughter got hugs before I hurried off to Carr's Creek. Boy, did I have some tales to tell Carolyn.

Even though Carolyn was glad to see me, she was aggravated that I hadn't been very faithful in my letter writing. Her hug was warm, but her eyes and the set of her jaw warned me that she was upset. Before we had been together for two minutes, she took me to task for my sins of omission. My explanation calmed her down a little before Miss Jennie called us back to the kitchen for cake and coffee with her and Mr. Paul. She, too, reminded me firmly that Carolyn had not received many letters from me recently and had become rather difficult to live with.

Telling them about my schedule settled the waters a little. By the time I finished telling about initiation, all three of them were whooping with laughter. By the time they had heard the saga of my trip home, they all felt sorry for me. Carolyn and I excused ourselves and returned to the living room. We discussed things at Auburn and Furman in a little more detail. She would graduate with a degree in education in June. She planned to get a job teaching and to continue to live at home. She made it quite clear that she still felt that I was not writing to her as often as I should, but she forgave me. I promised to do better and we turned the conversation to happier subjects. Just being with her was enough to make me want to celebrate Thanksgiving. Even when she was mad, she was wonderful.

Friday and Friday night were relatively peaceful. Saturday afternoon, I went by to see Bonnie. The conversation got around to Bonnie's life and her plans for the future. She had done nothing since her graduation from high school except help her mother a little around the house, run a few errands for her father, and play. As for the future, she seemed to have no real plans except to become Mrs. John T. Riddle.

That just wasn't going to work and I knew it. Sternly, I scolded her. She had not been using her time to prepare herself for the future. She knew that I still had to finish more than two years of school. She apparently wasn't planning to do anything except fritter the time away. I certainly didn't want to see her sit around and dry up. She should get busy building a future.

Intuition apparently warned her that Carolyn was going to be tough competition. When she asked about Carolyn, I told her that Carolyn had developed a plan for her life and that she was working energetically toward achieving her goals. As hard as I was working to get my degree in veterinary medicine, I didn't even want to think about spending my life with someone who had no ambition, no goals, and no get-up-and-get. That last statement really got her attention. She wilted like a cut flower under a hot sun.

Oh, no! I hadn't meant to hurt her. When I hugged her, she was trembling like a frightened child. She wanted to talk about marrying me while I tried desperately to steer the conversation toward her getting an education and building a future for herself. Realizing that I wasn't getting anywhere, I asked if I could come back to see her at Christmas and if I could see Miss Mae for a minute. She assured me that I would always be welcome, dried her tears, and called her mother.

Miss Mae came in and hugged me. She and I had a special love for each other. She had been mighty good to me and I respected her. We chatted briefly before I had to leave—"escape" would have described my feelings more accurately.

There must have been something in the air that day. Carolyn and I spent that evening just sitting and talking in her living room. In the course of the conversation, she mentioned that after her graduation in June, she planned to apply for a teaching job so that she could keep busy while I was away. Her intent was as clear as Bonnie's had been.

Surely I wasn't going to have to fight the same war twice in the same day! Hoping that a frontal attack would make her back off, I said slowly, "It sounds like you are planning to marry me."

She hesitated for a minute and then returned the fire. "I thought we had had a mutual understanding since the summer we finished high school."

Oh, $%! I should have known she would get tough. I brought up those two nights I had surprised her with other dates while I was at Clemson. She fired back that they were sons of her mother's friends—she had been nice to them at her mother's request! Whoa!

With a full head of steam, she rolled over to the offense. "We've talked about me. Now let's talk about how many girls at Auburn you're chumming up with!"

Ouch! With a wink and a teasing voice, I answered, "Enough to get around. With the way Auburn's social life is set up, if I don't accept invitations to a few sorority dances and parties, I'll be black-balled. I can't be a leader if I'm not active on the campus, sugar! You know my degree comes first. You just don't understand about campus life."

The fire in her eyes was getting brighter. Teasing wasn't going to get me out of this one. I tried conciliation. "When you see my spring grades, you'll know that my books take precedence over everything."

With steely control, she snapped, "Your books, your social life, and your goals are first in your life. I'm second. We are talking about two different things and two different sets of rules."

When I explained that my social life was simply an escape from my books, she parried, "Books my foot! I know you too well to believe that!"

The gist of the ensuing conversation was that I was going to date casually and she could do whatever she chose to do. She exploded, "That's not fair. Here I sit down here in the country with nothing to do but study and go to church while you have a ball!"

I had heard a different story from our friends, but I just said quietly, "Then you should be a very bright, very Christian girl by the time I get out of school!"

Both of us realized that we were not solving anything and dropped the subject. I showed her the bus ticket Papa had bought for me. The bus would leave at nine o'clock the next morning. While she was at Sunday School and Church, I would be on the first leg of a nine hour ride. I hugged her tight and assured her that she had nothing to worry about. Her response was, "Well, please convince me that I don't have to worry by writing more letters."

This girl was something else. For the sake of peace, I promised her that I would write even though I knew it was an empty promise. A lingering kiss, an embrace that neither of us wanted to end, and I was on my way back to the farm.

Why did life always have to involve choices? I loved both of these girls and their families. They had been a part of my life for a very long time. Why did they both have to get the marrying bug the same day? As many things as there were to do and to worry about, why did they both have to try to pin me down on the same day? At least let me get my degree and have a way to support myself before I decide on a wife!

In a way, the bus trip was a bore. It was a relief, too. At least nobody on the bus was trying to make me decide anything and I didn't have to worry about catching rides.

CHAPTER 28

The period from Thanksgiving until Christmas was hectic. The tensions at home were just a prelude to the wars at Auburn.

The Sheppards had sold the house and the cows to the Hilland family. Mrs. Sheppard held a meeting with all of the boarders to tell us what had happened and to introduce us to the Hillands. The transfer of ownership had been planned so that it would not disturb us boarders or our jobs. Mrs. Hilland assured us that things would go on just as they had been. We took her at her word.

Evidence that we had made a mistake mounted quickly. The Hillands and their two pretty daughters moved into the house when the Sheppards moved out. Things didn't run very smoothly in the house or in the kitchen and dining room. We figured that as soon as they got settled, the Hillands would solve the problems. When the Hillands bought a very expensive car, both the quantity and the quality of our food took a nose dive. Our situation went from bad to intolerable. Meetings with Mrs. Hilland brought threats rather than solutions. In desperation, all of the boarders decided to move out if things didn't improve. Instead of trying to resolve our difficulties, she presented us with higher bills for room and board. Among other things, she charged Tom and me fifteen dollars each for our room and thirty-five dollars each for our board. She did this despite the fact that both of us had done our work to earn our room and board. When we tried to work out an agreement, Mrs. Hilland was just impossible.

Keeping up with my work and my studies was tough enough without having to battle Mrs. Hilland. I got a friend who was an attorney to help us. As soon as she received her first letter from the attorney demanding back pay, Mrs. Hilland got hysterical and did all sorts of wild things. She wrote letters to our parents claiming that all of us were drinkers and gamblers who never paid our bills because all our money was squandered on booze and gambling. Her worst and most despicable stunt was offering me her younger daughter as a roommate. That made me mad enough to give her a lecture on child abuse, white slavery, and morality.

Her letter brought me a "what in the *** is going on?" letter from my daddy. Papa's letter also contained Mrs. Hilland's letter to the Riddles. I showed both letters to Mrs. Sheppard and asked her what to do. After listening in horror to my side of the story, Mrs. Sheppard wrote a letter to my parents assuring them I had done nothing wrong and that Mrs. Hilland's accusations were false. That letter brought me another letter from Papa enclosing letters from the dean praising my character and my grades, the letter from Mrs. Sheppard, and a letter to Mrs. Hilland asking how I could be both a superior student and a drunken gambler. Between my lawyer friend, our parents, and Mrs. Sheppard, we finally put enough pressure on Mrs. Hilland to make her back down and shut up. The shutting up wasn't achieved until I threatened to add harassment to my already ominous lawsuit.

When Mrs. Hilland finally realized that she was in serious trouble, I didn't have to take her to court. As many stupid bungles as she had made, I probably could have won a sizeable damage suit. If I had, there were twenty others who were just waiting to nail her again. It seemed wiser to concentrate on my goals, to find another place to live, and to forget this crazy woman and her antics. My housemates agreed with me. Before Christmas vacation, all of her boarders had found new places to live. Tom and I decided to move to Mr. Wright's dormitory which was just down the street. Most of us moved into two houses within a block of The Sheppard Chateau.

To add to the uproar, the Japanese attacked Pearl Harbor. Now instead of talking about the war in Europe, our country was actually involved in the war. The specter of the draft hung over all of us. Like many of my classmates, my draft classification was 1-A. All across the land, men were volunteering or being drafted into the armed services. I made up my mind to continue to learn as much as I could as fast as I could. Until they drafted me, I would keep striving for my doctorate in veterinary medicine. This was the period in which we observed a first at Auburn—Dr. Mudhenck actually laughed out loud in anatomy lab.

We were dissecting the hindquarter of the horse. He came along, covered the tags naming the muscles and asked Bill Spence to name them orally. Bill named the muscles quickly and accurately. Dr. Mudhenck nodded approvingly as Bill rattled off, "Semitendenous, semimembroneous, and semispencious." On the last one which was the anus, Bill enunciated very carefully, "semi-spencious," accenting it so that he gave the impression the muscle had been named for him! Who but Bill Spence would have a muscle in a horse's anus named for him? All of us including Dr. Mudhenck roared with laughter. When he realized that the other students saw him laughing, the old grump covered his face with his hand and hurried into his office. If anybody ever heard him laugh again, I never knew about it.

Finally the last quiz and the last class were over and I was on the train heading for Greenville. Carolyn met me at the station at nine o'clock that night. When I got off the train, it was Christmas for sure. Carolyn looked like a beautiful Christmas doll, a light snow was falling, and the Salvation Army Band was playing carols. I hugged Carolyn and kissed her quickly on the nose—even that much display of affection in public was bound to raise eyebrows!—threw two quarters into the Salvation Army Kettle, and walked down the street to her parents' car. With one arm around Carolyn and my suitcase in my other hand, I felt like King John with his queen and his scepter!

Walking and riding through the streets was sheer joy. The decorations were beautiful, Carolyn and I were together, and Christmas was in the air. We went a slightly less than direct route to Carr's Creek so that we had a few minutes to savor being together.

Miss Jennie and Mr. Paul had cake and coffee waiting for us. The four of us had a delightful visit—almost like the return of a son to the family. They had really out-done themselves on the decorations in the house. This was a perfect Christmas. I was so happy I had to pinch myself to be sure this was all real. Pretty soon Carolyn and I excused ourselves and retreated to the living room. All too soon, curfew arrived and Carolyn drove me out to the farm. It would have been nice if I could have kept my Christmas doll. Unfortunately, I had to kiss her goodnight, hug her tight, and then watch her drive off into the night.

Christmas was in the air at the farm, too. Love and joy surrounded the family and the animals. I joined the family around the fireplace in the sitting room. The firelight danced as we laughed and talked and enjoyed each other's company. Somehow we got to the subject of the fraternity initiation. By the time I finished building up those tales, they were whoppers. The family members had laughed until their sides ached. Interspersed with news and tales, we discussed plans for the holidays. Among other things, we planned to track rabbits through the snow. The uproars at Auburn and in Europe seemed far away.

When I got to Dr. Grear's clinic the next morning, Christmas seemed to have been replaced by Halloween. Dr. Grear had been drinking. He was too drunk to practice veterinary medicine and too sober to be quiet and go to sleep. I slipped into the back room and made a quick phone call to Jackie, his wife. My gut tightened as she said, "John, nobody on earth can do anything with him when he gets like he is this morning. Just stay with him and try to keep him from hurting himself or anybody else. I hate to tell you, but he has been waiting for you to get home so that he could really tie one on."

This was quite a predicament. Dr. Grear was a wonderful person and an excellent vet when he was sober. Unfortunately, he worked too many hours with too little rest and never allowed himself a vacation. When fatigue and depression caught up with him, he retreated into an alcoholic haze. That spelled trouble because he continued to work and refused to eat. While I was trying to decide what to do, Dr. Grear's voice roared and slurred, "Charlie, old boy, you treat 'em here; Dr. Riddle and I will go get 'em on the road. Come on, Doc. Let's go see all the pretty animals and make 'em feel real good."

Jackie usually drove him when he made his road calls. He had insisted that she stay at home today and he was certainly in no state to drive. Thank God, he threw the keys to me and got in on the passenger side of the car. The day was filled with all the frustrations created by dealing with a drunk. He insisted that I keep up with the money, treat the animals, and keep him well supplied with gin, chasers, and cups. He had enough sense to stay in the car and to keep his mouth relatively shut while we were at the various farms. I explained that he wasn't feeling well and suggested that folks not go over to the car to speak to him so that he could rest. Everybody knew that he worked too hard so that ruse was reasonably effective. Dr. Grear put on a royal show on one of our trips back to the clinic. A very nervous lady had brought in a Boston terrier which was suffering from eclampsia. (Heavy loss of calcium from having a litter of puppies had produced acute seizures.) While I was administering a massive dose of calcium to the pet, I worked at calming the lady down. Both were progressing very well when Dr. Grear decided to take over. He brought out a bottle of blue calcium tablets, poured out twelve tablets into his hand, and ordered the lady to give her dog two of the tablets three times a day. Realizing that he was drunk, she looked at him sternly and asked, "Are you sure you know what you're doing? I don't want you to poison Petunia."

"Of course we aren't going to poison Petunia! These pills might be good for you. As bad as I feel, they could even help me." With all of us watching him, he crammed all twelve of the tablets into his mouth and began to chew them up. First his saliva turned blue, then he began foaming at the mouth. As we gaped in disbelief, he started blowing blue bubbles. This was too much—all of us burst out laughing. With an audience for his antics, Dr. Grear put on a comic performance that would have made show business history if we could have filmed it. Finally we gave the lady some pills for her dog, picked up the list of road calls, and started out again.

Some of his other performances weren't amusing. As time passed, his mood changed from funny to resentful and combative. That evening while I ate supper at a local restaurant, he sat at the table with me and continued to drink. When his wife's brother, James, tried to get him to stop drinking and to go home, he got mad. Dr. Grear stood up, poured his glass of ice water over James' head to cool him off, and sat back down to resume his drinking. When we finally got him home, Jackie asked me to spend the night so that I would be available to handle any emergency calls that came in during the night. I drove their car out to the farm, explained the situation to my family, got a few things together, and drove back to the Grear's house.

The pattern continued through the holidays. I used their car for short periods during the evening for dates. It was convenient to have my own transportation even though the medicinal smell of the car wasn't very romantic.

Other than my dates, I was on call twenty hours a day. Not all my calls were for veterinary services. Jackie was frustrated and lonely. She saw me as her personal assistant as well as an assistant veterinarian. Jackie needed companionship, I needed sleep, the animals needed medical care, the family and my girls wanted my company, and Dr. Grear needed to be watched until we could sober him up. Life was certainly becoming a juggling act.

One night Jackie brought me some small yellow capsules that Dr. Grear was taking in addition to the copious quantities of gin he was drinking. Nembutal! She didn't have the vaguest notion what they were. It was my unpleasant task to explain to her that if he continued to refuse food, to drink, and to take nembutal, we had two choices—put him in the hospital or plan his funeral. She did what she had to do while Charlie and I handled the practice. There were several other veterinarians in the area who were very gracious about answering my questions by phone or accepting emergency calls from our clients when the cases were beyond my capability. Between the two of us, Charlie and I could cope with almost everything without outside help. Charlie's support was magnificent. That man was too good to be real. I lost count of the times he did something well and then told everybody that I had done it. Charlie was building my reputation as a vet and my confidence as well. If God rewards earthly good works in heaven, Charlie must surely have had a royal reception when he got there.

By the end of the holidays, I had more than one thousand dollars of Dr. Grear's money after I had covered all my road expenses and paid myself two hundred dollars. Jackie wouldn't take the money—she said that Don would have a fit if she did. While he was rubber-kneed and loose-tongued drunk, Dr. Grear had told me to keep it as a Christmas present. That had obviously been the gin talking rather than a business arrangement. Finally I deposited it in a separate account at the bank until Don could get straight and tell me what to do with it. Jackie thought that I should have paid myself more. We agreed to let Dr. Grear handle that question, too, when he got well.

This was one time I was glad to get on the train to go back to Auburn. The stress of handling all the responsibilities for the good doctor had been a heavy load. What little celebrating I had done had been squeezed in between calls. Even though Carolyn, Bonnie, Mama, and the family understood that I had to help the Grears, we were all thoroughly frustrated that we had so little time together. Goodbyes were short and tinged with disappointment.

CHAPTER 29

When we got back to Auburn, we were delighted to find that the Hilland family had packed up and moved out of town. Tom and I were living at Mr. Wright's house. He was as full of mischief as the boys who lived with him. Sometimes we thought that he enjoyed our pranks and practical jokes more than we did. Everybody laughed when I answered the phone, "Jot-em Down Store!" and Mrs. Sheppard asked to speak to John Riddle. Quick as a wink, I asked her to wait for a minute, called my own name loudly, and then answered the phone as breathlessly as though I had run down the stairs. That sort of foolishness went on all the time.

Since Mr. Wright did not serve meals, we ate at The Magnolia Inn where Bill Spence, Harry Morgan, and a number of other vet students lived. The arrangement was good for all of us.

Nothing particularly interesting happened during the rest of the semester. Without our hassles with Mrs. Hilland, we were free to finish up the loose ends of our school work and to struggle through exams. When grades were posted, I was still in first place. Tom teased me that I would be an educated son of a *$#! by graduation if I kept up the pace.

During registration for second semester, I noticed that there were enough blanks on the registration card to sign up for ten courses. After some concentrated figuring, I devised a schedule that would let me take ten courses. When I presented it to the dean's secretary, she stared at it. Her brother was in my class at vet school and she knew how tough it was to get through the usual six courses. She warned me that the dean would probably not approve my schedule. She took the card into his office. When she returned saying that Dean Suggs wanted to see me, I steeled myself for a tail-chewing and entered the inner sanctum.

Dean Suggs greeted me cordially. He pulled my academic record from his drawer and looked at it for a minute before stating that he would hate to see me over-extend myself and drop my average. I assured him that I planned to stay at the top and that I was confident that I could make an "A" in each of the ten courses. That

set him back in his chair! Floundering a little, he told me that nobody had ever done such a thing. My rebuttal must have sounded
good because he decided that I should think about it during the
five day break between semesters and come back to see him. Well,
at least he didn't say, "No."

With my finances in bad shape, I decided not to go home between semesters. The morning after the other students left for the
five day break, we had six inches of snow. This was the first snow
Auburn had gotten in twenty-eight years. The landscape was hushed
and beautiful. Without a car moving on the street nor anyone walking on the sidewalk, it was also very lonely. Homesickness and misery were beginning to pound on me when the phone rang. When
I answered it, Dan Brown, a friend from South Alabama, asked
if I were going home. When I said, "No," Dan was jubilant. He
asked me to see if I could borrow a .22 rifle and join him and his
three brothers to hunt rabbits. That sounded great. In a few minutes
the arrangements were made and Dan, Doug, Steve, and Ray were
trooping up the steps. I was worried because I had neither shells
nor money. They assured me that they had more shells than we
would need. As full of anticipation as any big-game hunters on
safari, we set out across the fields behind Mr. Wright's house.

The Browns and I had a lot in common. We had all grown up
on farms, we were wise in the ways of the woods and the fields,
we were financially poor but rich in resourcefulness, and we loved
to hunt. I thought I was the best shot around until Ray came along.
That rascal could out-shoot me without even trying very hard. All
of us were good hunters. A whole day tromping around the woods
and fields was like heaven after weeks of being confined to classrooms and labs.

Tracking small game in the snow was fun for all of us. We hadn't
gotten permission to hunt because we didn't know who owned the
land. It wasn't posted and nobody objected to our presence so we
just did what we would have done at home. By the end of the day
we had killed sixteen quail, eight squirrels, and twenty-six rabbits.
That much game is a lot to carry, but we hauled it all back to my
house. The laundry room was warm and it had hot and cold water
so we used it to dress the game. When we had finished that job,
we went over to see Mrs. Nowlin at The Magnolia Inn.

To our delight, Mrs. Nowlin bought every bit of our game and
paid us one hundred dollars! We had made twenty dollars apiece
having fun! Now that was the way to live.

By the next day the snow had melted too much to track anything. We spent the day rambling around the fields and woods anyway. We had fun even though we didn't kill much game. After dressing the few rabbits and quail we had, I insisted that the Browns take them to their boarding house.

My cure for the lonely evenings was Sandy. She was a pretty little brunette with all the playfulness and friendliness of a puppy. We went to the movies or took long walks in the snow. Just to keep the record straight, I told her about Carolyn. Sandy told me that I was the first college boy she had dated. We had a great time together. Moonlight and snow created a romantic atmosphere. Sandy decided that she was in love and I decided that we had a problem. She was too much fun to give up, too sweet to hurt, and definitely not a replacement for Carolyn. Why do women always have to complicate situations by falling in love?

Tom came back from his visit to his home full of tales of his adventures, aggravated that he had missed the snow, and rattling a little extra cash in his pocket. He promptly hunted up a poker game and increased his assets. Sometimes I wondered if he came to school to become a veterinarian or to hone his gambling skills!

Dean Suggs gave his approval to my taking ten courses with the understanding that I would drop some of the electives if my grades started to slide. Sandy reluctantly agreed to accept me on my terms—we would be good friends and have fun together, but we would not get serious. It was going to be a busy semester.

Two of my classes were so far apart that I had to run to get to the second one on time. Luckily, one of my friends who had a car took both classes and gave me a ride every day. Taking ten classes was a challenge. Even better was the realization that I could handle it. I was working hard, but I certainly wasn't working any harder than Mama was doing back home.

One weekend I had some time on my hands so I went up to the fraternity house. Some of the brothers taught me to play bridge. Wow! That was a game to sink my teeth into. By the end of the first afternoon, I was a bridge addict. The more I learned, the more I loved it. From then on, my spare time was devoted to bridge.

At mid-semester I still had all "A's" and all was right with my world. Dean Suggs met me in the hall and we went down together to check the grades posted on the bulletin board. He asked if I were having a hard time. He smiled at the negative answer and encouraged me to stick with it and to be the first student ever to take ten courses at once.

Carolyn and Bonnie were disappointed when I decided not to go home for the Easter holidays. There was no way I could keep up with ten courses and make enough money to pay for tickets between Auburn and Greenville and I was too proud to ask Papa for more money. Since it wasn't much longer until summer vacation, I assured them both that we would make up for lost time during the summer.

The rest of the semester went by in a blur.

I took Sandy to the spring dance. Her mother bought her a gorgeous dress and I gave her a pretty corsage. As usual, I was wearing my friend's tuxedo. Sandy looked like a dream and danced like an angel. Those big eyes were so full of love, I almost lost control. Please, dear Lord, let this girl fall in love with somebody else soon. I can't handle this kind of pressure much longer! My head knows what I have to do; my heart and my body are having trouble! In spite of my worries, it was a wonderful evening.

The lady who managed The Magnolia Inn sub-let rooms on the weekends and during holidays when the regular occupants weren't there. One weekend, she sub-let Gerald Wilson's room to a regular army sergeant. Bill, Harry, and I had just finished studying for an anatomy test when Tom came by on his way home from his Friday night poker game. He had won quite a bit of money and enjoyed several drinks. It soon became obvious that he was itching to get into something. Looking around the room, Tom spotted the spurs that Harry had just finished polishing in preparation for his polo game the next afternoon. Tom's eyes lit up with mischief as he asked, "Which room is ole Gerald Wilson's? Me and these spurs are gonna pay him a little visit."

Harry answered, "Room eleven," and we watched Tom pick up the spurs and stride out of the room.

Following him quietly down the hall, we saw him enter Gerald's room. Apparently Tom jumped on the occupant of the bed in the dark room, and began raking the spurs down his sides while he yelled, "Whoa, mule, whoa!"

That two hundred and fifty pound sergeant came out of that bed like an explosion, throwing Tom up in the air and against the wall. By the time I could reach in and turn on the light, Tom was hollering, "Get me out of here before this *%#! kills me!"

The sergeant, still half-asleep, was muttering, "Somebody better explain what's going on mighty quick or I'm going to break every bone in that son of a #%$!"

By this time most of the occupants of The Magnolia Inn were standing in the hall laughing fit to kill. Thinking fast, I jerked Tom out into the hall, stepped into the room, and closed the door. The sergeant settled down when I explained Tom's mistake. He agreed to forget it if we would keep Tom under control, or at least out of his room, for the rest of the night. I assured him that we would take Tom home immediately.

Now I could remind Tom that I had saved his worthless hide twice!

Shortly after the spurring episode, Tom and I were awakened by a loud bang as though something heavy had dropped right outside our room. Bolting out of our beds, we looked everywhere for the source of the noise. We found nothing. The next night the same thing happened shortly after we got to sleep. Again we found nothing. By the time this had occurred on ten straight nights, Tom and I were furious, frustrated, and determined to solve the mystery. We went up to our rooms, pretended to get ready for bed, and turned off the light. Tom hid downstairs and I hid upstairs. In about thirty minutes, the weight crashed down. I couldn't see anything.

Tom had seen Rick DeJarnett go outside, look up at our window and then return to his room shortly before the crash. Flinging Rick's door open, Tom caught him winding a cord. Grabbing the cord, Tom traced it up the stairs. Rick had run the cord through staples driven under the edge of the bannister and tied it to a weight. He could sit innocently in his chair and snatch the cord. When the weight tripped, the cord would come loose. Rick would quickly pull it back through the staples and hide it before anybody could see it. After we figured out the system, Rick admitted his guilt. We assured him that we would take care of his rear the next day.

On the way home from lab, I went by the fraternity house and borrowed a four inch paddle. When Rick got home, we called all the residents to witness his punishment. I blistered his fanny with ten Clemson-style swats. Tom decided not to paddle him if he would agree to run errands for the rest of the year. We agreed to shake hands, to remain friends, and to sleep undisturbed for the rest of the year.

A few weeks later Bill and Harry came down to our house to

study anatomy with us. As we studied, Bill asked what time we went to bed. We answered, "About eleven," and thought no more about it. About fifteen minutes before eleven o'clock, they wished us a good night and left. Tom and I got ready for bed. I climbed up on the top bunk, Tom finished shining his shoes, turned off the light, and got into his bottom bunk. Just as I dozed off, the door opened and a smoke bomb came spinning into the room.

That thing was spitting smoke, sparks, and flames as it spun crazily around the floor. Tom hollered, "John! John, you've got to get up and throw that thing out the window!"

I yelled back," To $!* with that! You throw it out! You're closer than I am!"

Afraid that we would set something on fire if we threw it out the window, I threw a towel over it while Tom raised the window. Tom bellowed, "Let's get out of here. This smoke is too much!"

We ran out and closed the door. All the other occupants of the house were standing at the bottom of the stairs laughing like a bunch of hyenas. They swore they didn't know who did it although they had seen a tall guy and a short guy run out the door. Aha! Harry was tall and Bill was short. Tom grinned as he put his thoughts into words, "It was Bill and Harry, sure as sin, and I'll bet those lousy turkeys are out there hiding in the shrubbery right now busting their britches laughing! Come on, John, let's get 'em!"

As we burst through the front door, they spooked like quail and ran down the street. I was fast enough to catch Bill and Tom's long legs soon caught up with Harry. Those jokers were laughing too hard to run anyway. Before we could even threaten them, we heard the sound of approaching sirens. Somebody had turned in a fire alarm. Those guys were going to drown our room for sure when they saw all that smoke. Now what?

Tom, still wearing his pajamas, ran over to the truck and told them what had happened. The chief was not amused. The firemen said very little and went on into the house as their chief lectured us about the seriousness of turning in false alarms. Conviction on that charge carried a hefty fine and a prison sentence. We knew that we couldn't prove that Bill and Harry were guilty and we didn't want to get them into that degree of trouble so we said that we didn't know who had thrown the bomb. The chief looked at his report, told us that the call had come from the Magnolia Inn, and asked if we knew anybody there. We told him that we knew almost everybody there. Still fuming, he told us that there would be a full scale investigation the next day. The firemen cleared our room of smoke with a high-powered fan and sprayed it with something to neutralize the odor. They took the remains of the bomb and the scorched towel with them.

The guys at The Magnolia Inn provided an alibi for Bill and Harry to keep them from getting caught. Tom and I held our threat to tell on them over their heads whenever we wanted them to do something for us. The investigation was dropped long before we dropped the threat.

Professional veterinarians belonged to The American Veterinary Medical Association. The AVMA handled everything from lobbying in Washington to getting out a monthly journal with all sorts of information useful to the practicing vet, to providing group insurance for members, their spouses, and their families. The veterinary schools had junior chapters of the AVMA on campus. The Auburn chapter had about four hundred and fifty members. One of its major functions was to arbitrate difficulties between the students and the professors. The officers were usually seniors and the faculty adviser was usually the most popular professor on campus. The officers and the adviser were elected by the members. It was customary for the fraternities and the independents to have separate slates. When the fraternities ran more than one candidate, the independents sometimes held the power to turn the election.

This spring when elections were held, the president was an Alpha Psi and the vice-president was an O.T.S. Somebody from O.T.S. nominated me for secretary and immediately somebody from Alpha Psi moved that the nominations be closed. When that motion had been seconded and passed, somebody else moved that the secretary be elected by acclamation. That, too, was seconded and passed. Whoa, hoss! I protested that this was a railroad job and wasn't fair. Their response was that I could take notes better and faster than anybody else and I should be secretary, therefore, I had been elected secretary.

Well, I now had another job whether or not I wanted it. Since I had been elected, I would do my best to be a good secretary, but I would be glad when the year was over.

Shortly after exams I went by the site of the new Alpha Psi House. That construction crew had really been turning out some work. The foreman saw me and said, "You boys will be living in this house this fall." I agreed that it looked that way.

We had a meeting to decide who would occupy which room when we returned to school. Somebody suggested that the juniors should live upstairs and the seniors downstairs. That suited everybody. Then we had to decide how to assign individual rooms. Somebody suggested that this be done by grades; the man with the highest grades got first choice, and so on down the line. I refrained from voting on that question although grades was the method of choice. As soon as the issue was decided, they started asking me which room I had chosen. Since final grades weren't in, I felt uncomfortable about taking first choice. Everybody insisted that my grades were going to be highest and that I should get on with the process. I chose the large room at the head of the spiral staircase with the proviso that everybody be very quiet coming upstairs so they wouldn't disturb my beauty sleep. That cracked them up. Tom had already asked if we were going to room together at the fraternity house. I had told him that after two years of living with him, I wouldn't know how to be satisfied with anybody else. He approved of my choice of rooms.

The only things left to do now were to pack up my gear, to talk to the dean's secretary about sending me a post card as soon as grades were posted, and to get myself and my stuff into Walter's car for the trip home. It didn't take long to finish all three.

Walter must have been as anxious to get home as I was. He put the accelerator down firmly and we were in Greenville almost before I finished my nap.

CHAPTER 30

One of the first things discussed after the greetings at the farm was that spring planting was running late because the weather had been bad. Mr. Charlie was short one tractor driver and that was delaying him further. When Papa asked me to drive a tractor for two weeks, I agreed to drive the tractor and to help with the planting before I started working for Dr. Grear. With that settled, we started catching up on all the news. Six months was the longest time I had ever stayed away from home and all sorts of things had happened. They were all tickled that I had found some hunting buddies and that we had used our country skills to make our spending money. When they asked about my grades, I told them that I had passed and that we would know how well I had done in a few days when the card arrived from the dean's secretary. They had gotten several snows since Christmas and lots of interesting things had occurred in the family and in the community.

Carolyn was just bubbling over with joy when I got to Carr's Creek. We had never been separated for six months and she declared that she couldn't believe how much I had changed. Under questioning, she allowed that all the changes were for the better. I couldn't think of any way to improve her, but I didn't mention that. My "other parents," Mr. Paul and Miss Jennie, had their usual coffee and cake ready for us. They visited with us long enough to find out the major events of the past six months. I was glad to see them, but I was gladder when they left us to catch up some of things we had missed for six months.

Carolyn was excited about her graduation from Furman. She would graduate on June 14. I would start working for Don on June 10. He had agreed that my job could wait until I finished helping Papa with the planting. We were both happy that he was in good shape and hopeful that he would stay sober during the summer. Working out a dating schedule around a veterinary practice was tough at best. When we had to work around his drinking bouts, there wasn't much left for dates. We didn't think we could handle a repeat of the Christmas holidays. Looking on the bright side, we started planning our summer activities.

One of the first things Mama noticed was that my work clothes were too tight and my school clothes were getting tight and worn-looking. When she said, "Boy, we had better go to town and get you some clothes right quick if you're going to look decent," I knew we might as well plan to go into Greenville.

When she finished getting the clothes she thought I needed, Papa looked at me and said, "Boy, it's cheaper to keep you in school than to keep you at home!"

I drove a tractor hitched to a tiller to turn the winter-bound land up to the sun. The heat from the sun would warm the soil enough to receive its seeds and fertilizer and to start the growing cycle. What I did with one tractor and tiller would have required eight men working with mule-drawn plows. The other tractor came behind me with a harrow and smoothed out the soil. Then I made another pass pulling seeding and fertilizing equipment. The good weather held and we finished the whole spring plowing and planting in ten days. Progress was wonderful.

Carolyn's graduation gift required another shopping trip. After a serious debate with myself over what to get, I chose a small cameo brooch as perfect in every detail as she was. Carolyn loved the cameo and I loved Carolyn. Life was looking good except that Carolyn was through with school and I had two more hard years to go. When she smiled and said that she would wait, I asked her what she was waiting for. Her answer was, "Dr. John!"

When I went by to talk to Dr. Grear about working during the summer, I had asked what he wanted me to do with the money I had put in the bank at Christmas. He told me just to leave it alone. He had plans for it.

The first days in the clinic were great. Charlie, Jackie, and Don were all glad to have me back and I was happy to be there. We decided that I would spend the summer living with the Grears so that transportation wouldn't be a problem and I could help with the late night and early morning calls. Farmers always seemed to have their emergencies between midnight and daylight!

During a slow period on the morning of June 14, I mentioned that it was Carolyn's graduation day. Don promptly told Jackie to call the florist and send an orchid or two to Carolyn and to have my name put on the card. When I protested the expense, Don growled, "Oh, ***! We're not going to let her down on her day of glory!"

We had to make a road call right after Jackie left to have her hair done. Don informed me that he was tired and that I would have to drive him. With my heart in my throat, I prayed silently, "Please, God, don't let him go on a tear like he did at Christmas!"

As we drove down the road, I asked Don why he and Jackie didn't take a little time off and take a trip. He could relax and get some rest and it would be good for both of them. His answer surprised me, "Now that you've mentioned it, I'll tell you what I'm going to do with the money you put in the bank. I've never been to a national convention of The American Veterinary Medical Association. This year I would like to attend the convention in Washington. If I leave you the house, the car, the clinic, and Charlie, can you handle it?"

I hedged a little and asked if he thought I had the ability to handle all of that. He snapped, "Ability? Just look at what you did when I was sick last year. You know more about veterinary practice right now than all those quacks in town! If you don't, I feel sorry for you!"

When I responded that I certainly knew more than the quacks, the deal was settled. We finished checking Mr. Breedlove's bull and drove to the bank. Don was stunned at the size of the account. When he asked how I made so much, I said, "Long hours and hard work—just like you!"

When he left the bank, his conversation jumped back and forth between the money and the trip. He was as excited as a little boy. When he asked how much I had been paid for my work at Christmas, he decreed that I was worth a lot more than $200.00. He decided to make it up by raising my salary to $50.00 a week. He went on to say that my work was worth more than $50.00 a week, but that was all he could afford to pay me. I assured him that I was glad to be getting $50.00 a week and that I would work hard to earn it. My experience was helping me in school and that was important, too.

After Carolyn's graduation, the summer flew by. The card came from the dean's secretary saying that I had made "A's" in all ten subjects. Hot dog!

My daddy got a special letter from the dean praising my accomplishments. Then Dean Suggs sent me a letter congratulating me and asking me to come by his office before I registered in the fall. Things were working out pretty well.

Don arranged with a veterinarian about twelve miles away to help me if I needed anything while he and Jackie were away. The days sped by and before I knew it, I was driving him and Jackie to the railroad station for their trip to the convention. They were as excited as children and it made me feel good to see them so happy. After giving me some last-minute instructions about ordering drugs, they were on their way.

With mixed emotions, I went back to the clinic. I still wasn't a licensed veterinarian, but I had learned a lot since the last time Don had left me with the practice. Charlie and I ought to be able to handle routine things. Professional help was available if we needed it. I really felt that we could make it for two weeks unless we had some sort of major disaster.

Charlie and I kept complete records of everything that happened at the office and I kept a separate record of the after-hours calls. We listed every call, the nature of the problem, the treatment, the results, and the charges. Realizing that Don's fees were much too low, I raised them. I also ordered two new drugs that I had learned about at Auburn. During the past year, whenever I had free time during clinic sessions, I had sat in the balcony and observed. Although all vet students were encouraged to do this, I was one of the few who did it regularly. I knew that the professors were very much aware of who was in that balcony. It never hurt anybody's grades for the professors to note his presence in the clinic balcony on a regular basis. You could learn a lot by watching and by asking questions while the clinics were in session. It sure was coming in handy now. I only had to call the neighboring vet once during the two weeks and that was just to ask a question.

Carolyn and I managed to have just three short dates while they were gone. Wouldn't you know that I got late calls all three of those nights! No wonder the pressure sometimes got to Don. When Don and Jackie came back two days early, I was glad to see them. They looked great as they stepped off the train. I met them at the station, drove them home, and insisted that Don take the rest of the day off. If he stayed rested and relaxed, I thought we could avoid a repeat of the Christmas disaster.

The next day we went over the records and Don was delighted. He wondered if anybody had complained about the higher fees. When I said nobody had said a word, he seemed surprised. I heard Jackie ask him later about the suggested fees I had written down for the clients who were billed monthly. He told her to charge what I had written. Many of the clients called him to praise my work. He was so happy he offered to pay me double for the two weeks. I declined and he insisted that he was going to do something to compensate me. I suggested that the thing that would make me happiest would be for him to take another week off before the end of the summer. That sounded good to him and we agreed that he and Jackie would take off for one more week before I left for school.

Later when Jackie and I talked, she mentioned that Don thought my raising the fees was the greatest thing that could have happened. He had a terrible fear of competition. He kept his fees ridiculously low for fear his competitors would take over his practice. She also said that he was very worried that after graduation I would set up a practice in Greenville and take away his clients. I assured her that I would never set up my practice in Greenville since that would be betraying the man who had made it possible for me to become a veterinarian.

Don showed his appreciation by giving me Wednesday afternoons off for the rest of the summer. The milk truck picked me up as it went back to the farm after finishing the morning deliveries. Those Wednesday afternoons became the best part of the week. I had begun to realize how tough it was to be on call twenty-four hours a day, seven days a week, fifty-two weeks a year.

The rest of the summer melted away. Don and Jackie enjoyed one more week away from the practice and then I was going to take off three days to get ready to return to Auburn. My last working day was miserable. I felt bad when I got up and the pain in my side just got worse all day. Finally Don looked at me, asked a couple of questions, and probed my side gently. I thought the pain would kill me. Rolling his eyes toward heaven, Don announced that I had appendicitis and that he was taking me to the hospital. Despite my protests, he took me straight to the hospital. Before I knew what was happening, my appendectomy was over and I was catching a whole lot of flack from the family about having my illness diagnosed by the vet! When he paid me for the summer's work, Don gave me a rather large bonus. At first I demurred. When he insisted that I had earned it, I decided that it would pay for a very special gift at Christmas. Without saying a word about it to anybody, I put the bonus in a safe place. Don made it clear that I would always have a job with him when I came home as long as I was a student. Jackie's description of his fears seemed to underline those last seven words. Both of us thought we would have another summer together before we would take separate paths. The world situation was going to change that although none of us suspected it when we wished each other good-bye and good luck.

Going back to Auburn this time was going to be different. My little brother Herbert was going with me. He had been accepted at Auburn as a five-year freshman. He would take both his pre-med requisites and his veterinary medicine courses at Auburn. With the country at war, he surely didn't want to go to Clemson nor to any other military school. That was almost a sure ticket to Europe and death in combat. The two of us raced around getting our trunks and suitcases packed and saying our good-byes. Lord, I always seemed to be saying good-bye!

Carolyn was going to be teaching at East Gantt High School this fall. She was getting ready to go to work and here I was going back to school. It didn't seem right, somehow, but that was the way it was.

Mama gave Herbert the money he needed for school. He had gotten himself a job waiting on tables to earn his room and board as I had done. He was going to live near The Sheppard Chateau and The Magnolia Inn.

Papa decided that I had earned the right to live in the fraternity house and to have all my expenses paid this year. He gave me enough money to cover all the expenses I knew about plus a special bonus to see that Herbert did as well as I had done. Herbert heard him and promised to do his best. We would be living across town from each other and probably wouldn't see each other very often, but at least each of us had a brother available when we needed one. That was a good feeling for both of us.

Mama and Papa took us to the railroad station. All too soon, Herbert and I were on the train heading toward Atlanta and Mama and Papa were heading back to the farm.

CHAPTER 31

As the Southerner pulled out of the station in Greenville, Herbert and I settled back in our seats. Soon the conversation turned to life at Auburn. After four years of hearing me talk about college, Herbert knew a lot more than I had known when Bly and Papa took me to Clemson. Even so, he still had a lot of questions and I suspected that buried somewhere deep inside were a few doubts and fears.

Lord, my ignorance had been painful! Maybe the Riddle method of training "rats" at Clemson would work for a little brother. I told Herbert what he could expect and advised him on how to handle problem situations. Assuring him that Auburn's hazing was nothing like Clemson's, I suggested that he go along with the "rat routines." The sooner he fitted into the environment and the less commotion he caused, the sooner the upper classmen would accept him as a person rather than a victim. I didn't want him to be as naive as Jason nor as arrogant as Coleman. If he could be more like Gleason, maybe things would work out well for him.

By the time we finished hashing out the pros and cons of being a good rat, supper was being served. When Herbert said that he was hungry, I decided to be a big shot and treat him to "dinner" in the dining car.

Since we were wearing suits and ties, I figured we might just as well act like rich boys. With a grin, I said, "Come on, let's eat like rich folks. We'll go down to the dining car and have a fancy meal. Don gave me some extra cash. I'll do the paying—you just remember that this is "dinner" instead of "supper" and don't act like a farm hand! And you be sure that Papa doesn't hear about this! He'll have a conniption fit if he hears how much money we're going to spend filling up our bellies."

The elegant atmosphere in the dining car was a little bit scary. From the waiters in their white coats and black ties to the white linen tablecloths and heavy silver, nothing looked anything like the dining room at the farm nor the restaurants we frequented in Greenville. We were escorted to a table and seated like royalty. Neither of us dared to breathe until the waiter handed us menus and left us to decide on our orders. We looked down the menus and then at each other. We didn't have the wildest notion what most of those things would taste like! Worse than that, as expensive as this meal was going to be, we were certainly going to have to eat it whether we liked it or not.

Finally I ordered the roasted Long Island Duck. Herbert looked at me like I had sprouted a second nose and then ordered exactly the same thing. As soon as the waiter left, I leaned over and said, "Shake hands with a millionaire, little brother!"

We had a big laugh and settled down to enjoy ourselves. The food was delicious and the waiter made us feel like millionaires, sure enough. It was the most expensive meal either of us had ever had, but shucks, Herbert wasn't going off to college every day. I remembered my first meal at Clemson in that little greasy spoon restaurant with those other bald-headed, miserable freshmen. This was definitely a better way to start a college career.

We had a blast being "rich boys" even after we changed trains in Atlanta. It sure felt good to have a brother to share the trip. I was glad that Herbert would never know the agony I had endured those first lonely weeks at Clemson.

It was about eleven o'clock that night before we got to Auburn. We took a taxi to Herbert's rooming house near The Sheppard Chateau. Now we had to settle down to reality. The driver waited while Herbert's landlady showed us to his room. We moved his things in quickly. He looked a lot less like a man of the world as I wished him goodnight than he had looked on the train. My own gut tightened as I remembered my first night at Clemson. Telling him to do what his landlady ordered and assuring him that I would see him the next day, I ran back out to the cab for a quick trip to the Alpha Psi House.

Holy cow! Our new fraternity house was gorgeous. I went right back to feeling like a millionaire. Some of the brothers helped me to get moved in. Old Tom was ahead of me for once in his life. He had already moved in and taken the lower bunk. My fifth year of college and I still had the top bunk! I did a little grousing about it while Tom swore that he was scared of heights and would surely fall out of the top bunk if he had to sleep up there. As always, I ended up sleeping in the stratosphere while Tom enjoyed the lower regions.

Not even the smell of fresh paint could spoil the thrill of living in a beautiful house with plenty of space for the first time in my life. Knowing that I wouldn't have to work for room and board this year made my dreams sweeter.

The dining room at The Alpha Psi House would not begin serving meals until Monday. I ate a quick breakfast at The City Cafe and walked over to Herbert's house. He had just finished serving breakfast. Like me, he was starting out by working for his room and board.

The two of us took a walking tour to acquaint him with his new home. We saw The Sheppard Chateau, Mr. Wright's house, and Vet Hill—the Anatomy Building, the old classroom building, and Cary Hall, the new main building. It was probably a good thing he didn't know how much work and struggle those buildings represented.

I saved the best until last. You should have seen Herbert's face when he saw The Alpha Psi House. That look was worth all the torment of initiation! The boy was impressed. I really had a good time showing him the house and introducing him to my fraternity brothers. By the time we left, he had Alpha Psi fever. He couldn't wait until he could move into the house even though he knew that it would be at least three years down the road. I reminded him to be sure that he played his cards right and got invited to be an Alpha Psi.

The weekend passed in a blur of getting settled, renewing friendships, catching up on the gossip, and honing my bridge skills.

Monday held the usual dull "hurry up and wait" routine of registration. Tuesday morning was the time for surprises.

Juniors and Seniors met in Cary Hall at nine o'clock. Dean Suggs called for attention and then called John Riddle to the podium. John Riddle! Good heavens, he was calling me to come up there with all the professors and the president of the university! I sat there like I had a bale of hay in my lap and straw in my head! When I finally persuaded my reluctant feet to carry me up to the podium, my heart was pounding like John Henry driving spikes in crossties. Dean Suggs recognized me for being the first student ever to take ten courses in one semester and the first to make ten "A's" in one semester. The students gave me a standing ovation. I thanked them and mumbled something about anybody being able to accomplish things if he applied himself. Dean Suggs told how reluctant he had been to approve my schedule and how my sincerity had won him over. He also said that he was especially proud of my success since he never expected to see anybody else do it. Finally he gave me a letter of commendation signed by all of the bigwigs on Vet Hill. I thanked him and fled back to the safety of my seat in the auditorium as applause thundered in my ears.

The next announcement was a blockbuster—the Fourth Service Area Command in Knoxville, Tennessee had decreed that we would have to join the Army if we were going to be allowed to stay in school. We would be fingerprinted and sworn in as soldiers in the Medical Administrative Corps—Reserve. That last word was beautiful! "Reserve" meant that we had not been called to active duty. Our draft cards would be changed from 1A to 1S, we would be classified as students in necessary studies, and we would receive certificates saying that we were second lieutenants in the reserve. At least for the present, we could continue our studies.

I had a good schedule even though we had changed from the semester to the quarter system. The professors were cramming into one quarter what they had been teaching in a semester. We spent mornings in the classrooms and afternoons in the clinics. We would rotate between large animal clinics and small animal clinics every two weeks. Clinics were what I had been waiting for even though juniors did very little other than observe and supply necessary muscle power on demand.

The third week of school was the time chosen for the traditional State Inspection Trip. Every year Dr. Robinson took the members of the Junior Class on a tour of the state to visit facilities which served the public such as the docks, municipal water systems, bakeries, dairies, and prisons. This trip was a high point of the school year. In order to get the proper mix of fun and learning, Dr. Robinson planned the week's activities down to the last detail. We learned a lot because we knew that we would have a major test on the facilities and their activities when we returned to Auburn. We played a lot because we were boys and because we were standing on the brink of military service in a global war. Some of our friends had already been wounded or killed in combat. There was always the specter of the call to active duty hanging over our heads. "Live today—you may be dead tomorrow!" was an ever-present temptation.

There were too many members of our class to fit into a bus and

too few to hire two busses. We solved that by renting eleven cars.
Dr. Robinson chose one student to be in charge of the boys riding
in each of the cars. I couldn't drive so soon after my appendectomy, but that didn't protect me from having responsibility. Dr.
Robinson put me in charge of our car and told me to pick the driver.
I chose Harry Morgan and told him that he could drive and help
me with the discipline. At almost six feet, four inches tall and weighing well over two hundred pounds, Harry was big enough to handle anything. I just prayed he wouldn't get his hands on any more
smoke bombs!

We had a good group and we left Auburn in high spirits. With
troopers in front of us and behind us to keep us together and to
get us through the towns, we felt like big shots. When we passed
through a town, the lead trooper would turn on his siren. Our sense
of importance would inflate as we drove through the cleared streets.

One of our stops was at Kilby Prison near Montgomery. The staff
there entertained us by staging two simulated escapes. As we watched
the bloodhounds track and tree the "escapees," my stomach tightened into an unpleasant knot. Watching men chased like animals
during field trials galled my soul. If "trusties" were treated this
way, how much more degrading was the treatment of the other
prisoners? I was glad to leave the prison.

During dinner the first night, Dr. Robinson gave us our room
assignments and laid out the rules: no drinking, no gambling, and
no staying out past midnight. At least the hotels didn't have bunk
beds—Tom and I would sleep on the same level on the trip! As for
the rules, they were bent a little and occasionally broken because
boys have to carouse a little even on field trips.

Our trip almost got cancelled that first night. Some devilish redneck showed more than a little bad taste when he sent a "woman
of ill-fame" to Dr. Robinson's room about eleven p.m. The good
doctor was neither pleased nor amused. In fact, he went very quickly
from embarrassed to furious. The "lady" retreated and the students assembled for a very thorough tail-chewing. Dr. Robinson
made it quite clear that a repetition of that sort of joke would end
the trip for everybody.

The days were packed to the brim with visits to bakeries, dairies,
food storage facilities, and all sorts of things. If there was anything
edible at the places we visited, you can believe we consumed it in
quantities. The bakeries must have showed a precipitous drop in
profits after our visit.

I was amazed at how complicated life could be when hundreds of people were concentrated into small areas. The municipal water and sewage systems were infinitely more complex than the well and the privies on the Riddle farm. The dairies held no surprises for me although most of the other facilities were much more complex than I had imagined. The food storage facilities at the state docks were particularly awe-inspiring to this country boy.

The last activity of the trip was a day of deep-sea fishing. Dr. Robinson had chartered two boats to take us out into the Gulf. We would rendezvous at ten o'clock, at noon, and at mid-afternoon. Wouldn't you know that Dr. Robinson put me in charge of discipline on one boat and himself in charge of the other? I attracted responsibility and work like a long-haired dog attracts fleas!

Of course, everybody wanted to go with me. Dr. Robinson solved that by calling the roll and assigning every other name to my boat. That would have worked fine except that Tom Talker got assigned to the wrong boat. He and his friends had planned to fish for luck with their cards and Tom was the only one of the gambling group assigned to Dr. Robinson's boat.

In payment for the use of my notes and my tutoring, Tom had paid all my expenses for the trip. With his usual generosity, he had given me some spending money as well. The luck of the draw was going to spoil Tom's trip unless I could get him switched to my boat.

Tom was shaking his head when I winked at him. After a quick conference with Dr. Robinson, Tom was swapped for Gary Lankford. The explanation I gave was that Tom was my roommate and we had planned to share our fishing equipment. That wasn't quite accurate because neither of us had any fishing equipment with us! I felt guilty about concocting such a tale, but I didn't want to spoil Tom's fun and I surely didn't want to be responsible for Gary. That clown would undoubtedly get stinking drunk and he would probably fall overboard before the day ended. When Dr. Robinson announced the swap, Tom was delighted, Gary looked betrayed, and my conscience hurt.

The list of names for each boat was prepared, the rules were read—no drinking, no gambling, no jumping overboard, stay out of the way of the crew, and fish as much as you please—and then we boarded the boats.

As we pulled away from the docks, Tom tapped me on the shoulder to demand an explanation of how I had made the switch so fast. He nearly busted his britches laughing at the tale I had told. He was even more impressed when he heard my reason for getting rid of Gary. "For a little guy, you think pretty big—I'm especially proud of you since you pulled this off before five a.m.!"

Knowing that Tom and his friends were going to gamble as long as they were breathing, I had gotten two rolls of bottle caps from a girl at a dairy during a tour. I brought them out and told the gamblers that they were to use the caps as chips and to keep the money out of sight. I made regular rounds during the trip to check on things. I also "cut the pot" on a regular basis to tip the crew members. The gamblers were kept well supplied with food and beer all day and the crew was tipped generously. That kept everybody happy. The only person who got seasick was a boy from Florida who had grown up on the coast. He recovered pretty quickly although his pride was grievously injured. All of our guys were having fun without creating problems. I knew there was a little booze aboard and that it was futile to try to keep everybody cold sober. As long as things stayed under control, I decided to ignore the drinking and the gambling.

As we approached the rendezvous point, Dr. Robinson yelled, "Have any of you caught anything yet?"

Without thinking, Bill hollered, "Yeah, Tom Talker just caught a straight flush!"

Ooops! Just then good old Gary saved my hide by falling overboard and having to be rescued by the crew. In the uproar, Dr. Robinson forgot about Bill's goof. He was embarrassed and I felt guilty for having pawned Gary off on him. After a little good-natured yelling back and forth, the boats separated again.

At noon we pulled into Pine Point to visit the oyster packing plant. Some of the boys had never eaten a raw oyster. I insisted that everybody try at least one. I can still see Joe with his eyes shut and his mouth open while I dropped an oyster into his mouth and held his chin to keep him from spitting it out. Once he swallowed the first one, he decided they were so good, he ate three dozen!

After touring the plant, we returned to the boats and continued to fish, play cards, or laze on the deck. It was dark when we pulled back into the dock. Tom and his friends hadn't seen the sun nor taken a break from their cards all day except for touring that plant!

Everybody had enjoyed the day and I could report that I had had no problems. I was careful not to state that there had been no drinking nor gambling—I just said that nothing had gotten out of hand. Dr. Robinson was satisfied with that. He had also had a pleasant day after they had gotten Gary back on board and bedded down to sleep off his booze. To work off my guilt, I helped to collect the money to buy a gift for Dr. Robinson. All of us chipped in to show him our appreciation for taking us on the trip.

By the time we got back to the hotel, we were too tired to do anything but fall into our beds. After a quiet night, we headed back to Auburn.

One of the traditional joys of being a junior was not having any more classes nor labs under Dr. Mudhenck. We did not share that joy. So much of the staff was being called to active military duty that he had been assigned to teach us embryology. Life can be rough and it can be awful—this was awful! Time hadn't improved him a bit. He was still as obnoxious as ever and still clearing his throat as regularly as a metronome.

The textbook he required us to buy, Embryology of the Swine Species, served no useful purpose. As far as we could tell, there was no relationship whatever between his lectures and the textbook. Taking his lectures down in shorthand was my salvation. I was one of the six in the class who were passing. The rest of the class were not doing very well and their averages were mostly in the range between forty and sixty. There was a lot of griping about the lectures not matching the book. The failures and the griping affected Dr. Mudhenck about as much as a lecture on morality would affect a bootlegger.

Lady Luck must have been guiding me the day I picked up a human embryology book in the Veterinary Library. That was where the old buzzard was getting his lectures! I went down to the bookstore, bought a copy of the book, and then passed the word around. Some of the other students bought it, too. Even after my discovery, there were still a lot of folks in deep trouble in that class.

There was so much going on at school, the days seemed to run together. Suddenly it was Thanksgiving. I had too much work and too little money to go home. Most of the Alpha Psi brothers were also spending the holidays at school. We decided to keep the house open.

I knew Herbert was homesick, but I managed to persuade him to hang on until the Christmas holidays. Being away from home on Thanksgiving was really hard on him. He was glad to get the extra money he made working at his boarding house even if it was a poor substitute for being with the family. I made sure that we spent a lot of time together. Herbert especially enjoyed the hours he spent at the Alpha Psi House. He was becoming a bridge nut, too.

Dr. Mudhenck must have been frustrated that he couldn't keep us overtime like he had in anatomy. We had a bacteriology class right after embryology and he had to dismiss us promptly. There was no accurate way to determine why he did anything. For whatever reason, he was flunking a whole bunch of people and there was an air of desperation in the class.

The days passed quickly and the desperation grew as the end of the quarter approached. One day the roughest, toughest boy in the class, Jack Landers, asked if he could speak on behalf of the class. When Dr. Mudhenck finished clearing his throat for the fifth time, he granted his permission. Jack asked what kind of exam we could expect. Specifically, he wanted to know whether the questions would be discussion, multiple choice, or true or false.

After some more throat-clearing and some more discussion, Jack pointed out that only six people were passing. On behalf of the class, he requested that Dr. Mudhenck either grade on the curve or give us a true or false exam. The class chanted, "True or false!"

Dr. Mudhenck agreed to give a true or false exam if every student in the class would prepare one hundred true or false questions and hand them to him within a week. The exam would be taken from those questions. We applauded and cheered. To be certain we didn't get too happy, he kept us until the last possible second. We had to run to bacteriology class.

Our professor was late, so Jack took the opportunity to explain that we could all pass Dr. Mudhenck's exam if we cooperated. He suggested that we start all the true questions with "a," "and," or "the," and start the false questions with anything other than an article. We all agreed to use Jack's system. Then Jack cemented the agreement by stating that if anyone did not follow the system or told about the agreement, he, Jack, would find him and beat the *%#! out of him. Not being sure that the bookworm of the class was entirely trustworthy, Jack walked over to him, shook his finger under his nose, and snarled, "This includes you, too!" The poor boy turned as white as a lab coat and nodded affirmatively.

Everybody devised questions according to Jack's system and submitted them. Dr. Mudhenck honored our agreement and used our questions for the exam. We all finished in record time which aroused his suspicions. He nearly had fits when he graded the papers. After seeing that the first dozen papers all had perfect scores, he called his assistant, Dr. Pritcherd, over to his desk and told him that there was something fishy going on. The two of them finished grading the papers and found that there were sixty-six papers and sixty-six perfect scores. One jump from apoplexy, Dr. Mudhenck stormed that he was going to see the dean and stalked out carrying all of our papers.

At the next class meeting, Dr. Mudhenck announced that there would be a delay in giving us our grades. Dean Suggs called a faculty meeting to discuss the problem. Not one soul could break the code. Dean Suggs ordered Dr. Mudhenck to pass the whole class with a "C" unless he knew that the student should have a higher grade. I got one of the two "A's." Dr. Mudhenck probably got ulcers!

The quarter ended with me still in first place academically and Herbert doing well in his classes.

CHAPTER 32

Second quarter began quietly. Its first major event was the "accidental" destruction of Dr. Mudhenck's car. He parked his old Essex near the top of the "down" side of Vet Hill. About half of our physiology class was standing outside the old Vet Building waiting for our professor to arrive. Dr. Mudhenck stalked past us without smiling or speaking to a soul. His coldness and his arrogance plus two years of bitter memories of his classes and labs were too much for Jack Landers. As soon as Dr. Mudhenck's coattail disappeared into the building, Jack walked over to the car, knocked it out of gear, and released the parking brake.

He stepped back with a satisfied smile as the car started its long roll down the hill. By the time that old Essex jumped the curb, it must have been doing close to forty miles per hour. The noise was impressive when the car centered the huge oak tree in front of the fieldhouse. "Sturdy as an oak" took on new meaning for us as the car flew apart like a fragmentation grenade.

It was hard for us not to cheer. None of us were really mean and nobody actually planned to harm Dr. Mudhenck. When the collision occurred, it affected us like an emotional catharsis, releasing more than two years of pent-up rage. Dr. Mudhenck had often made us wonder if he had any human emotions. He showed no more feeling in dealing with students than he showed the animal corpses in his labs. Harshness, sarcasm, and icy indifference were his trademarks. Warmth, kindness, consideration, or caring of any kind simply were not permitted in his teaching. Perhaps his terrible experiences in Nazi Germany had warped him. In any case, he aroused hatred in his students even though he was a brilliant teacher. He taught us material that was vital to our success as veterinarians and brutalized us emotionally in the process. Perhaps his emotional brutality boomeranged to destroy his car and our innocence,

Somebody went into the building and told him that his car had rolled down the hill. Redfaced, shaken, and angry, he assumed that he had forgotten to set the parking brake. Nobody disagreed. Several of us expressed at least perfunctory sympathy and a few of us walked down the hill with him to survey the wreckage. As the model plane builders say, he had "re-kitted" his car. No two pieces were still attached to each other.

Dr. Mudhenck resigned at the end of the school year and left Auburn. There were a number of stories that circulated: somebody in our class had threatened him....he was afraid of our class....Jack Landers finally told him about the exam code and what the students really thought about him. I don't know Dr. Mudhenck's story and I can't understand how such a brilliant man could be so harsh and cold. Maybe the horrors of his past had replaced his emotions like formaldehyde replaced the body fluids in the animals in anatomy lab leaving only a dead shell rather than a living thing.

Another big event for me occurred in the small animal clinic. I was sitting in the balcony with the other juniors watching Dr. Masters and a surgical team perform a Caesarian-section on a Boston Bulldog. The dog had more puppies in her womb than she could carry. During the surgery, the puppies shifted and put pressure on the diaphragm. The dog was near death when Dr. Masters ordered the seniors to inject a respiratory stimulant. He had made his incision and had both his hands full. All six of the seniors tried unsuccessfully to hit a vein. Dr. Masters got frustrated and furious as the dog's condition deteriorated. Looking up into the balcony, he bellowed, "Can any of you juniors hit a vein before we lose this dog?"

Several people answered, "Johnny Riddle can do it!"

Now what was I supposed to do? Not wanting to be a show-off, I sat still, kept quiet, and hoped he hadn't heard them. About that time, Dr. Masters looked me squarely in the eye and said, "Riddle, get your*$#! down here and show this bunch of seniors what they ought to have done!"

Even though the dog was near death, I knew the seniors were not going to appreciate my help. One of them made a snide remark as he handed me the syringe. The remark reinforced my resolve to save the dog. My mind spun with the realization that there was no way I could hit the veins in the dog's legs; the seniors had already stuck them too many times. Seeing the dog's tongue hanging out reminded me of an emergency I had watched Don Grear handle. Getting a firm grip on the syringe, I ordered the senior out of my way, stepped forward, grabbed that tongue, and hit the vein on the first stick. When I asked what to do next, Dr. Masters snapped, "Push that *** plunger!"

"All the way?"

"All the way and hurry!"

The injection made the dog start breathing again. Unfortunately, she kept getting faster and went into convulsions. Between the dog's tongue and my friends' tongues, I had really fixed my grade and my reputation! Dr. Masters told us not to get excited, the reaction was expected, and the convulsions would stop momentarily. He sent me back to my seat after telling me to hand the syringe back to that *# senior.

The balcony exploded in cheers and applause. Still under pressure to get all those puppies out, Dr. Masters snapped, "Shut your %$#! mouths!"

The rest of the procedure was routine. When the surgery was finished, he left the seniors to clean up the dog and to put her in intensive care. As the observers filed out of the balcony, Dr. Masters met me at the door and said, "Riddle, I want to see you in my office in thirty minutes!"

He must be mad at me—but why? For showing up the seniors? For using an unusual procedure?

When I knocked on his door, the tone of his voice warned me that he was fuming. There sat the six seniors who had helped him during the afternoon clinic. He had already made mincemeat of their egos. Now he wanted them to hear what he had to say to me.

The next few minutes were surprising. First he complimented me on my procedure. Then he asked how I knew about it since he had never heard of it. I told him a little about working with Dr. Grear and having watched him use it. After praising me for saving the dog's life, Dr. Masters chewed the seniors for not using their heads, and dismissed us all.

I felt good about saving the dog and bad about making the seniors look boneheaded. If only he had praised me privately instead of rubbing the noses of the seniors in their mess, things would be less awkward. As we walked out of the building, the seniors assured me that they held no animosity toward me. They understood that I had done what had to be done. That was a relief.

About the middle of December, we got another nasty surprise. The President of the United State ordered all of the veterinary students in the reserves to begin a physical fitness program under the supervision of the army. We would be organized into military units in January.

You never heard such fussing and moaning. Most of the students were soft city boys and they knew that hurting times were coming. I wasn't worried. I ran and did so many calisthenics, my fraternity brothers teased me about still having Clemson blood in my veins. I was as hard as I had been when I left Clemson. Bring on the army, I can handle it!

Finally the Christmas holidays arrived. Herbert was happier than a dog with a steak. Not even the prospect of a seven hour bus trip dampened his enthusiasm. Watching him reminded me how happy I had been to go home that first Christmas at Clemson. I slept most of the way home. Herbert was too excited to care what anybody did as long as the bus kept rolling.

We had two weeks of vacation and we made the minutes count. I worked with Dr. Grear and took just one morning off. That was the day I went into Greenville and bought Carolyn a diamond solitaire with the money from my summer bonus. I hadn't gotten around to asking her to marry me, but I figured that the diamond would persuade her to say, "Yes!"

When I got home that evening, Mama was flouring chicken for supper. She looked startled when I asked her if I could see her in her room for a minute. Quickly dusting the flour from her hands, she straightened her apron, washed and dried her hands, and followed me into her bedroom. You could have cut the tension with a knife, but Mama didn't ask questions. Her apron was straight and her hands were clean; Mama was ready for whatever came.

This surprise was for Mama only—the rest of my rowdy tribe could find out about it tomorrow. I closed the door and showed her the ring. Her eyes glowed with happiness and a few tears as she hugged me. She laughed when her inquiries revealed that Carolyn was not expecting the ring and that I had learned the correct size when Carolyn got her Furman ring. With her highest accolade, "John, you always seem to do things just right," Mama agreed to keep my secret.

It took all my self control to hide my secret when I got to Carr's Creek. My little school marm looked like a Christmas doll with shining eyes, curly hair, and dimples. As soon as we were alone in the living room, I slipped the diamond on her finger. It worked! Miss Carolyn Carr was the most surprised young lady you ever saw. While she was recovering her speech, I asked her if she would marry me. Her somewhat unromantic response was, "What do you think I have been waiting for all these lonely nights? You bet I will!"

Okay, it wasn't exactly like the movie scripts. Who cared? We decided to get married on December 20 of the next year. It was her parents' anniversary and it just seemed to be the right time.

With that settled, Carolyn ran out of the room. What was the matter now? I had given her a ring, we had set a wedding date, and instead of falling into my arms passionately, that silly girl had run away! Before I could figure it out, Mr. Paul and Miss Jennie came in to congratulate us and to wish us joy and happiness and all that stuff.

Aside from some hassling from my brothers about being hooked, the rest of the holidays passed in a happy blur. Carolyn was ecstatic, Don was sober, the family was well, and I was getting close to my goals. 1942 was getting off to a good start.

Then I was kissing everybody goodbye again because Herbert and I were on the way back to school. The two weeks had passed in what seemed like the blink of an eye.

CHAPTER 33

One of the first things I did after getting back to Auburn was to visit Dean Suggs. We started to discuss the American military situation and he handed me a letter to read. Oh, no! Dean Suggs would be Colonel Suggs as of March 15. Before I had absorbed that fact, he told me that Dr. Masters had also been called to active duty. As of January 28, Capt. Masters would be leaving the campus. I hadn't even been aware that these men were in the reserve. If they were calling up professors and deans, the situation was really getting bad.

Still reeling from these two revelations, I gaped as Dean Suggs told me the new regulations concerning the student reserves. Under the new military system being instituted on campus, we would be required to drill, to attain military level physical fitness, and to participate in other military training programs so that we could move into an active duty situation on very short notice. We would take our physical examinations prior to January 15 and report to the drill field at two o'clock on the afternoon of January 16 to begin our training. Furthermore, we would attend school all summer with only one week of vacation between quarters.

Wham! There went my plans along with those of hundreds of other young men. At least we hadn't been called up yet. I thought I had left military training when I left Clemson. Now the devilish stuff had followed me to Auburn! I had enjoyed two and a half years without a drill. If I had handled it before, I could handle it again.

I was relieved that Herbert was not affected by the regulations. He was too young for the draft and he hadn't gotten into graduate school. My head was whirling as I left the dean's office. Surely I wasn't going to get this close to my DVM and then be thwarted by the army!

The whole campus was in an uproar and rumors were rampant as to what was going to happen. What happened to me was no rumor. I joined the milling, mumbling mob on the drill field on January 16. An hour later I was Acting Major John T. Riddle, commanding the whole *** battalion. Major Smith had come down to the drill field, asked for a show of hands of those who had had previous military training, asked a few questions of those people, narrowed the questioning to me and before I realized what was coming down, he had given me the rank of acting major, pushed me into the driver's seat, and put the reins in my hands. When he asked if I had a preference as to who my assistant would be, I chose Tom Rodgers. Tom was a transfer from Virginia Military Institute and I felt that he would do a good job as my adjutant. Tom was given the rank of Acting Captain.

Before the dust cleared, we were organizing the four hundred veterinary students into a working battalion complete with companies, platoons, and squads. Those who had had previous military training were asked to stay and the others were dismissed until two p.m. the next day. Those who stayed became the company officers and sergeants. By four p.m. all the slots on the organization charts had names in them and we were ready to roll.

During a break the next morning, Tom Rodgers and I went down to look at the obstacle course. That *%# thing was a replica of the one at Clemson. Tom gawked at the hazards—V.M.I. did not have an obstacle course. If we were going to lead the battalion, we were going to have to get them through the obstacle course. I dared Tom to run it with me. He accepted the challenge without much enthusiasm and we started out.

The first hazard was that miserable wall. I showed him how to go over the wall even though I thought for a minute that I was going to bust my gizzard doing it. I aggravated Tom a little by telling him that with his long legs he ought to be able to fly over the wall. He ran at the wall, made a flying leap, and missed the rope. On his second try he caught the rope, but he couldn't pull himself up.

Provoked, he turned to me to ask what he had done wrong. I told him that he had to run up the wall rather than just pulling up with his arms. At my suggestion, he stood off to the side and watched while I did it again. On the next try, he made it over. He spooked when I landed right beside him. Laughing, he said, "I've got to try it one more time to be sure I've got it down pat."

He sailed over the wall on his first try and he was ready to take on the rest of the course. With nobody watching and only each other for competition, we went through all of the hazards like boys playing follow the leader. When we finished, I dared him to run the two miles back to the drill field. We made it back with very little trouble except for being hot and winded. Tom thanked me for teaching him how to get over the wall and suggested that we not mention that we had run the course. I agreed to keep quiet about it.

The next day at drill, we finished the organization process and Major Smith explained the rudiments of drill, military courtesy, and battalion structure. Then he ordered me to call the battalion to attention and to receive the reports. As we went through all that rigmarole of orders, salutes, roll calls, etc. I felt like a cross between an idiot and a kid playing soldier.

Then the major created chaos. He decided that we should begin drilling. These guys didn't know the difference between "Right face!" and "Left face!" and we were going to drill them all at the same time! Praying that not too many got stomped to death, I assigned the companies to the far corners of the field, cautioned them not to march into nor over each other, and ordered them to their respective areas.

Tom, Major Smith, and I watched them march/straggle to the corners of the field. Seeing the situation deteriorate from a semblance of order to ill-tempered confusion reminded me of freshman drills at Clemson. I requested and received the major's permission for Tom and me to go down to the field and to assist the floundering lieutenants. As we went across the field, I told Tom that we could probably save some lives if we did a quick exhibition and explanation of the basic commands. Tom could give the orders and I would demonstrate them. Remembering the success of the Riddle Method at Clemson, I insisted that we give everybody the idea that we were there to help rather than to hassle since they were all obviously miserable anyway. Tom agreed that it might work.

We went from platoon to platoon putting on our little show and pointing out to the lieutenants such things as when and how to give a command. Like a miracle, order followed in our tracks. When we had finished with the last company, Tom and I rejoined Major Smith on the reviewing stand. Absolutely amazed at the progress the battalion was making, he asked why we hadn't chosen military careers. I told him that I could do more good for my country and the world as a veterinarian than I could do as a soldier. Tom expressed similar sentiments. Shaking his head, Major Smith ordered me to return the battalion to the area in front of the reviewing stand.

I blew my whistle, yelled a command, and watched with satisfaction as my troops marched toward me with minimal mishaps. This was working better than I had dared to hope. Major Smith congratulated them on their progress and announced that he would step out of the picture as soon as we mastered the drill procedures. Just before he ordered me to dismiss them, he announced that I would have a surprise for them the next week.

After dismissal, Major Smith gave me my orders for the rest of the week and told me that we would start running the obstacle course the next Monday. Tom and I just smiled as he explained the purpose of the course and how we would get the battalion through it. Surprise was written all over the major's face when I told him that Tom and I had already run the course and that we anticipated no problems.

The rest of the week went smoothly and our civilian mob began to look like soldiers. Tom and I ran the course together on Saturday and Sunday to be sure that we had every detail down pat for Monday.

When I called the battalion to order on Monday, I told them that we had figured out a way to short-cut the drilling and playing soldier if all of them co-operated. They cheered enthusiastically. You can be sure that Major Smith was not within earshot at the time!

When roll call and reports were finished, I told them that we would run the obstacle course and then run the two miles back to the drill field. Ouch! The cussing, griping, and complaining were awesome.

Calling them back to attention, I made it clear that my short-cuts would work only if they quit bitching and gave me their full cooperation. Once the army regulars were satisfied with our progress, they would leave and then we could implement our short-cuts. In the meantime, I would not order them to do anything that Capt. Rodgers and I had not done three times in succession. That stunned them into silence.

After explaining that we would march in double file using the route step, I ordered them to fall in and march to the wall.

Their reaction to the wall was quite similar to mine at Clemson. Their faces and eyes showed their doubts and fears. The army first sergeant concealed behind the wall stared in disbelief while I explained how to go over the wall and then demonstrated the process with Tom. The two of us ran forward, grabbed the ropes, and went over at the same time.

After a brief discussion with the sergeant, Tom and I walked back around the wall. I explained that the men would come forward by twos and that each man would have two tries to get over the wall. Those who failed would have to keep coming back every day until they had mastered it. I would demonstrate how to scale the wall once more, then I would run the rest of the course ahead of them. With a reminder that we had to be back at the drill field by six o'clock, I encouraged them to do their best, and scaled the wall again.

I ran the whole course, had a brief visit with the regular army man at each hazard, and was waiting when the battalion began straggling across the finish line. They really bitched and moaned when I ordered them to march at double-time back to the field. The sergeant from the wall and I started out at the head of the column. After half a mile, the griping from the ranks was getting very loud and the pace was slowing down. I told the sergeant that I would drop back and check on each platoon and then catch up with him again. In typical army fashion, he snapped, "Like *! you will!"

I did drop back, yelled encouragement and a threat or two at the troops as each platoon passed, and then I yelled that I had to catch that fat sergeant. The man was stunned when I pretended not to see him and passed him with a burst of speed. When he hollered at me, I slowed down to double-time. He huffed and puffed as he quizzed me about my stamina and admitted that he had been sitting around, drinking beer, and getting fatter than his grandpa's hog.

Most of the battalion made it back to the drill field in pretty good shape. I pulled out four men who were clearly unable to make it. Two were grossly over-weight and the others were asthmatic. I gave them permission to rest as much as necessary and to set their own pace. The next day I arranged for them to get disability certificates from the doctor.

In choosing my officers, I had made a real effort to create a balance between Alpha Psis, Omega Tau Sigmas, and independents. It worked out very well in building a sense of loyalty to the battalion and in avoiding internal rivalry. I ordered them to use the Riddle method of training their men and to avoid the usual military harassment. Our military training advanced at a brisk pace.

It wasn't long before we were mastering the obstacle course and drilling impressively. As promised, the regular army men left the campus. Now I could institute my short-cuts. On a rotating basis, each officer and each platoon was excused from drill one day per week. This was handled on a verbal basis. Nothing was ever written down about it and the army never caught on to what we were doing. If they had, we would have caught all kinds of flak for being A.W.O.L. (absent without leave.) Another short-cut was to walk back from the obstacle course until we got within a quarter mile of the drill field. At that point, we would all start running and yelling and charge unto the field as though we were attacking an enemy position. The short-cuts were marvelous morale builders. We all had a sense of being in this thing together and putting one over on the army.

In a stirring ceremony on the drill field, we bade farewell to Dean Suggs. All of the members of the veterinary school student body were there wearing white smocks and white pants. I made sure that the detail which presented his going-away present included one Alpha Psi, one O.T.S. and one independent. We had a little problem when Dean Suggs stood right in front of the place where I had hidden his gift under the bleachers. We had bought him a large leather clothes bag which was awkward to maneuver under the bleachers. I finally managed to drag it out without hitting him while my fellow students struggled to keep from laughing. After the usual round of speeches and handshakes and a rousing cheer of good wishes, the ceremony ended.

As we marched across the field with the sun sparkling on the dew, I thanked God that I was still in school and prayed for the safety of this man who had meant so much to all of us. (That was the last time I saw Col. Suggs. Years later I heard that he and Capt. Masters both came through their military duty unscathed.)

The new dean was a Clemson graduate. He and I became good friends and shared many a laugh about the scrapes we had gotten into at Clemson. He taught one of my classes and provoked a lot of snickers with his habit of keeping one hand in his pocket, apparently holding on to a very private portion of his anatomy. All of us were convinced that if you took his pipe out of his mouth and his hand out of his pocket, he would not be able to lecture!

All of us had written letters home explaining that we had been ordered to attend classes during the summer. In April Carolyn's loneliness got to be too much to bear. I received a letter stating that she was arriving on Friday afternoon to spend the weekend at Auburn. Whoa! Fraternity, military, and scholastic duties were moved to the back burner as I made the necessary arrangements to entertain my bride-to-be.

My fraternity brothers got the word that they would be perfect gentlemen or they would drill until they dropped seven days a week. After some scurrying around, I got everything lined up from a borrowed car to a room at the Old Pitts Hotel. My fraternity brothers and my friends were incredibly generous in helping me to get ready.

When Carolyn stepped off that train, I thought my heart would explode with happiness. We had been separated for three and a half months: it had felt like three years! After a quick trip to the hotel to freshen up, we toured Auburn. From The Sheppard Chateau to Vet Hill, she could see the places she had heard about for so long. It was probably a blessing that the anatomy lab was locked. Even peeking through the window, the sights and smells were too much for Carolyn. We enjoyed touring the other parts of the campus before dinner.

Carolyn was to be a dinner guest at The Alpha Psi House. Even after all my threats, I was a little concerned that mischief would motivate some of my brothers to play tricks. Carolyn was absolutely awed by the house, the grounds, and the brothers. The house was gorgeous and the Alpha Psis could not have been more charming. Mrs. Stover, our housemother, really turned on the Southern hospitality. If Carolyn had been royalty, nobody could have been nicer to her. She freshened up in Mrs. Stover's room and peeked up the stairs at my room. It would have created instant scandal if we had even considered having her go up to my room.

The hours passed in a happy blur as we discussed the changes in my life from the farm to Clemson to The Sheppard Chateau to Mr. Wright's house to the Alpha Psi House. Neither of us was happy about my having to attend school during the summer. We consoled ourselves by dreaming about the future when we would be married and by reminding ourselves that we were blessed that I had not been drafted and shipped overseas. It seemed that almost before I hugged her hello, I was kissing her goodbye.

From Carolyn's visit to the end of the quarter was just more of the same old grind. I began to feel that I had been in school forever and that I wasn't ever going to get through. The added burdens of the military program and my extra-curricular activities meant that I never got quite enough rest and I was always on the go. Nonetheless, I finished the quarter still in first place academically. By the time Herbert and I got on the bus to go to Greenville, I was ready to sleep the whole way.

CHAPTER 34

Our brief visit at home seemed to run on a fast merry-go-round. My older brothers teased me about not ever finishing school. They thought I must really be having a high old time to stay in school seventeen years. Lord, if they only knew!

Laughing, I asked if I could please have their permission to go to school for just nine more months. By then, I would have my doctorate in veterinary medicine and a wife. That last word really turned on the ribbing.

Herbert knew that none of them had any idea how hard my life had been. After reminding them how far I had come since Papa and Bly had taken me to Clemson that first time, he suggested that they should walk a mile in a man's shoes before they judged him. At last the hassle subsided.

Carolyn and I spent every possible minute together. She and I swapped "war stories" about her teaching children the joys of learning and my teaching veterinary students to play army. Carolyn made it quite clear that she had no desire to pursue a long-term teaching career. I understood because I was more than ready to quit playing Maj. Riddle.

Since I would have just one week off at the end of the summer and then not get home again until Christmas vacation, we had to start planning our wedding. After a very brief discussion, I decided the wisest thing for me to do was to go along with whatever Carolyn and Miss Jennie planned. What did I know about a church wedding? My brothers had all just gone to the preacher's house to get married. Our church was one hundred years old and we would be the first couple to be married in it. Nope, I didn't know any more about weddings than I had known about college.

The next order of business was to visit the clinic and explain to Don, Jackie, and Charlie that our summer plans had been scrapped. Instead of working with them, I would be attending school in order to retain my reserve status. They were all disappointed. Don and Jackie had planned two vacation trips. Jackie was afraid he wouldn't go anywhere if I weren't there to handle the practice. With all my heart I hoped that he would not return to taking his vacations in a bottle.

Jackie and I had developed a very close relationship during the previous two years. She was probably going to miss her assistant more than Don was going to miss his assistant vet. We had a long talk while I encouraged her to insist that Don take their planned trips. Charlie could handle routine things and he could call on a neighboring vet in emergencies.

Don was too busy to talk very much. There was an uncomfortable tension between us. Perhaps each of us felt that he had both used and been used by the other. In any case, our days of practicing together were over. We would remain friends, but we would no longer be members of the same team.

Almost before we realized we were at home, Herbert and I were back on the train, rolling toward Auburn. Herbert was quiet—so quiet I knew something was bothering him. He was worried about a lot of things—his future, my future, my marriage, being at Auburn after I left.

We discussed all of his worries in detail. He would work toward his DVM and ignore the war unless he were called to active duty. Carolyn and I would get married at Christmas. When the Christmas holidays ended, she would return to her parents' home and her teaching; I would return to Auburn and my studies. After my graduation in March, I would get a job. By the time her teaching job ended in June, I would be able to provide a home for her. There was just no practical way to have Carolyn at Auburn—we had agreed to accept that fact. As for Herbert, he had followed my path through Simpsonville High School, including being president of the student body. He could do the same thing at Auburn.

Herbert protested that I had set too fast a pace at Auburn. We chewed on that until he convinced himself he could handle Auburn, too.

This time he bought our dinner in the dining car. I teased him royally about passing me on the way to dinner. Little brother was growing up.

It was almost eleven o'clock by the time the cab dropped Herbert off at his house and me off at the Alpha Psi House. Tom was already there. It didn't take long for us to decide to keep our room at the top of the stairs rather than exercise the senior privilege of moving downstairs.

We had to settle into our routines in a hurry. The urgency of the war effort touched everything.

When fraternity elections came along, I requested not to be elected to any office. Whistling into the wind would have been just as effective. When the secretary was elected,—or railroaded,—I was stuck again.

When the Junior Chapter of the A.V.M.A. held its elections, Tom nominated me for president. This time, there wasn't even a second nomination. The president was elected by acclamation.

Well, I could still hope they would replace me as cadet commander. With our hurried up schedule, I was already carrying a heavy load. Before the meeting ended, Dean Winters announced that I had requested a vote on the officers of our reserve unit. Another dream went down as the same officers were re-elected. How was I going to get everything done?

Drilling and developing physical fitness in the fall, winter, and spring were tough enough; in the summer heat, they were killers. As we organized the freshmen into platoons, and re-organized the other platoons, I overheard some comments about myself. "He's tough, but he's fair." "He won't tolerate goofing off or smarting off, but he won't ask you to do anything that he can't do twice." "Just do what he says, and you'll be all right." If I could live up to those comments, I would do very well.

During our first drills, I watched carefully to see who was having problems. Two freshmen were clearly physically unable to make it. I pulled them from the ranks and sent them to the infirmary to get medical disability deferments. The other cadets fussed and groaned, but they could handle it. As the heat got worse, I realized that mid-afternoon drills and running the obstacle course were just asking for trouble. I got the dean's approval to shorten or to cancel training sessions when the temperature soared. You never saw nor heard such jubilation as we had on the days we didn't have to drill nor run the obstacle course. I got our unit into shape and kept them in shape, but I surely didn't want to kill anybody with heat prostration. As long as we achieved what the army required, nobody checked on how we did it. We managed to keep our rotating days off system, too.

Our senior year was under way with a new acting dean and a new pathology professor. Dean Winter and I had already gotten off to a good start. Dr. Conklin had just graduated from Michigan State

University. He was an excellent teacher who made it clear that he would not drop any bombs on us as long as we didn't pull any stunts on him. We missed our professors who had gone to war and we rejoiced that Dr. Mudhenck had left for heaven knows where.

As seniors, we had a very active role in clinics. Dr. Wolfe conducted the large animal clinics. Dr. Cane conducted the small animal clinics. Juniors and seniors rotated biweekly between the two. ·

Dr. T. P. Wolfe, the large animal surgeon and clinician, had a well-deserved reputation as a character. Short, stocky, bald-headed, and as set in his ways as any old maid, he ruled his territory by the Wolfe Code. No one wore any jewelry to his clinics, goofed off in his presence, presented a target for his barbed wit without drawing fire, or laughed when he displayed his displeasure by shaking his shoulders as though he were trying to dislodge his head. (There may have been an occasional surreptitious prayer that he would dislodge his head!) He called his students by their last names and expected immediate and unquestioning responses to his commands. For some reason unknown to us, he seemed to feel some animosity toward the Jewish boys in our class—they were frequent targets of his wit and his ire.

Right after demonstrating the proper use of the balling gun (a hollow tube and cup device used to administer capsules to large animals), Dr. Wolfe handed a capsule to Ira Steinberg and told him to give it to the horse in stall number four. It appeared obvious that he wanted to see if we understood how to use the balling gun. Poor Ira hesitated and then asked how he should administer the capsule. Typically Dr. Wolfe snapped, "I don't give a *how you do it! You can give it to him by mouth, stick it up his other end, or mail it to him! Just be *sure he gets it!"

Being able to anticipate what he wanted was very important in getting along with Dr. Wolfe. He would pour one ounce (the standard dosage) of medicinal crystals into his hand and ask a student how much he had. The proper response was "A dose." Heaven help the student who responded, "An ounce." Because Papa and my older brothers had taught me the value of anticipating, Dr. Wolfe and I got along very well. He included me in his clinical demonstrations much more frequently than anyone else.

One afternoon when I was helping Dr. Wolfe perform a C-section on a small sow, I had a real challenge. Dr. Wolfe had made his incision in the base of the U-shaped uterus. I moved the pigs down the uterus while he removed them and handed them to the drying gang. We emptied one horn of the uterus and then the other, counting the pigs as we delivered them. When the count reached fourteen, Dr. Wolfe straightened up and said, "Well, that's all."

I had felt one more pig so I said, "No, sir, I don't think so."

The silence was electric as Dr. Wolfe turned beet red, shook his shoulders violently, and snapped, "Well, you check her again, and you had better find or manufacture another pig!"

I didn't want to make him look bad, but I knew there was something else in that uterus. Lord, I hoped it was a pig! As I located the pig and moved it down toward the incision, Dr. Wolfe asked, "Well, Riddle, what have you got?"

When I said, "A pig, sir!" he snapped, "Well, bring it on out before it gets grown!"

When that little pig popped through the incision, he was the prettiest pig I'll ever see and the most surprising one Dr. Wolfe had seen. Dr. Wolfe straightened up and said sternly, "Anyone can make a mistake. If you people don't learn anything else today, remember this!"

While Dr. Wolfe stripped off his gloves and headed for his office, I started suturing the sow. The other assistants and observers started buzzing as soon as he got out of earshot. "Weren't you afraid to correct Dr. Wolfe?" "What if you had been wrong?" "Why didn't you just keep quiet and let him find it in autopsy?" "You're gonna catch it now for showing him up!"

Still suturing, I explained that having done what I thought was right, there was no use worrying about the consequences. The suturing took almost an hour. When the clean-up crew took over, I went to the prep room to clean myself up. I met Dr. Wolfe coming out of his office. We discussed the procedure and I assured him that I had not intended to show him up. He was adamant in his insistence that I had not shown him up and that he would have given me a zero if I had missed the fifteenth pig. He went on to predict that I would become a great clinician.

Much of the dinner table conversation at the Alpha Psi House that night concerned the ramifications of my disputing Dr. Wolfe. Predictions ran from my impending take-over of the clinic to other less desirable fates. When the teasing grew wearisome, I turned the discussion to the reasons we were studying veterinary medicine.

After supper I went up to our room to type my notes while Tom went over to the O. T. S. House to play poker. About 9:45, I finished typing and began to wonder whether I should join Tom. Just then somebody called me to the phone. By the time I got downstairs, the whole house was in an uproar—the caller was Dr. Wolfe! It was a relief to hear him ask if I would help him with a cow's calving problem at a nearby dairy. I agreed to go with him and decided to trick my curious fraternity brothers. When somebody asked if Dr. Wolfe had kicked me out of school, I said, "Yeah, y'all just come on up and watch me pack."

Several boys followed me up to my room and stared incredulously as I put on a fresh pair of lab coveralls "so that I could leave in appropriate clothing." They followed me out to the front lawn where I "waited for a taxi."

They nearly fainted when Dr. Wolfe drove up. With a "Goodnight, suckers!" and a big smile, I got into Dr. Wolfe's car. As we drove the eight miles to the dairy, I noticed that he was wearing a suit. He introduced me to the farmer and gave no indication of changing his clothes. I asked if he wanted me to make the examination. He did. I asked the farmer to bring me a bucket of very warm water while I got the obstetrical roll from the car. After washing the cow's genitalia, I soaped my arm to the shoulder for lubrication, and inserted it into the birth canal. The calf had its head and one forefoot in the birth canal and the other forefoot folded back along its chest. No matter how hard the cow strained, she wasn't going to be able to deliver that calf without help.

I got Dr. Wolfe's bag from the car and asked him to get a 1½ inch 20 gauge needle and a 5 c.c. syringe while I got the bottle of novocain. After applying alcohol and iodine, I injected the novocain into the epidural space. I cleaned and repacked the syringe and needle while Dr. Wolfe explained the procedure to the dairyman. The cow relaxed, I resoaped my arm, re-entered the birth canal, and looped a 30 inch obstetrical chain around the retained foot. After having the dairyman get a handle so that he could pull the chain, I handed him the chain. He pulled while I guided the foot into the canal. When the two feet were parallel, I hooked the other end of the chain around the second foot. Then the dairyman inserted the handle in the middle of the chain and continued pulling. Soon we had a fine, healthy calf and a recovering cow. Within forty-five minutes we were on our way back to Auburn. The very relieved dairyman was delighted at not losing either the cow or the calf. He had been afraid of losing both of them.

As he drove, Dr. Wolfe quizzed me about where I had learned to use an epidural anesthetic and the obstetrical chain. He had not taught us to use either. I told him about growing up on a dairy farm and about working with Don Grear. We talked for half an hour after we got back to the house. Dr. Wolfe wanted me to accompany him on all of his ambulatory calls. Realizing that this was both a compliment and an invitation to accusations of favoritism, I suggested that we take another senior with us each time. That was fine with him... if I would choose the senior each time!

Good grief! More responsibility for me. He averaged calling me five times per week. Each time, I pretended that he had requested whomever I chose to go with us. Before long, all of the seniors had been included on a call. This went a long way toward smoothing relationships between Dr. Wolfe and the students.

He was our Alpha Psi adviser, but that didn't soften his treatment of us. When we made mistakes, he gave us "Hail Columbia." When we left ourselves open, we caught his barbed wit. In spite of all this, he was an excellent teacher and adviser.

Dr. Wolfe wasn't the only one I disagreed with in clinic. Dr. Cane gave wonderful lectures and drew excellent illustrations. Unfortunately, his experience was much stronger in academics than in actual practice.

A young cocker spaniel with distemper created a bad situation. We students diagnosed the disease as distemper; Dr. Cane insisted it was rabies. After clinic, I went by his office and requested permission to explain why I disagreed with his diagnosis. He promptly asked if I had ever seen a case of rabies. When I told him about seeing more than sixty cases in my work with Dan Grear, he clearly doubted me. Adding that I had seen rabies in dogs, horses, cows, and one man really soured the situation. Dr. Cane had never seen a single case of rabies, but he insisted the dog was rabid. He marked the cage, "Suspected rabies! Do not destroy in case of death." That irritated me. I predicted that the dog would be dead of distemper complications before morning.

I was right, but disaster continued to stalk us. Luke, the old black janitor, either didn't see the sign or couldn't read it. He incinerated the corpse before we could amputate the head and send it to the state laboratory. Poor Luke caught old manner of ruckus from Dr. Cane. Ten of us students caught fourteen anti-rabies shots in the abdomen. For the second time, another man's mistake had cost me the discomfort and the risk of the anti-rabies serum.

To make matters worse, after he had ordered us to take the shots and we had started the series, Dr. Cane called Dr. Grear to check on my story. When he called me into his office several days later, I figured he was going to chew me out for disagreeing with him. Instead, he told me about calling Don and admitted that if he had confirmed my story earlier, none of us would have had to take the shots! My thoughts were unprintable.

Dr. Cane repeated some of the nice things Don had said about me, assured me that he would never doubt me again, and promised to give me all of the breaks if I didn't tell the rest of the class about his error.

The nerve of this guy! With difficulty, I controlled my fury enough to tell him that I didn't want any breaks and I would keep quiet and continue to do my best work. He went on to add that he had been checking my academic and extra-curricular records in the dean's office and that I really should be teaching him.

That was too much. Despite my aching belly, I assured him again that I would continue to do my best. After suggesting that he could check on my competency as a vet by talking to Dr. Wolfe, I excused myself.

By the time I rejoined my group in the clinic, my self-control had slipped badly. Blind with rage, I kicked over a trash can and knocked over a tray of instruments. Stunned, my group insisted on knowing what had riled me. Realizing that they were not going to hush, I told them as briefly as possible. They, too had aching bellies and they seemed to understand. I was still boiling when I got back to my room. Tom and I talked until I cooled down.

Money was still a problem for me. One of the veterinary students who had flunked out started a taxi service in Auburn. By the time I was a senior, he had built a very successful business. Occasionally he hired me as an extra driver. It was an easy job, he paid me well, and most of my fares tipped me generously. My first fare was Doc Parrish who still lived over on East Thatch Avenue. We had a fine visit and enjoyed reminiscing about old times as I drove along. His tip was more than the fare! Tips were always good when the passenger wanted to go to Opelika to buy whiskey or when somebody wanted to send a cab to Opelika for the same purpose. My biggest tip came one night when a man sent me to Opelika to buy a fifth of Four Roses. He made it clear that time was important and he would reward a quick trip. I made the fourteen mile round trip in sixteen minutes. After he paid the fare, he and his friends tipped me twenty dollars! Mama would have had a fit—and given me a fit—if she had ever heard about that. I was sorry when my friend recruited enough full-time drivers not to need me any more.

Picking up and selling lost golf balls and occasionally ushering at a ball game added a few more dollars. Tom still paid generously for the use of my notes and sometimes paid me for other chores I did for him. By careful management, I managed to get by without taking on a regular job or asking my parents for more money. Bless their hearts, they had no idea how much money I needed. They thought they were providing everything I could possibly need and I was not about to ask them to sacrifice anything else for me.

In spite of classes, clinics, calls with Dr. Wolfe, military affairs, and studies, I squeezed in as much play as possible.

Lester Young and I had a standing bridge game every Saturday afternoon with Tom Talker and Joe Stearner. Lester didn't believe in wasting time. He frequently opened his bidding with four no trump. Using the Blackwood convention, that rascal made more slams than any bridge player I ever saw. Tom didn't fool around playing anything just for fun—the boy had to gamble! To make it interesting, we played for steak dinners. Tom and Joe usually had to buy the steaks.

One memorable Saturday afternoon, Harry Morgan and I decided to play a round of golf before my bridge game started. Two other seniors joined us for the short walk from the fraternity house to the first tee. Just then Dr. Conklin walked past. Impulsively, I asked the others if it would be okay to invite him to join us. They responded, "If you've got the guts to ask him, we'll play with him."

I called to him, issued the invitation, and he accepted. By the third green, he was sharing Harry's bottle of Jack Daniels. Dr. Conklin handled the golf clubs better than the Jack Daniels. I was matching them drink for drink with one important difference—my cup contained straight Coca Cola or straight Seven-Up. After a few more holes and a few more drinks, Dr. Conklin was just one of the boys. By the ninth hole, he was feeling so euphoric that I offered to walk home with him. By the time we reached his house, he was hugging my neck and bragging about what a fine group of seniors we were. After thanking me profusely for including him in our game, he finally let me go.

After a quick run back to the house, I showered, put on clean clothes, and started our bridge game. Before we finished the second rubber, Dr. Wolfe called me. A cow had milk fever and we had to go out right away. I handed my cards to one of the brothers and went out to meet Dr. Wolfe. He wasn't feeling well and wanted me to drive. Good grief! I was becoming the faculty nursemaid!

When we reached the farm, the farmer said that his cow was down in the pasture. While Dr. Wolfe sat in the shade of a tree, I carried the medical bag and followed the farmer a quarter of a mile across open fields and pastures. A quick examination showed that the cow was in a normal position and showing no signs of metritis nor mastitis. I gave her a massive injection of calcium solution and she started shivering as though she were freezing. By the time I explained that this was a normal reaction, the cow was definitely recovering. I waited five minutes and then stepped on her tail. She jumped up and started back to the barn. The farmer and I followed her as he asked questions and I answered them. By the time she was back in her stall, I had finished explaining the proper follow-up care.

Dr. Wolfe grunted and said, "Yeah, I know," when the farmer told him what a good doctor I was. His response would have been exactly the same if the cow had died and the farmer had claimed it was all my fault. While Dr. Wolfe collected his fee, I cleaned and repacked the equipment. We got back to the house in time for me to play a few hands of bridge before supper.

The quarter ended in a flurry of activities. Finally Herbert and I were in Walter's car for the week's break between summer and fall quarters.

CHAPTER 35

Carolyn was going to meet us in Greenville. She was anxious to show me the slightly used 1936 Chevrolet sedan her father had bought for her. Herbert and I were delighted that we would not have to ride the milk truck nor wait for one of our brothers to pick us up.

Walter must have been as anxious to get home as we were. In just under six hours we pulled up beside Carolyn's car. In less than five minutes our gear had been transferred to her car, arrangements to meet Walter the next Sunday morning had been made, and we were on our way out to the farm.

It didn't take long to drop off Herbert and our baggage, hug Mama, gobble a piece of cake, greet the other family members who were available, and get over to Carr's Creek to see the silver that Carolyn had bought with the money she had earned as a teacher. The new Mrs. Riddle was obviously planning to do a lot of high-toned entertaining! It looked like she had bought enough silver to start a store and it was all beautiful. I was proud of her.

With a little prodding from Miss Jennie, we finalized the plans for the wedding. Papa agreed to be my best man. I knew he was pleased when he volunteered to buy a new suit for the occasion. Mama was worried about her role as mother of the groom. Love finally won out over her shyness, and she, too, planned to buy a new outfit for the wedding. Carolyn's cousin Mildred would be matron of honor and my sisters would be her bridesmaids. Two of my friends would usher. Carolyn's best friend from Furman would play a violin accompaniment to the pianist. Miss Jennie and Mr. Paul would have the reception at their home. Between the time squeeze, my very austere budget, and gasoline rationing, we could not go away for a honeymoon. Carolyn had solved that, too. Her aunt's neighbors were going out of town for a week and we could rent their house for our honeymoon. Having a church wedding was getting more complicated by the minute! Now I understood why the little white frame Reedy Fork Baptist Church had stood for a hundred years without having a wedding within its walls! Well, if

217

we were going to be the first couple to be married in it, we were going to have to do it right.

Carolyn and I had plans for every night of the week. It created a small uproar when I told her that I had to attend to some personal business on Tuesday night. That was going to be the hardest thing I had to do in preparation for the wedding—break off my relationship with Bonnie. I wasn't ready to discuss it with Carolyn nor anybody else. I flatly refused to explain what the personal business was and I insisted that it had to be done Tuesday night. Although Carolyn was annoyed, she didn't press the matter. Bonnie was delighted when I called and asked for a date. Just like old times, we went for a ride up to Paris Mountain. With my arm around her, I told her how beautiful and charming she was and how fervently I hoped she would be happy. The sparkle in her eyes went out and her shoulders stiffened as she waited for what she suspected was coming. Quickly I told her that Carolyn and I would be married in December. When she started crying, I almost joined her. She was a sweet girl and we had had a lot of great times together. Oh, Lord, I didn't want to hurt her. I tried to tell her that she would find somebody much finer than I who would make all her dreams come true. She didn't agree with me and the tears came faster. In desperation, I took her home, asked her to give my love to Mrs. Brady, and gave her a kiss that both of us would remember for a long time. My heart ached as I left her crying, but what else could I do?

Carolyn was not pleased when she figured out what my personal business had been. She knew that it had to be done, but she didn't like it one bit. She was more than slightly miffed when I asked her how many evenings she needed to break up with her old boy friends. She glared at me as she said, "None!" and the edge on her voice would have cut through cold steel. This discussion was only going to lead to trouble. I ended it abruptly by kissing her. Love worked its magic again. Her irritation faded swiftly and we went on with our plans and dreams for the future.

Somehow I squeezed in a short visit with the Grears. Don wanted to know what that telephone call from Dr. Cane was all about. The expressions on his face were classic when I told him that wretched story. He assured me that he had straightened Dr. Cane out thoroughly and that he would do it again any time it became necessary.

Those were the only sour notes in a wonderful week. In a flash, Carolyn was taking Herbert and me to meet Walt for the trip back to Auburn. I reminded her that the next time she sent me back to Auburn, she would be Mrs. John T. Riddle. She blushed and smiled as she acknowledged that she had been thinking about that.

The miles passed quickly. When we got back to Auburn, it was like stepping into a whirlwind.

My fraternity brothers wanted to know if I had gotten married like so many others were doing. The war was forcing a lot of our friends to grab what little they could of love and marriage before they were shipped overseas. I assured them that Carolyn was worth waiting for until we could have the kind of wedding we had planned. We would get married in December—not before! On Monday we registered for classes, clinics, and labs. On Tuesday, Dean Winters met with the whole vet school to welcome us back and to inform us that we would continue the Army Reserve Program. In the midst of the moaning, cussing, and fussing, I requested permission to speak. I asked the students if they wanted to change their officers. The chorus of "No's!" was deafening. Still hopeful, I requested and received a vote on the officers. When we were all re-elected, Dean Winters gave us a pep talk and assured each student that the officers were just as reluctant as anybody to continue the program. Like it or not, it had to be done. I surely didn't like this Major Riddle stuff, but I seemed to be stuck with it.

Before the organizational meeting for the battalion that afternoon, I had a meeting with my officers and Dean Winters. We agreed to handle the program just as we had done before. As soon as everybody was in shape, we could go back to the rotation program. The army hadn't caught on to that, and we were going to ride it as long as possible. I challenged the officers to run the obstacle course with me. Tom Rodgers and I made it over the wall on the first try—some of the others had to try it two or three times. With the wall conquered, the rest of the course seemed easy. We raced through it and then galloped on back to the drill field. We were ready to shape up the troops.

The merry-go-round was spinning faster and faster with clinics, classes, drills, meetings, and calls with Dr. Wolfe.

One of the highlights of the fall quarter was being tapped for membership in Phi Kappa Phi. Only four members of the vet school were tapped for this honorary fraternity—the four with the highest scholastic averages. There were no meetings and no dues. We were awarded beautiful keys and impressive citations and honored by a standing ovation from the vet school student body. The citation read, "Phi Kappa Phi is a national honorary society organized for the purpose of encouraging scholarship and original study among students. It is comprised of professors, graduate students, and undergraduate students who have distinguished themselves by scholarship and intellectual services to their Alma Mater. Taking its membership on the quota system from the various schools on the campus, this senior honor organization brings to its members at Auburn the equivalent distinction for generally outstanding work that Phi Beta Kappa brings to its members on campuses having A. B. Schools. However, Phi Kappa Phi is unique in the fact that it considers the extra curricular activity of its candidates in addition to mere scholastic achievement."

Most Auburn students, like those at Clemson, wore their academic and social keys on a chain hooked into a belt loop. Not wanting to be a show-off, I added my Phi Kappa Phi Key to the other keys in a corner of my trunk. I was very proud of each of them, but together, they made a display that could only be considered ostentatious.

Things were going entirely too smoothly. Leave it to Dr. Wolfe and a white mule to create an uproar. When we reported to clinic, Dr. Wolfe had us guess the weight of a tremendous white mule. It was important for us to be able to estimate an animal's weight fairly accurately in order to prescribe proper dosages of medication. He insisted that each of us write down our estimate of the mule's weight and emphasized that the estimate must be written down. As soon as we wrote down our estimates, I stuck mine in the pocket of my coveralls. He ordered me to ride the mule over to the Federal Research Laboratory, have her weighed, and bring her back with a statement of her weight. On the half-mile ride, I figured out what was sure to happen. If my guess was accurate, Dr. Wolfe would swear that I had written it down after the mule was weighed. When I slid off the mule and led her onto the scale, the attendant weighed her. My estimate was right on the money. I took the slip of paper out of my pocket, showed it to the attendant, and assured him that Dr. Wolfe would call him in a little while to verify whether I had written down my estimate before or after the weighing. He laughed as he said that I had obviously spent some time around mules and assured me that he would tell Dr. Wolfe that he had seen my written estimate.

There's no way to hurry a mule, but I did my best. When we got back, I slid off the mule just as Dr. Wolfe came out to ask her weight. When I told him she weighed 1300 pounds, he replied, "That's exactly what I thought!" Teasing, I asked if he had written down his estimate. When he said, "No," I told him his estimate didn't count. Ouch! That was the wrong thing to say. He shook his shoulders fiercely, mumbled something, and then asked what my estimate had been. He hit the ceiling when he saw it and swore that I had written it down after she was weighed. Very carefully, I suggested that he call the Research Center and verify that the attendant has seen my estimate and that it had been done before the weighing. Shaking his shoulders furiously, he stalked into his office and made the call. I could hear him mutter, "Umm, huh, umm huh!" He came out, apologized for doubting my word, and then verified that he and I had been the only ones to guess correctly. Still provoked, he asked, "John, how come you are always so *@ lucky?"

As clinic ended, he called four names to meet in his office— Riddle, Morgan, Spence, and Talker. Puzzled, we looked as each other and tried to figure out what we had done wrong. As we walked into his office, he burst out with a Santa Claus laugh and said, "Boy, I just don't know what makes you so lucky!"

Whew! At least he wasn't mad. He had a proposition for us. One of his clients had a herd of slightly over a hundred calves that needed to be castrated and wormed. He would pay us one hundred dollars to do the job, the school would provide the medication and equipment, and we could drive Dr. Wolfe's car out to the farm. All right! We weren't about to turn down that kind of deal. We agreed to go out on Saturday morning to do the job and pledged to keep quiet about it around the other students.

Saturday morning found us in coveralls, ready to get the job done. The farmer had put them in a lot which had no catch shoot. There was no way those half-wild calves were going to stand still voluntarily until we castrated them. While the others were wondering out loud how we were going to catch and restrain the calves, I volunteered to lasso them one at a time if somebody else would grab the rope and throw it around a post.

The responses were predictable, "Oh, shoot, we've got a cowboy in our midst!'' ''When in the #* did you get to be a Carolina cowboy?''

Not wanting to waste the day gabbing, I bet each of them five dollars that I could lasso the calves. That galvanized them into action. Predictably, Tom was the first to take the bet and the others followed his lead. Lassoing, like riding a bicycle, is something that you master once and never forget. I had lassoed many an animal on the Riddle farm and I knew I could still do it.

As the others waited doubtfully to grab the rope, I swung the lasso and it settled gracefully around a calf's neck. They grabbed the rope, wrestled the calf down, performed the castration, applied the screw-worm medicine, and released the bawling calf while I lassoed the next one. The work was hard and hot. Before long we pulled our arms out of the sleeves of the coveralls. That was a mistake. The Alabama sun broiled our backs and shoulders like so many steaks on a grill. By the time we finished at noon, I couldn't bear to have anything touch my shoulders. My $25.00 pay plus $15.00 in bets helped my budget remarkably, but my back and shoulders hurt for days.

When we got back to the Alpha Psi House, there were a lot of questions about where we had been. We told them we had been on a secret mission. They all allowed that it must have been a rough secret since we were all scratched up and had assorted cuts and bruises as well as our sunburns.

Almost before the sunburn healed, Dr. Wolfe called just prior to drill to insist that Morgan and Riddle meet him on the sidewalk in front of the fraternity house in fifteen minutes. He needed some help dealing with a killer mule. Even drill was preferable to battling with a killer mule! Well, be that as it may, we had no choice. Dr. Wolfe had called and that was that. I called the O. T. S. House, told Tom Rodgers that the battalion was all his for the afternoon, and went out to join Harry on the sidewalk.

In a mellow—or desperate—mood, Dr. Wolfe apologized for interfering with drill and then told us about the mule. He was lame and totally unmanageable. There was no way to get a twitch-stick on his nose and Dr. Wolfe really didn't know quite how we were going to deal with him. The farmer thought there was a nail in the mule's foot. He could get a bridle on him and that was as far as he could get with control devices.

Oh, boy! This was the era before animal sedatives and tranquiliz-

ers. Man-handling, brute strength, and restraints were our only tools for handling unruly or frightened animals.

Dr. Wolfe introduced us to the farmer and both of them warned us to be careful because that mule had never been conquered. We discussed the situation and watched the mule for a little while. I challenged Dr. Wolfe to guess the mule's weight. This time, he beat me. Harry's guess was 1,000 pounds, mine was 1,100 pounds, and Dr. Wolfe's was 1,150 pounds—the exact weight! Dr. Wolfe was grinning broadly when I told him that even a blind hog could pick up an acorn occasionally! Harry held his breath until Dr. Wolfe laughed and complained that I sure had been riding him hard lately.

The farmer got the bridle on the mule and Harry thought he could get a twitch on him. He tried manfully but unsuccessfully. Dr. Wolfe asked if I had any ideas. I remembered watching Don Grear and his brothers put an Indian War Bridle on some killer mules and I thought I could do it. Dr. Wolfe was ready to try anything.

I got a manilla hemp rope, and rigged it so that I could jerk it through the mule's mouth. The pain would shock him into submission. It seemed cruel and yet it was kinder than letting him die slowly from an infected hoof. It worked! As the mule went down, Harry grabbed a hoof knife and a pair of grips. By the time he had pulled out the ten-penny nail and cleaned out the hole, Dr. Wolfe had iodine and cotton ready to pack the hole and a tetanus shot ready to administer. In less than five minutes, we were finished and the mule could be released.

On the way back, the car was mighty quiet. Finally they asked where I had learned that technique and what it was called. I told them it was called an Indian War Bridle and about the times the Grears had used it. Dr. Wolfe allowed that he wished he had known about it a long time ago—it would have helped him over some rough spots. Then he added that he would like for me to demonstrate it in the clinic if I didn't mind sharing a trade secret. I assured him that sharing knowledge was a part of the learning process for me.

Just before Thanksgiving, the weather was beautiful. It seemed that God had set his big thermostat and climate control unit to please everybody. About that time, two Alpha Psis showed up from the vet school at Cornell. They proved themselves by giving the president the password and we proved ourselves by overwhelming them with Southern hospitality. Before they left, they told us that their school had sent them down to see if we really handled as many cases in our clinics as we reported. Since the Cornell clinics were extremely small, their students saw and dealt with very few cases. We took them on a tour of the campus and showed them our clinics as well as our other facilities. They absolutely gawked at the size of our clinics and the number of animals in our cages and stalls. They were clearly envious of our program. Both of them seemed to be great guys and we enjoyed showing them that not everything in the South could be classified as poor and deprived! It would have been great to hear the tales they told about Auburn's facilities and Auburn's Southern belles and parties when they got back to Cornell.

It was about this time that we got a killer mule in the large animal clinic. With no warning, Dr. Wolfe announced that John Riddle would give a special demonstration on restraining unruly large animals. Harry Morgan brought out a mule with a painful growth on his foot. That big rascal was kicking and spooking at everything in sight. With a deep breath and a prayer, I again rigged an Indian War Bridle. It worked this time, too. We were able to anesthetize him and perform the surgery to remove the growth. Later, Dr. Wolfe acknowledged that he had put me on the spot to see how I handled pressure. He erupted with his Santa Claus laugh and told me he was convinced that I could handle anything, anywhere, under any circumstances.

Sandy was still my Auburn girl. We attended most of the fraternity and sorority parties and dances as well as occasional movies. She knew about Carolyn and about my engagement. We often talked about the necessity of keeping our relationship casual. She was a real little doll.... we had a lot of fun together. My fraternity brothers teased me a lot about two-timing my fiancee, but what else could I do? It just wasn't possible to have Carolyn come to Auburn every week and I couldn't maintain a leadership position nor be a well-rounded student if I didn't participate in social activities. Sandy and I had a comfortable relationship; I couldn't be with Carolyn anyway;.... this just seemed the best solution. As my wedding day got closer, I began to sense that Sandy's heart was getting control of her head. Those big beautiful eyes were saying things that her lips could never say. Well, I could give her a beautiful swan song.

As president of the Jr. A. M. V. A., my date would be first lady of the annual ball. I invited Sandy and she accepted. Her mother bought her a beautiful dress and I gave her a lovely corsage. As we led off the first dance, she floated out onto the floor. If I hadn't held on to her, she might have floated right up to the ceiling. There was no denying the presence of trouble. Sandy's eyes were misty and everything about her fairly shouted that her romantic notions had over-powered our "Nothing serious, ever!" agreement. Oh, Lord, why do girls always have to complicate everything by falling in love?

Well, I wasn't going to spoil her big event. We could deal with the practicalities later. Tonight she could be the princess of the ball. With that settled in my mind, I settled down and enjoyed my lovely princess and the ball.

A few days later we had a party for the new Alpha Psi pledges, including Herbert. I invited Sandy to come over and help us entertain the pledges and their dates. I picked her up early and left her in the parlor to play hostess while I went up to my room to get a clean handkerchief. Tom, Harry, and Bill were all in the room sharing a few nips of Jack Daniels. Just teasing, I threatened to send Dr. Wolfe up to check on them. Reminding me how drunk they had gotten Dr. Conklin, they dared me to send up Dr. Wolfe and then allowed that I didn't have the guts to do it. That was too much. Ordering them to tidy up the room in preparation for Dr. Wolfe's arrival, I went downstairs and asked Dr. Wolfe if he would like a little toddy. He looked a little startled, smiled, and said, "I believe I would."

We went upstairs to join the fellows. When we asked Dr. Wolfe what kind of toddy he preferred, he settled on Scotch and soda. I sent Bill downstairs to get more ice and to explain to Sandy that I was going to be tied up for a little while. After a drink or two, Dr. Wolfe really began to unwind. Eventually, he got around to saying that after grading three of my papers, he had never bothered to read another one—he just graded them "A" or "A+!" I was glad I was drinking Coke or I would have been sure I was hearing things! When he started predicting my future, I excused myself to rejoin Sandy.

I picked up a cup of punch for Sandy and took her outside. As she sipped her punch on the lawn, I told Sandy what was happening in my room. She looked surprised and asked, "Have you been drinking, John?"

I assured her that I hadn't and handed her my cup of Coke. She tasted it, laughed and said, "I didn't think you had, but I just had to be sure."

In a few minutes somebody called me and said Dr. Wolfe was looking for me. He just wanted to tell me goodnight and to thank me for being the first brother ever to invite him into his room or to offer him a drink. He left in a euphoric mood. My mood was getting heavier by the minute. My wedding was three weeks away and I just had to break off my relationship with Sandy. When I rejoined her, she started asking questions about Dr. Wolfe. Delighted to have a safe subject, I told her all sorts of experiences that Dr. Wolfe and I had shared. By then it was time for us to bid the pledges and their dates goodnight. When we found him, I teased Herbert because it was now definite that I would miss his initiation in the spring. He was counting the days until he became a brother.

My heart grew heavier with every step as we made the rounds telling everybody goodnight. I knew, and Sandy didn't know, what had to be said on the way home. As we walked slowly toward her sorority house, I told her about the wedding plans. She was girlish enough to cry and woman enough to turn it into a joke. Her parting shot was, "I always knew you had good taste and good judgment or you wouldn't have dated me!"

At the door, we talked for a minute or two more, she smiled through her tears, and I left quickly. One more second, and I might have cried, too. As the song says, "Breaking up is hard to do!"

When I got back to the Alpha Psi House, nearly all the guests had left and most of the brothers had gone to bed. Making a quick check through the house, I met our housemother. She looked at me quizzically and asked, "What's wrong, John?"

My too-quick, "Nothing," didn't fool her any more than it would have fooled my mother. She invited me to sit in the kitchen with her while she had a cup of tea. She drank her tea while I played with a glass of milk and told her about Sandy and my wedding. Like Mama, she soothed my feelings and sent me to bed feeling better although there was no way to make me feel good. A part of my life had just ended.

When I got to my room Tom and Harry were waiting to tell me that Auburn was going to offer me a job as Associate Professor of Large Animal Medicine and Surgery. I thought they were either teasing or repeating something that the Scotch had made Dr. Wolfe say. I assured them that in three months I would be long gone from Auburn.

The weeks flew by in a blur. Suddenly it was the Monday before my wedding and I still had not requested permission to leave school on Thursday. I was on my way to the dean's office when a sign shattered my day: "NO STUDENT WILL BE PERMITTED TO LEAVE THIS SCHOOL UNTIL THE END OF THE SCHOOL DAY ON SATURDAY, DECEMBER 19, 1942!" Wham! Well, nothing ventured, nothing gained. I might as well ask and see what happened.

Wearily, I walked on down to Dean Winter's office and told him that I had the biggest problem I had encountered in school. When he asked about it, I told him what was wrong, and he started laughing. He could and would solve that problem right quick. He dictated a memorandum to his secretary and the wedding plans were back on track! Then he asked about my future ...from the wedding to my long-term career plans... and mentioned that Auburn was going to offer me the assistant professorship that Tom and Harry had told me about!

That was a shock! I finally told him that I had dreamed of a mixed practice since I was twelve years old and that I really felt that it would look ridiculous for a twenty-two year old professor to be teaching men who were older than their professor. After thanking him for his help and for his faith in me, I left quickly.

This time I made a quick trip to the bank to borrow enough money to buy a dark blue suit, black shoes, and a felt hat for the wedding. Carolyn might not marry me if I showed up in overalls! It didn't take long to get the loan and to make my purchases.

When I left Thursday wearing my new hat because it wouldn't fit in my suitcase, half of the brothers had to see me off on the train. Before they got through hugging me, patting me on the back, and wishing me well, my hat got knocked off and crushed under Harry's size thirteen shoe! He wanted to buy me a new one, but the train pulled in and I had to get on board. As I mounted the steps, the gang started singing "Auld Lang Syne." This was as bad as breaking up—another part of my life was ending and tears were mighty close.

The train's wheels clicked on the tracks as fast as my thoughts raced through my head. From remembering the past to anticipating the future, my thoughts raced around and around. The next thing I heard was the conductor announcing the stop at Greenville.

CHAPTER 36

Carolyn was waiting when the train stopped. In less than two minutes she would be in my arms. In less than 72 hours she would be my wife. Squashed hat and all, I jumped down the steps and ran to meet her. As soon as I kissed her, she started rattling off wedding plans. Details, details, and more details. I could perform surgical procedures on animals, I could organize and train a battalion, I could maintain the highest average in the vet school, but this twenty minute ceremony was about to overwhelm me.

When Carolyn realized how nervous I was getting, she stopped for a minute and then said, "Just be at the church for rehearsal at 8:00 Friday night and get to the church by 3:30 Sunday afternoon for the wedding. I've already bought the license and we (members of the family) can handle everything else."

That sounded simple enough. I had no idea my feelings would ride such a roller coaster. We had dreamed of marrying for so many years—why was I coming unglued now?

My brothers teased me, Carolyn was alternately anxious to see me and too busy with wedding plans to be bothered, and Mama fed and soothed me.

Finally the magic hour arrived. Just as I stepped up to the altar, there was a terrible roar....the whole building trembled....the windows rattled....the congregation gasped.... and I wondered whether to stay and get married or to run like the devil. Just as suddenly as it had begun, the noise subsided. Then it came again, subsided again, and came back a third time. Were the Father, the Son, and the Holy Ghost all trying to tell me something?

Papa touched my shoulder as though he were gentling a skittish horse. The preacher smiled reassuringly. I found out much later that one of my high school buddies who was stationed at Greenville Air Force Base had "buzzed" the church three times in a C-47. Thanks a lot, ole buddy.

Mama smiled nervously and I tried to smile back. She really did look nice in her new blue dress and fancy hat. If Mama could make it through the wedding, I darned well could, too.

Just then the wedding march began. The door at the back of the church opened and my sisters came in followed by Carolyn's cousin. They were looked mighty pretty. Then the pianist and the violinist really came down on their instruments and Carolyn appeared. If Mr. Paul hadn't walked down the aisle with her, she might have floated away. From her little blue hat and soft blue dress right down to her toes, she was beautiful. When she smiled at me, all was right with the world.

Somehow we got through the ceremony with no further dramatics, the preacher pronounced us man and wife, and suddenly we were outside on a gorgeous December afternoon. Everybody had such a good time at the reception, I thought they would never leave.

Finally we were on our way to our honeymoon house. Hearing a weather forecast on the car radio, I asked Carolyn if she had plenty of antifreeze in the car. She assured me that Will, her father's tenant farmer, had taken care of it.

We picked up the house keys from Carolyn's aunt and unlocked the house. It was beautiful. Somebody had even put in fresh flowers for us.

Carolyn went back to the bedroom to change her clothes. I sat down in the living room to wait for her. In a little while, she came out wearing a pale blue gown and negligee looking just the way I had dreamed she would look. Just as I scooped her into my arms, somebody started knocking on the door. Now wait a cotton pickin' minute, that wasn't in the script.

Reluctantly, I answered the door. Carolyn blushed and I fumed as my brothers Donald and Joe and their wives and my sister Blanche and her husband trooped in and sat down. Of all the bad jokes!

They sat around and talked until I was ready to kill all of them. Finally I sent Carolyn to the bedroom and turned on my slightly tipsy male guests. "You-all can stay as long as you want to stay— just be sure to turn off the lights and lock the front door when you leave! I'm going to bed now!"

Whew. They took the hint and left.

At last, my bride and I were alone. The weather outside turned nasty and the temperature dropped to 25 degrees that night and to 12 degrees on Monday night. We didn't even notice the weather.

Tuesday morning we drove into Greenville to buy groceries. We were driving up Main Street when the radiator started steaming. Before I could find a place to park, the horn started blowing and wouldn't stop. I slammed on the brakes, jumped out, and raised the hood. The steam was pouring out, the horn was blasting, people were staring, Carolyn's face was as red as a neon sign, and I was totally out-done. I couldn't see the * horn, let alone the wire leading to it. I felt like a fool standing in the middle of the street steaming my face and freezing my behind.

Finally the steam cleared enough for me to disconnect the horn and to drive slowly to Mr. Julian's garage, two blocks away. He repaired all of Papa's vehicles and I knew that he could handle this mess. That * Will had forgotten to put in the antifreeze, as sure as shooting.

At last we pulled into the garage. Mr. Julian looked at our version of the Stanley Steamer, shook his head, and said, "Mr. Riddle, you have a busted block." He could have added, "To match your budget."

With a sinking heart, I replied, "Yes, sir, I know that. How much is it going to cost to fix it?"

He looked at it, scratched his head, and said, "$54.50 is the best I can do for you." Then he added, "Do you know that your horn is disconnected?"

Trying to smile, I said, "Just touch the wire to the connection and you'll see why it's disconnected."

He touched it, heard it, and found the short-circuit caused by the steam. He would fix that, too. We could have the car back on Friday.

Carolyn called Mr. Paul and he came to pick us up. All of us were ready to strangle Will. After a little while, we simmered down and realized that he had meant no harm—he had just forgotten the antifreeze in the confusion of getting ready for the wedding.

I had to borrow $75.00 from Mama to fix the car and to get back to school on the train. Marriage was already becoming an expensive proposition.

We picked up the car on Saturday. On Sunday, Carolyn took me to the railroad station to meet the 3:00 train. Every time I looked at her, she was more beautiful. When the conductor called, "All aboard," I kissed her goodby. She started crying and I came mighty close. Leaving her had always been hard, but this was torture. She waved from the platform and I waved from the window as long as we could see each other.

Since Herbert had gone back to school on Friday, I was making this trip alone. As the train sped along, I tried to figure out what to do. I had to repay the bank...repay Mama...support myself and my wife...prepare to support a family....I had three job offers and I didn't like any of them....I didn't want to be a lieutenant in the army—my whole life had been geared to establishing a veterinary practice, not to filling a battlefield grave. . . . Teaching at Auburn would be too confining....Testing cows in South Carolina for the government would be too monotonous....Where could I establish a practice?...How could I get the money to set up a practice?....Surely in three months something would turn up.

Sleep must have slipped up on me because the next thing I heard was the conductor announcing our arrival in Auburn.

When I got back to the Alpha Psi House, seven new juniors told me there was a big party going on in my room. That was the last thing I needed. When I got up there, I discovered they were celebrating my wedding. That was all right. Before the party ended, I asked Playboy when he was going to sober up. He rolled his eyes toward heaven and slurred, "Boy, I'm going to stay drunk for the duration."

"Of school or the war?" I inquired.

"Whichever lasts longer, son. Whichever lasts longer," was his answer as he poured himself another drink.

I unpacked my clothes, drank a couple of Cokes, and then told those clowns to clear out because Carolyn had already taught me the value of going to bed early. With a few more pats on the back and a few more rowdy comments, they left me to try to sleep in my lonely bed and to dream of my lovely bride.

Right after registration, the dean called me into his office. After chatting awhile about the wedding, he asked if I would continue leading the battalion until graduation. I agreed to do so. Then he said that there had been a tie between me and Billy Flynn for Outstanding Senior. I requested that the honor be given to Billy since I had already received so much recognition. Finally he showed me a letter from Mr. LeRoy Brownfield, Secretary of the Cobb-Marietta Chamber of Commerce, in Marietta, Georgia. Mr. Brownfield requested help from the vet school to locate a student who would set up a mixed practice in Marietta. The student would have full support from the Chamber and from the community in setting up his practice. Encouraged by Dean Winters, I called Mr. Brownfield. From the first "Hello," we hit it off. I arranged to go to Marietta that Thursday night. On Friday morning I met Mr. Brownfield and a number of prominent citizens of Marietta and Cobb County. After taking an automobile tour of the county, I knew where my future home would be.

When I got back to Auburn, I discussed it with Carolyn, with Dean Winters, with the Fourth Service Area Command, and with Dr. Sutton, a Georgia veterinarian whose sons were Alpha Psis. Everybody agreed that this was the place for me. I felt like I was going to heaven.

The weeks flew by. Carolyn and my brother Grover arrived on the train for my graduation. Grover stayed in my room and Carolyn and I stayed at the hotel. The graduation ceremony was held on the stage at the Tiger Theatre in Auburn. It seemed a strange place to hold a graduation and yet there was an appropriate drama in the whole situation. Graduation would be the great equalizer— whether our grades were straight "A's" or barely passing, we would all have the same degree. Nonetheless, the habits we had built, the attitudes we had developed, the friends we had made, and the knowledge we had gained, would determine to a great degree the course of the rest of our lives.

John T. Riddle, age 15, and Sonny Boy beside the Riddle home in Greenville County, S.C.

John T. Riddle, Clemson freshman.

John T. Riddle watering cows behind Sheppard Chateau.

John T. Riddle presenting a gift to Dean Suggs at Auburn.

John T. Riddle wearing new western outfit purchased by Tom. Auburn's new Vet Building is in the background.

Auburn Vet School Juniors on Municipal Docks at Mobile, Alabama.

John T. Riddle on rail of Bay Maid during cruise at end of inspection trip.

Alpha Psi officers in front of new fraternity house: l-r Roland Clanton, Vice President, John T. Riddle, Secretary, Lamar Blalock, President, Walter Glazner, Treasurer.

Dr. Riddle in his office at The Veterinary Clinic in Marietta, Georgia just prior to his retirement.